"Are you struggling with your teen's behavior, worried about your relationship, or wondering how to respond? If you've ever asked yourself 'What were they thinking when they did that?', Dr. Wolf's book is a must-read. His incredible insight into everything from the typical to the most challenging of teen behaviors is right on the mark. He is able to make sense of what, how, and why teens do some of the things they do. You will want to keep this book close at hand, as it will provide pearls of wisdom and hope as you journey through the teen years. An easy and enjoyable read, this book will actually help you keep smiling as your teen matures into adulthood."
—Sandra "Sam" Fabian, Community Outreach Program Manager, Children's Hospital of the King's Daughters

"This book is vital reading for all parents wanting to ensure their relationship with their teenage child is as good as it can possibly be. Dr. Wolf humorously applies psychological insights from more than thirty years of counseling teens to detail communication techniques . . . that can make a significant difference in strengthening parents' everyday conversations with their adolescent."
—Joanne Cunard, professor, School of Education, St. Joseph College

"*I'd Listen to My Parents if They'd Just Shut Up* reads much like a coach's playbook. Effective coaches are masterful at developing and bringing out the best in people. An old saying teaches, 'The clearer the target, the surer the aim.' Dr. Wolf's new book clarifies the role of the parent and the teen as if it's common sense—learn to disengage, listen, and set the emotional tone and atmosphere for mutual respect. Good coaches provide balanced feedback that helps people clearly see what they should keep doing, stop doing, and start doing. This book illuminates that teens don't care how much a parent knows until they know how much we care."
—Sandra Jarvis, a "Boomer" parent

"Direct and to the point in his usual humorous style, Dr. Wolf has zeroed in on the things teens say that are the most difficult for parents to hear and respond to . . . he has the rare ability to take complex terms from clinical psychology and present them in ordinary terminology that parents can relate to and use immediately. This is very helpful to many parents who often feel that they, alone, are lost and wondering where they went wrong."

—Elizabeth A. Ayres, Ph.D., family therapist

"As a parent of a seventeen-year-old son, I was challenged by Dr. Wolf's book to react consciously instead of unconsciously to my teenager . . . I felt as if he wrote this book while observing my family through my living room window, and it made me laugh out loud. I highly recommend this book to all parents of teenagers."

—Siobhan Morgan, parent of teenager

I'D LISTEN TO MY PARENTS IF THEY'D JUST SHUT UP

Also by Anthony E. Wolf, Ph.D.

*Get Out of My Life, but First Could You
Drive Me and Cheryl to the Mall?*

The Secret of Parenting

Why Did You Have to Get a Divorce? And When Can I Get a Hamster?

*It's Not Fair, Jeremy Spencer's Parents
Let Him Stay Up All Night!*

"Mom, Jason's Breathing on Me!"

Why Can't You Shut Up?

I'll Be Home Before Midnight and I Won't Get Pregnant

I'D LISTEN TO MY PARENTS IF THEY'D JUST SHUT UP

What to Say and Not Say When Parenting Teens

ANTHONY E. WOLF, Ph.D.

HARPER

NEW YORK • LONDON • TORONTO • SYDNEY

HARPER

HarperCollins books may be purchased for educational, business, or sales promotional use. For information please write: Special Markets Department, HarperCollins Publishers, 10 East 53rd Street, New York, NY 10022.

FIRST EDITION

Designed by Michael P. Correy

Library of Congress Cataloging-in-Publication Data

Wolf, Anthony E.
    I'd listen to my parents if they'd just shut up : what to say and not say when parenting teens / Anthony Wolf. — 1st ed.
        p. cm.
    Summary: "Practical, dialogue-based advice for parents of teenagers from the author of the bestselling *Get Out of My Life, But First Could You Drive Me and Cheryl to the Mall?* Anthony Wolf applies his philosophy and humor to a wide variety of everyday situations, showing both the way interactions tend to go (not so well) and why, then offers parents a script and guidance on how to achieve the most satisfying outcomes. Wolf deals with all the things that have dramatically changed in society to affect parenting in the twenty-first century, especially the role of the Internet and electronic devices of all kinds in kids' lives."— Provided by publisher.
    ISBN 978-0-06-191545-1 (pbk.)
    1. Parent and teenager—United States. 2. Parenting. 3. Adolescence. I. Title.
    HQ799.15.W653 2011
    649'.125—dc22

                                                              2011008901

11 12 13 14 15   OV/RRD   10 9 8 7 6 5 4 3 2 1

To Mary Alice, Nick, and Margaret

CONTENTS

Preface

As a child psychologist I often hear parents of teenagers express their frustrations over the way that their children talk to them. They are utterly bewildered by how argumentative their children can be compared to past generations of kids.

By way of example, here's a typical parent-child interaction in the 1950s:

> "James, would you please take the trash out to the curb?"
> "Sure thing, Mom."

And a typical parent-child interaction today:

> "James, would you please take the trash out to the curb?"
> "Mom, I'm really tired. I'll do it later."
> "No, James—I want it done now."
> "Why does everything have to be when you want it? I'm not your slave."
> "Why do you always have to give me a hard time whenever I ask you to do something?"
> "Why do you always have to give me a hard time?"

Invariably today's parents think, *He is so disrespectful. He talks back to me all the time. What is his problem? What am I doing wrong?*

Although the latter, less-than-pleasant variation of an age-old conversation has been going on for just about half a century, parents still don't get it—there is one significant reason why teens today are not as immediately obedient and talk back to their parents in a way that was unthinkable just a few decades ago. Simply put, this generation is *not* afraid of their parents. And there is one important reason why this is true: we parents no longer use harsh punishment when raising our children. There are no more hard smacks across the face or use of a switch or belt. All of that is now considered child abuse.

This move away from harsh punishment was an excellent change for kids *and* adults, a real step forward for the whole human race. We—at least most of us—now believe that while harsh punishment may have produced behavior that was better for the moment, overall, as a regular part of child raising, it makes a child more, not less, likely to treat others harshly.

This changed attitude toward harsh punishment represents a whole new view of parenting and child development. Let me give an example.

Imagine that a mother is with her six-year-old daughter and eight-year-old son. The two children start bickering. The bickering escalates to the point where the boy hits his sister on the arm, causing her to cry. Their mother intervenes.

She smacks her son sharply on the arm.

"Don't hit your sister," says the boy's mother. *"Do you understand? DON'T . . . HIT . . . YOUR . . . SISTER."* And the boy's mother punctuates each word with a smack. *There, that will teach him, she says to herself.*

Not long ago, most people watching that scene would have probably agreed: *"Yeah, that will teach him."*

But today we recognize that yes, that will teach him all right—it will teach him that if he wants to hit his sister, he had better not do it when his mother is watching. We also recognize that if this is his mother's typical parenting style, the boy will ultimately be *more*, not less, likely to become a hitter himself. Having been hit, the hitting becomes a part of him. For unlike in the past, we now believe that it is not only what you say to a child, but also how you treat him that shapes a child's behavior and who he becomes in the future.

This new way of looking at child development has caused the revolution in parenting that has now produced almost two generations of children who are not afraid of their parents. This really is a brand-new phenomenon in the history of parenting.

I strongly believe that the children reared in this new school of thought have gone on to become kinder and gentler people as a result.

Not everybody agrees, of course, as continual back talk can be difficult to deal with. But it is where we are in our parenting evolution to date, and where this book picks up in an effort to move our progress even further along.

As I said, today's kids do not fear their parents. And big surprise: when children are not afraid of their parents they talk back far more frequently and are not nearly as obedient to a degree that we never could have imagined just a couple of generations ago.

Well, duh! What did we think was going to happen? Children today do not behave at all like previous generations because the main leverage parents had over them in the past has been removed from the parenting arsenal. Yet despite this seemingly obvious point, today's parents still expect their kids to behave in a way that is only possible when using methods that were sensibly abandoned two generations ago. Essentially, the standard for proper child behavior never changed even though parenting practices did change. These days, when children don't behave the way they are expected to (which is inevitable when harsh punishment is removed from child rearing practices), parents feel that they have somehow failed.

I don't understand. I do my best. But it obviously isn't good enough. . . .

Not only do today's parents have unrealistic expectations for their kids' behavior, but in their never-ending attempts to get their kids to live up to outmoded standards, they are also holding themselves to unrealistic standards . . . and inadvertently making matters worse, not better.

> *"Alexander, please try to remember not to track mud through the kitchen."*
>
> *"You're always yelling at me about something."*
>
> *"I don't always yell at you. I just don't want mud tracked into the kitchen."*
>
> *"You're a neat freak. You don't know what it's like living in this house. Would you get off my case. Please."*
>
> *"Alexander, don't talk to me that way."*
>
> *"What way?"*
>
> *"Listen to your words. Listen to your tone of voice. It is so disrespectful. A teenager shouldn't talk to his parents that way."*
>
> *"I'm not talking to you in any way. You're the one who's disrespecting me."*

"I'm not disrespecting you."

"Yeah, you are. You're always nagging at me about something—like now, for instance."

So parents, let me ask you a straightforward question: Why would anyone want to continue interacting with someone who is exceedingly unpleasant? What is the most reasonable and logical response to that behavior? I believe the answer is that you would want to end that kind of interaction as fast as you can. Certainly, what you would not want to do is prolong the agony by continuing a fruitless discussion, as that would only fan the fire. Yet this is exactly what parents of today's teenagers repeatedly do—this, and so many other things that cause themselves and their kids great frustration. I see it all the time in my practice, which is why I'm now offering up hope and some practical tips to help you deal with the day-to-day challenges we all face when raising teens.

This is a book about parenting twenty-first-century teenagers—it's about who these kids are and the rules that apply to raising them in the world as it exists today. This book is designed to be as helpful as it can possibly be. It will provide you with very specific advice about how to best deal with your teenager in all of the most perplexing situations.

It will offer useful word-for-word responses and will also steer you clear of responses that are definitely *not* useful. In each of these scenarios, it will provide an explanation as to why certain responses work while others don't. It will help you discover a new way of successfully interacting with your teen.

Last, this book will talk about how, beyond the changes in parenting and in adolescent behavior, the world in which today's teenagers live has changed. Most notably, it will address how the exploding and ever-changing world of electronics is affecting the nature and scope of their experiences. When they are not in school, most of their waking hours are spent in an electronic universe of words, sounds, and images. Our kids are often engaged in using more than one medium at a time, which has had a profound effect on how they communicate with us, both good and bad. In many ways it is a new world. And yet, in many ways, the world of teenagers has changed very little.

Above all, this book is intended to make living with and rearing your teenage child a significantly more enjoyable and memorable experience. So let's get started.

I'D LISTEN TO MY PARENTS IF THEY'D JUST SHUT UP

Introduction

THE PARENTING REVOLUTION

Before I get into providing specific advice, I need to discuss certain truths about child development and the nature of adolescence that underlie all of the guidance I offer in this book.

Having read what I have written so far, you are probably wondering: *If the removal of fear from child rearing was the direct cause of the dramatic increase in back talk . . . and if this guy is saying that the removal of fear from child raising was excellent . . . is he then saying that the onslaught of back-talking little monsters we've produced is not such a bad thing after all?* My answer is yes, that's exactly what I am saying.

Fortunately, this increase in bratty behavior—as unpleasant as it sometimes can be—is not nearly as bad as it seems. This is because a particular fact of human psychology places the bratty behavior in a more benign light. Further, this same fact of human psychology suggests ways to dramatically reduce the amount of fussing we experience day to day in our relationships with our teens. (Mind you, it will not eliminate the fussing entirely, as that would require returning to the old harsh-punishment model of parenting, but it will help.) Let me describe this particular universal fact of human psychology to you.

THE BABY SELF AND THE MATURE SELF

I have noticed a remarkable phenomenon. If I am at the home of a friend or a relative, I always ask the host if there is anything I can do to help. Or if we have guests at our house, I ask if there is anything that they would like to make them more comfortable. If they request something of me, I willfully comply. I do it easily, happy for the opportunity to be useful.

As of this writing, I have been married for many years to a wonderful woman. I am very happy in my marriage. But if just Mary Alice and I are at home and Mary Alice asks me to do a rather simple favor for her—let's say we're both in the same room, and Mary Alice asks if I wouldn't mind getting her a glass of water with a little ice in it (our refrigerator has an ice dispenser that makes this quite easy to prepare), I invariably find myself engulfed by an incredible and sudden tiredness. Just the thought of the slightest exertion leaves my body overwhelmed by a leaden heaviness that makes completing this task impossible.

Maybe I have chronic fatigue syndrome. I really can't do it. I can't.

Not only that, but a sense of being very much imposed upon also comes, unbidden, into my head.

Why can't she get it herself? As she perfectly well knows, I had a very hard day, considerably harder than hers—which, by the way, she never seems to understand. She thinks her days are harder than mine. She should be asking me if I want a glass of water with some ice in it, for goodness' sake. Omigod, I am so tired. Nobody understands.

You, dear reader, might feel at this point that I am acting like a big baby. But I totally disagree, which only shows that you don't understand either. *Why is everybody always on Mary Alice's side? I don't get it. A big baby? Hardly.*

But this phenomenon doesn't just apply to me, as you will see from this next example:

If we were to take a video camera and follow sixteen-year-old Lindsay through a typical day at school, where she is a very good student, always handing in her homework on time, we'd see that she is very polite and responsive in class. She belongs to many school clubs. All of her teachers agree that she is a model student. She is also a good, sensitive listener to her friends.

After school, we'd watch as Lindsay goes to her friend Tara's house. There she and Tara work on a project for Spanish.

"Bye, Mrs. Timmerman," Lindsay says to Tara's mother as she leaves.

"Bye, Lindsay dear," says Tara's mother.

I'm so glad Tara has such a nice friend, thinks Tara's mother.

We continue the video. It is later that same day; Lindsay is now at home.

"Mom, get Jared the hell out of my room!" she shouts before bursting into tears.

A little later. Lindsay is in the kitchen.

"Somebody drank my Diet Pepsi. I can't believe it. Nothing is mine. I can't have anything of my own that people don't feel free to take. I hate this house!" Lindsay screams this last part.

And a little later still:

"Mom, where the hell is the red towel? You know it's the only one I can use. Where the hell is my red towel?!"

My point in sharing these two perplexing examples is to illustrate a universal fact of human psychology among both children and adults: we all have two distinctly different modes of behavior—really two different selves. One is a domestic self that just wants to unwind and be fed. In an attempt to completely relax, that self will tolerate absolutely no stress whatsoever. I call it the "baby self." Its domain is at home and with immediate family members—those with whom we feel the safest and the most comfortable. But there is another side to us: what I call the "mature self." It functions at a completely higher level. It will go out into the world, work, endure stress, and even delay gratification in order to achieve a goal. It has patience and self-control. And these two—the baby self and mature self—function side by side over the course of a day, going back and forth, switching gears. I have always pictured this phenomenon like a boxer who goes into the ring, does what he needs to do, then comes back to his corner, collapses and gets the nurturing that then allows him to go back into the ring for yet another tough round.

Initially, children are all baby self. But soon the mature self begins to appear. Over time it grows until gradually it takes over more and more of our functioning. But it never takes over completely. Even the most mature among us has a baby self that asserts itself from time to time.

"I thought you were going to work on bills."
"No, I decided to take a nap."

"You're sulking because we're eating at a restaurant that wasn't your choice."

"No, I'm not."

"Yeah, you're sulking."

It is only in the baby-self mode that we and our children get the deep nurturing we all need. Without our baby selves—and without a safe place for our baby selves to rest—life would be way too hard. Our stress levels would be intolerable. This is especially so with children.

"Mom, I'm home. . . . Why are we out of salt and vinegar taco chips? I didn't eat the last ones. . . . Mom, I can't find the remote. Where's the remote? Mom!"

Were there no opportunity for baby-self nurturing, there would be a stunting of emotional growth. Children need a place where they can fully be a child. And that place is with us, their parents.

Baby selves are generally good. They are cute, lovable, funny, and affectionate. But sometimes they are not so cute. Especially when baby selves are not getting their way. Then baby selves are not so cute at all.

"But why? Why not? Why? You have to give me a reason. Why not?" they goad us on.

WHO WITNESSES THE BABY SELF MOST OFTEN?

Another fact of human psychology well known to parents is that their mere presence is enough to bring out the baby self in their child.

Having stayed after school for extra help, Paula is with her algebra teacher, Mrs. Hendrickson.

"Well, Paula, I hope this extra time after school has helped you grasp what we have been doing in algebra."

"Oh, yes, Mrs. Hendrickson. Thank you. It's hard, but I think I'm getting it now. Thank you for staying after school to help me."

At that moment, Paula's mother appears in the classroom.

"Hi, dear. They said it would be okay if I came in to get you."

"Mom! Why are you in here? You weren't supposed to come in. I said I would meet you in the parking lot. Don't you ever listen to what I say? Mom! Really!"

My goodness, thinks Mrs. Hendrickson. *I've never seen this side of Paula.*

This phenomenon, of course, is true of how we relate not only to our children but also to our significant others.

"Dad, why do you always lose your temper with me and Mom and never with anybody else, except when you are playing golf?"

Just the presence of our nearest and dearest brings out the baby self in us.

Alex, for instance, is always a good sport. He never complains during his basketball games or at practices. But as soon as he is in the car with his father for the drive back home, he lets loose. His remarks follow a game where he scored two points in limited playing time.

"Coach P. is such an asshole. He gives Billy so much playing time, just because Coach P. is friends with his parents, and Billy sucks. And when I do get in and was open like today, that little dick, Clement, never passes. He just wants to shoot—and he can't shoot for shit. I'm going to quit basketball. I mean it." (Which he never does.)

Let me ask a question that might help put your reaction to your child's baby self in perspective: If it is good—even necessary—that there is a place for your teenager's baby self, and if the baby self can be babyish, childish, and even downright unpleasant at times, wouldn't you rather that your child's baby self rear its unruly head at home with you rather than when he is out with others in public? Of course, you don't have a choice because of the aforementioned psychological fact that whenever a parent is anywhere near their teenaged child, that child's baby self will appear. But if you did have a choice, wouldn't home be the better place for your child's baby self to hang out?

WHICH SELF IS YOUR CHILD'S REAL SELF?

There is another important question all of this stuff about baby selves and mature selves begs, and that is: Which of these two—the baby self (the one you get to see) or the mature self (the one others see, the one who has the same name as your kid and looks like her, but doesn't match your description in any other way)—is the better indicator of who your child really is? And, more important, which of these two is the better indicator of who that child will become as an adult?

Fortunately, with the vast majority of teenagers, the answer is the mature self. And there is very strong proof of this. By the end of high school—if not before—teenagers tend to change. They become nice—not just to everyone else, but even to you—and they go out into the world and become perfectly good citizens. This is what has already happened with well over a generation of back-talking teens, who now make up a large portion of the adult world. And that world continues pretty much as it always has. Contrary to parental worries, the world has not been, nor will it be, taken over by a horde of barbarians as a result of this parenting style.

And this change—from back-talking teen to more or less mature adult—comes about not because parents, in the home stretch of high school, just before the finish line, are finally able to shape up their surly teenager, as they imagine they will.

"It was a tough task but finally—just in time, let me tell you—we were able to shape Carlton up. We had to put in a full court press right at the end, but we did it."

Not at all. It happens because, as part of normal psychological development, teenagers move into the next major developmental stage: young adulthood. The good parenting that most parents do—but often do not realize they have been doing—kicks in. All the years of love, teaching, and, at times, being willing to set unpopular limits and make unpopular demands, bear fruit. Their mature side will prevail.

"Hello, I like you. I think you're a good parent. You always have been, even if at times crazed. Also, I just want you to know that I agree with you, I drive too fast and I'll try to control my speeding from now on. Also, if I spill something in the refrigerator, I'll make sure I thoroughly clean up the mess."

"You will?"

"Well, actually, I don't know if I can promise the part about cleaning up the messes in the refrigerator."

And all of this happens automatically as part of normal psychological development. It is not because on the last day of his son Barkley's adolescence, his father finally figured out the lecture that would do the trick.

"Listen here, Mister. If you think for one minute that you can keep behaving the way you do toward me and your mother, well,

think again, Buster! You will never be able to get married. You will never be able to hold down a job. Well, just think about that."

And Barkley, impressed by his father's words, says,

"Gosh, Dad. I feel bad for you and Mom. What you say makes complete sense. I only wish you had told me sooner so that I could have been better toward you two. Of course I'll change. You'll see. Thanks, Dad."

No, it is not because of that.

But if it is true that most teenagers—even pretty obnoxious ones—grow into good citizens who are friendly to you, what does that say about the often unpleasant baby-self behavior that you have to endure over the course of your child's adolescence?

For one, baby-self behavior does not necessarily mean that there is anything especially wrong with your child. Nor is there anything necessarily wrong with the way you have been parenting. Mainly, your teenager's unpleasant baby-self behavior is nothing more than that: unpleasant behavior comes out because at home and with you, he or she feels safe enough for that to happen.

"NEVER GIVE UP!": THE BABY SELF'S MOTTO

Fortunately, as mentioned earlier, there is something that you can do to significantly decrease the unpleasant back talk and fussing that you experience with your teenager. This relates directly to one overwhelming characteristic of baby selves: when a baby self is not getting its way, a baby self will say anything, do anything, to change that. But, failing to get its way, a baby self will go on and on forever. And I do mean forever.

"No. I'm sorry, Sarah. No, and that's final. Do you understand me? That is it."

"But why? You don't understand. Why not?"

"Sarah, we've already been over this. No, I'm sorry. No."

"But why? Why not?"

"Sarah!"

"But why not? You have to give me a good reason. It's because you hate me, isn't it?"

"Sarah, that's ridiculous, I don't hate you."
"Yes, you do. Then give me a good reason."
"Sarah, I've given you a good reason."
"No, you haven't. All you've given me is a stupid reason."
"Sarah, I do not want to hear any more about it."
"But why not? Why?"

And should Sarah's mother go into another room, Sarah and her baby self would follow. Even if Sarah's mother put a closed and locked door between herself and her daughter, that wouldn't stop the pleas from coming.

"But why not? Why? Why not? Mom, are you listening to me? Can you hear me? Why not? Mom!"

When baby selves are not getting their way, they do not let go. It's as if they cannot move forward. They are stuck. They just hold on. They simply won't relent. What baby selves abhor beyond anything else is to separate, to disengage. When baby selves are not getting their way, they cannot let go.

This, more than anything else, is the basis of most of the advice in this book.

You cannot say *"Stop. Shut up. That's it. Finis. Enough, and I mean it. This is going to end—now. I mean it. Finis"* to a baby self who is not getting her way and seriously expect her to back off.

It is not going to happen.

And, of course, if we let it, the baby self who will not quit will ultimately bring out our own baby self, who will not let go either.

Here's a perfect example of such an exchange between a father and his teenaged daughter:

"Don't you dare talk to me that way, young lady."
"I'll talk to you any way I want."
"You just better watch it."
"What are you going to do, hit me? You would like that."
"You're just going to have to control your mouth before somebody does smack you."
"You're just mad because you can't control me anymore."
"You're going to have to learn to respect adults. How do you think you're ever going to make it in the world with a mouth like that?"

"I'm going to do fine. I certainly don't need your fucking approval."

"You are really pushing it."

"You're pushing it."

There you have it: two baby selves in action, and neither is anywhere close to letting go.

So what does this fact about baby selves say about parenting teenagers? What it says is that when going against your teenage child's wishes, the greatest wisdom is to say what you have to say, do what you have to do, and then stop—because they will not. An overwhelmingly valuable skill in the parenting of today's teenagers is learning to disengage—sooner rather than later.

ADOLESCENCE: A NECESSARY STAGE

Before talking any further about how to deal with your teenager, it is extremely useful to understand that much of your child's behavior is the direct result of a powerful and inevitable developmental phenomenon: the advent of adolescence. Much of your child's defiant behavior with you is not about their reaction to you personally, but rather it's about the nature of adolescence itself. It is also not something that you can change. But fortunately it is something that does end, albeit in its own time when it is good and ready and has run its course. Not a moment before.

Adolescence is the convergence of a number of major developmental changes within a relatively short period of time. Teenagers begin to inhabit new bodies. They do not just get bigger, but with the advent of their secondary sex characteristics—developing breasts and hips with girls, losing baby fat and growing new body hair with boys—they rather swiftly take on a much more adult look. If a teenager you know but have not seen for a few months goes through a growth spurt, you'll probably recognize the phenomenon before you'll even recognize the teen. It is very striking.

"Who is this person? Randy, are you you?"

"Yeah? What? Why?"

With their new bodies, teenagers suddenly become far more aware of and far more self-conscious about how they look.

Prior to adolescence, a ten-year-old boy confronting a mirror would likely prompt this exchange:

> *"What is that thing called?"*
> *"It's a mirror, sweetheart."*
> *"Oh, I never noticed it before. What is it used for?"*

But once he becomes an adolescent, this same boy knows very well what a mirror is for.

> *"Omigod, I think my nose turns a little to the left. Mom! Does my nose turn a little to the left?"*
> *"Your nose looks like your nose."*
> *"Mom, I'm serious!"*
> *"I can't see anything. It doesn't look like it turns either way. It's fine."*
> *"No, Mom, look at it!"*

They are very serious.

Another change among adolescents is that they not only get smarter but they also make whole new cognitive advances that enable them to understand things in a much more adult way. Suddenly you have to watch what you say because what used to go right over their heads is now something they pick up on far more readily.

> *"Aunt Theresa sure has had a lot of boyfriends since her divorce from Uncle Ed. Is she a slut?"*
> *"Lainie, don't use that word."*
> *"So she is?"*

The third and most dramatic change of all is that they develop sexuality. They now not only have the ability to reproduce, but they also have sexual feelings in a way that they simply did not before. Their world is transformed. Much of what was neutral to them now becomes sexualized. This new dimension makes everything in their lives forever different. This is a very big change indeed.

"Dad, why do they call it a breast of chicken. That's so weird."

"I don't know, Lawrence. I never thought about it. That's what they call it."

"It doesn't look like a breast. It doesn't have nipples."

"That's enough, Lawrence."

"It feels weird touching it if it's a breast."

"That's enough, Lawrence."

THE ALLERGY ALL TEENS DEVELOP

There is one last change—a purely psychological one—that warrants discussion before we move on. It's a change that, more than anything else, determines why adolescents act as they do, and especially why they act as they do with their parents. That change—a part of normal human development—is the adolescent mandate: *I must see myself as an independent, adultlike being. It is no longer acceptable for me to experience myself as a dependent little kid.*

The advent of this mandate makes sense, because in just a few years they will have to be out on their own, where they will not be successful if they still feel like dependent little children. This need to see oneself as an independent, adultlike entity is fine. It is necessary. But there is just one problem with it: up until this time there was this person or persons for whom they had strong love, attachment, and dependency feelings— namely, their parent or parents. But now those strong love, attachment, and dependency feelings make them feel like a dependent little kid. And that is no longer okay. In fact, it is a big problem. The result is what we recognize as adolescence.

The following example illustrates the point:

Fifteen-year-old James is sitting by himself on a couch in the family room watching television. He is very relaxed until his mother, who says nothing, enters the room. Immediately his body tenses. He is no longer relaxed. He starts moving around nervously on the couch. *I thought maybe I left my glasses in here, but I guess I didn't*, his mom thinks as she turns and leaves the room.

James immediately goes back to being relaxed. He'd have the very same reaction in any similar circumstance where he is alone in a room that his mother enters. She comes in, he's agitated. She leaves, he's back to being relaxed.

This is not a conscious process. His mother's mere presence brings out in James the strong love, attachment, dependency feelings that he has always had toward her. Previously these feelings were not an issue: he loved his mother. He still does. But now, as part of the normal, newly arisen adolescent mandate, all of this is no longer okay.

His mother's appearance in the room creates inside of James an internal conflict, a very real physical tension. And this is true for both boys and girls. Just the presence of a parent creates this tangible discomfort. Were we to watch through a one-way mirror, we would see: parent not there; child in relaxed state. Parent there; child feeling tense and fidgety.

But let's say that in this particular instance, James's mother does an even worse thing: after entering the room, James's mother fails to leave quickly. And not only does she stay, but she speaks too. She says her son's name.

> *"James."*
> *"What?"* he says in an aggravated tone of voice.
> *"Don't talk to me in that tone of voice."*
> *"What tone of voice?"*
> *"That tone of voice."*
> *"I'm not talking in a tone of voice."*

But he is. And they go on from there. Why is he being so rude? After all, his mother was only saying his name. Again, it is not intentional on James's part. His mother's coming into the room had made him quite tense. But now she's not only in the room, she's *staying* in the room. And not only is she staying in the room, but now she is actually speaking to him! Under such trying circumstances, under such considerable stress, it is very hard to speak in anything other than a tense, unpleasant-sounding manner.

> *"You speak to me as if you don't even think I'm human."*
> *"I am too speaking to you like you're human."*

But—like I said—he's not.

Now let me turn this incident into an outright horror story. Let's say that on this particular occasion, James's mother decides that she is going to have some quality mother-and-son time. And so, after entering the room, she goes over to the couch and sits down next to her beloved son. What's worse, she puts her arm around him. This, as we know by now, is just too much for poor James. He gets up and leaves. His mother is heartbroken. She's devastated. She feels so rejected. She was just reaching out to her darling son. What had she done wrong?

For an answer, let us go back in time to when James was ten years old. As in the scene just described, James's mother comes into the room and sits down next to her son. And, as above, she puts her arm around him. But this time he is just ten. And, as a ten-year-old, James is quite relaxed. He likes his mother sitting next to him. In fact, at ten years old *he* might well have been the one to initiate the closeness, putting his head on his mother's shoulder before she motioned to do so.

And let's say—as more often than not is the case—in the intervening years between James at ten and James at fifteen, James's mother had not done anything especially wrong. She had been a good mother. She had not made any major parenting mistakes. What happened to change this loving ten-year-old child into a fifteen-year-old who literally could not stand being in the same room as his mother?

The answer, of course, is the dawning of adolescence. As part of their normal development process, the vast majority of teenagers develop a temporary allergy to their parents.

Everything about their parents aggravates them.

"Dad, do you have to breathe that way?"

And the child's poor father, who had previously paid no attention to his breathing, is self-conscious about it for the rest of his life.

Your tone of voice, which had always been a source of reassurance and pleasure, now seems infinitely irritating.

"Mom, do you have to talk that way?"
"What way?"
"The way you do. Can't you talk some other way that isn't so irritating?"
"But it's the way I've always talked my whole life."
"Well, can't you change it?"
"But it's the way I talk."
"See, there it is. The way you just talked. It gets on my nerves."

And, as discussed earlier, just your being there is a problem.

"Must you?"
"What?"
"Be here."

Finally, one of the most difficult things all parents of teenagers swiftly learn is that their child considers just being seen with them in public to be the ultimate humiliation.

Leanna and her mother are at the mall.

"Pretend you don't know me."
"What?"
"I just saw Jessica and Kimmy go into that store. Pretend you don't know me."
"But I'm your mother."
"Omigod, I'm going to have to hide. I'll see you later. This is so humiliating."

They are allergic to you. It is the quintessential adolescent dilemma. What are they supposed to do about all the unacceptable love, attachment, and dependency feelings that are created just by your very existence, let alone your presence? Especially when other people see it too?

There are two classic teenage solutions—one preferred by boys, the other by girls.

The boys' way involves absence. They simply choose not to be there. They're out of the house or in their room with the door closed. And when they are there, they are evasive or they mumble. They're as invisible as they can be even though they're present.

"Michael, did you put your dirty clothes in with the laundry?"
"Mmbf."
"I didn't understand you. Did you put your dirty clothes in with the laundry?"
"I don't know."
"What do you mean you don't know? Michael? Where'd he go? He was standing right here. Michael?"

The boys' solution to the unacceptable love, attachment, and dependency feelings they have toward their parents is simple—they create as much distance as possible. In their room. Out of the house. And even when they are with you, they are as uncommunicative as they can be. It is very much like a wall going up.

The girls' way, by contrast, involves combativeness. It's as if they are telling themselves, *Anything you say I will disagree with or yell at. And in regard to your irritating presence, I will regularly let you know how irritating it is.*

> *"Renee, did you put your dirty clothes in the laundry?"*
> *"Why do you always have to be at me about stuff when I'm in the middle of doing something?"*
> *"But you're not doing anything."*
> *"I am too! Just because it doesn't look like it. That is so rude! Everything has to be when you want it. You are so inconsiderate of anything that is going on in my life! The whole world does not revolve around your convenience."*
> *"Revolve around my convenience?"*
> *"What? Are you implying something? Are you saying I'm inconsiderate? What do you mean?"*

If you are a girl you deal with unacceptable love, attachment, and dependency feelings toward your parents by simply declaring your independence moment by moment and by doing it in their face. *"What do you mean? Are you criticizing me? You are the most difficult mother in the world!"*

What can be so maddening is that with many teens this allergy seems to wax and wane. Some of the time—perhaps because they are temporarily feeling a little more secure about themselves, about their own independence or about their own integrity—they seem to tolerate, maybe even like, being with you.

> *"See, Mom? Isn't this nice? Just you and me talking? We should do more of this."*
> *"We should?"*

But it is truly unpredictable. It comes and goes.

"Renee, what do you think would be nice for supper?"
"What? I don't care. Why ask me? Whatever you make, I'm probably not going to like it."

It leaves you questioning yourself time and again. *She was so nice ten minutes ago. What did I do?*

"I thought we were friends."
"Why would I want to be friends with you?"

Like I said, it comes and goes.

REMEMBER NOT TO TAKE IT PERSONALLY

To keep your sanity, just remember this: it is not personal. It is adolescence. It is part of normal psychological development. Much of the time, the person your child is responding to is not you at all but a projection of you that comes from deep inside of themselves: an image of you as the parent who won't let them go—even though it is they who can't let go of you! The parent who is so much a part of them, they wish they could expel you from inside of themselves. The parent who, simply by existing, makes them feel like a little kid.

"Mom, omigod, there's that look that you have. It is so annoying. If you only knew! Why are you looking at me?"
"Actually, I was looking at the lamp."
"Yeah, right."

But take heart, sooner or later adolescence ends. As part of normal psychological development, your teen will move into the next major developmental stage. They will become young adults. During their adolescence, they will have gotten genuine psychological distance from you. You no longer compromise their sense of psychological independence. The adolescent allergy evaporates. They become nice again.

"Hello. What's for supper? Mom, you're hair looks nice."
"Renee, is that you?"

"What are you talking about?"
"You're friendly, my darling."

It can seem like a miracle. But it's not. While adolescence is incurable—there really is nothing you can do to change it—it does pass with time.

I imagine that about now you are asking yourselves the obvious question: *"So if back talk is inevitable, allergies to me and my spouse are to be expected, and my kids will likely grow up to be good, productive citizens despite this phase of 'normal' development, how do I cope in the meantime?"*

For starters, you have to treat adolescence like a cold—or any other illness that has to run its course. You must do your best to reduce the symptoms. As you will read in the following pages, the key to having a more pleasant time with your teenage child largely rests in learning the skill of disengagement.

Let me get right down to it with a discussion of that most basic of all parent-child interactions: saying "No."

One

THE IMPORTANCE OF SAYING "NO"

Saying "no" sounds so easy, right?

> *"Mom, can I have thirty-four dollars? Please?"*
> *"No, I'm sorry, dear."*
> *"Oh, okay."*

> *"Dad, would you drive me to the store right now?"*
> *"No, I'm sorry, son, I'm busy."*
> *"Oh, okay."*

> *"Mom, can I stay out until two-thirty in the morning on Saturday?"*
> *"No, that's way too late."*
> *"Oh, okay."*

If only it were that simple. But sadly, a parent's first attempts at saying "no" usually go more like this:

"Dad, I need ninety-two dollars for a new pair of sneakers. The ones I'm wearing are falling apart and don't fit right anymore."

"No. I'm sorry, Liam, we just got you a new pair two months ago, and those look fine to me. And, besides, ninety-two dollars is a lot to spend on a pair of sneakers."

"You don't understand. The ones I have are totally geeky and don't fit. How can you know whether they fit or not? You're not the one who's wearing them!"

"No, I'm sorry, we don't have the money right now. I'm not going to give you ninety-two dollars for sneakers."

"You don't have money to buy your son a pair of shoes when his are falling apart?"

"Liam, your sneakers are not falling apart."

"You don't understand what it's like to have to wear these stupid sneakers to school every day, and they are falling apart! It's really embarrassing! The truth is that you're too cheap, and you're being unreasonable!"

"I'm not being unreasonable. You don't need new sneakers."

"You are being unreasonable. You don't understand. I can't wear these sneakers to school. They are too dorky. I'm embarrassed to let my friends see them."

"Your sneakers look fine."

"No, they don't! You think they do because you don't know anything. You don't even remember what it was like when you were a kid!"

"Liam, what I remember or not has nothing to do with getting you ninety-two-dollar sneakers."

"Yeah, it does, because you don't know anything!"

"Liam, don't you talk to me that way."

"I will if you're being a jerk, which you are!"

WHY SAYING "NO" IS SO DIFFICULT

The difficulty with "no" is that, with today's teenagers, the conversation never ends with an easy "okay" the way it might have years ago. Instead, your "no" unleashes a flood of words and emotions that is so unpleasant and continues over such an extended period that it completely drains your time and energy. Saying "no" is definitely the most difficult and taxing part of being the parent of a teenager. But it *is* one of the most important parts, despite what your kid tells you.

"Saying 'no' is so difficult for my parents because it means they have to be difficult with me, which they wouldn't have to be if they were just reasonable sometimes, which they're not. And if they didn't treat me like a six-year-old, which they do, and which they wish I still was but—excuse me for living, I hate to disappoint them—I'm not."

Teens Argue

Once you have said "no" to a teenager, whatever you may say subsequent to that "no" really doesn't matter all that much. The only thing your teenager hears is whether or not the "no" still stands. As long as you continue the conversation, all of their words following your "no" are going to be about trying to change your "no" to a "yes."

> *"No. I'm sorry, Liam, we just got you a new pair two months ago, and those look fine to me. And, besides, ninety-two dollars is a lot to spend on a pair of sneakers."*
>
> **Hmm,** thinks Liam, *Dad has given three different reasons for his "no." Let me think: Which reason is the best one to start with? Or maybe I should use a completely different strategy of attack. Hmm. Let me think.*

Of course, this all happens within a split second.

Don't be fooled; they are not interested in weighing the pros and cons from your perspective in order to come to the most reasonable conclusion. They are not interested in understanding your reasons for the "no" other than as starting points for their arguments. Nor do they care whether a particular "no" is fair or not. To them, all "nos" are unfair. Period.

"What's your point? If my dad was ever fair I would be the first to admit it. But since he never is fair, not once, I don't understand what it is that you are trying to say."

What this means is that you cannot expect to deliver a "no" and then get them to understand. You cannot say "no" and then say words that are somehow going to make your "no" palatable to them. It's not going to happen.

As I said, you're not likely to hear your kid reply, *"I hate to admit it, Dad, but now that you've really explained it to me, I see where you're coming from. I wish I could get cooler sneakers, but I know money is tight. I'm really disappointed, but I understand that I'll have to accept it. Actually, my current sneakers are perfectly comfortable. I lied about that."*

After delivering a "no," never expect that your words are going to convince your teen or are going to produce a reasonable, amicable resolution.

Once Liam's dad says, "No," Liam proceeds to do what any good future lawyer would do—he begins looking for only the points in his father's case that he can best refute with a good counterargument.

I know what I'll do: I think maybe my best strategy is to follow up on my first point about my sneakers not fitting. None of the reasons that Dad gave can really refute that. Yes, that's where I'll start.

Teens are superb litigators. Their brains are very good, very fast, often swifter than our own; what gives them an immediate advantage over us in any argument is that they are not bound whatsoever by the truth. *"You don't notice it, Dad, but the truth (which it totally is not) is that the sneaker for my right foot hurts all along the outside when I wear it. I actually limp sometimes, but I compensate so you don't see it too much."*

A basic adolescent arguing tactic, well known to the parent of any teen, is the way that, in a remarkably short period of time following a "no," you find yourself caught up in a quagmire of side issues, defending a full range of points that hadn't been part of the original discussion at all. Now you're on the defensive, confronting one new argument after another as to why your "no" is thoroughly unacceptable—and criminal as well.

> *"Dad, you say I can't go to the concert. Let me ask you a serious question. Why is it that you literally seem to want to ruin my life? It's not my fault that you were unpopular as a teenager and can't stand it that I might actually have a nice time occasionally. You always say how you weren't so lucky? But I think you're jealous. That's why you say 'no' so much. You don't like that I should have a really good time. It's not right that I should have to pay for your bad memories about your adolescence."*
> *"What are you talking about?"*
> *"I'm talking about how I'm paying for your crappy adolescence."*

Teens Never Give Up

But it is not a teen's skill or "sliminess" in arguing (and by *sliminess* I mean they don't have to believe at all what they are saying) that presents the number one challenge with saying "no."

Let's say that, for all of Liam's arguments and counterarguments, for all of his clever ploys, his father does not change his mind. He stands firm and says, "No, I am sorry, Liam. I'm not going to give you the money for the sneakers," Liam will very likely fall back on what kids always fall back on when confronted with a "no"—the most powerful weapon in their arsenal: sheer, unrelenting, mind-numbing persistence.

"But why not? Why not? Why not? You haven't given a reason. Why not? Why not? You've only given sucky reasons. You have to give a reason. Dad! Dad! Why not? Why not? Dad, you're being a dick. Why not? Dad! Why not?"

Obviously this is an exaggeration, but it is not really that much of an exaggeration. Actually it's not an exaggeration at all. It's an abbreviation. Liam would go on far longer than what I described above. Suffice it to say, teens on the losing end of an argument can go on for a very long time.

As I said before, teens in an argument never quit. Let me give you a different example. This one involves Olivia and her mother.

It's Tuesday night at around 7:22 P.M.:

> *"Mom, can I go over to Lydia's for a sleepover Friday night?"*
>
> *"No, I'm sorry, dear, I'm just not comfortable with you and your friends and a sleepover."*
>
> *"But why not?"*
>
> *"I know you guys mean well, but sometimes when all of you get together, what happens is that the whole gets to be more than the sum of the parts."*
>
> *"What the hell is that supposed to mean? That's the stupidest thing I have ever heard. The sum of the parts?"*
>
> *"Don't get fresh with me, Olivia."*
>
> *"Well, what am I supposed to do if you are being completely unreasonable and treating me like a six-year-old? You don't trust me. You always think we're going to end up doing something. That somehow I'm going to end up having sex with some boy, even if there aren't going to be any boys there."*

"That's not true, Olivia."

"Yeah, it is true! I have a crazy person for a mother. My life is a wreck ever since you married Randall! It wasn't my idea for you to marry him."

"No, Olivia, you cannot go to the sleepover. That is it."

Later that night, at 8:14 P.M.:
Olivia's mother has just gotten off the phone with a friend. Enter Olivia.

"But, Mom, that is so unfair! Nothing bad is going to happen. It's not my fault you have sex on the brain! Nothing is going to happen! I promise nothing bad will happen. Nothing bad will happen!"

"No, Olivia. And I mean it."

At 9:08 P.M. that same night:
Olivia's mother is brushing her teeth. Enter Olivia.

"Mom, I just talked to Lydia, and she said that her mother said that she was really comfortable with the sleepover. She didn't understand what you were worried about. What are you afraid we're going to do? Mom, it is so unfair!"

"Olivia, no! No, and I'm not going to change my mind. No, and that settles it. No. I do not want to hear any more about it. The answer is NO! Got that? NO!"

But since the sleepover is not until Friday night, Olivia continues the debate well into the next day.
Wednesday at 5:15 P.M.:
Olivia's mother is coming home from work. As she enters the house, she is greeted by her daughter.

"But, Mom, our whole group is going. I just can't not go, Mom!"

"Olivia, what do I have to say to make you understand?"

"You could say yes."

My point in relaying this story, of course, is that even if your answer is a "no" whose prohibition extends into the future, and even if your initial "no" was incredibly firm and clear, you will hear more about it from your child as long as the "no" is still relevant to them.

Teens Rage

We've already covered the subject of most teenagers' great debating skills and their extraordinary persistence. But there are two last major weapons—sheer passion and energy—that will be easily recognized by most parents as part of the teen armory. In fact, outrage, pulled up from the very center of their being, accessible at the drop of a hat and able to accelerate from zero to 60 mph in just under a second, is among their favorite tools.

"No, Tanya, I'm sorry."
"But what do you mean, 'no'? You can't! You can't say 'no'! You can't!"
"That's what I just did, Tanya."
"But you can't! You don't understand! You can't! You are so mean! I can't believe you're saying this! You are such a bitch! I can't believe you! You are such a bitch! You're a bitch! That's what you are! You're a bitch! You can't do this!"

All of which Tanya is screaming at her mother.

When not getting their way, teenagers can bring forth a vast reservoir of emotional intensity with amazing speed and force. Being on the receiving end of this deluge can be extremely overwhelming and draining, to say the least.

What can make all of the above even more maddening is that, shortly after such a huge outburst—one that leaves you shaking and exhausted for the rest of the day—many teenagers seem to be fine. They go on about their business, oblivious to what had just taken place between you and them only a disconcertingly short time later.

"What's for supper?"
"What do you mean, 'what's for supper?'"
"Just what I said, 'What are we having for supper?' I really hope it has nothing to do with ground beef."
"How can you be asking me what's for supper?"
"Because I'm hungry. Is there a problem with that?"

They really don't get it. Were someone to mention, *"You just had a major fit at your mother. You were really mad and upset. You were screaming at her. Don't you remember?"* The reply would be, *"Yeah, I remember. She was being a bitch then. I was mad at her, which I should have been because she was being a bitch. But I'm not mad now, I'm hungry. Is that a problem?"*

WHY YOU SHOULDN'T CAVE IN

When dealing with your teenage child, you want to be able to say "no" and have it hold up. You want to be able to say "no" without always getting into a huge battle. But to do so is not easy. Kids bring a stockpile of weapons to the discussion. Perfecting a strong "no" is essential. You need to develop one with some real force behind it. The number one mistake in parenting a teenager—a mistake that you will keep paying for—is allowing them to wear you down too often. Sometimes, despite your greatest efforts, it will happen. You're human. It is not a big problem if it is the exception rather than the rule. But if their persistence bears fruit too regularly, if you do cave in and your "no" becomes a "yes" too frequently, it will truly become a disaster. Because under those circumstances your child will learn the following terrible lesson: *If I'm fussing and I'm not getting my way, and I keep on fussing and I'm still not getting my way, what that means is that I haven't been fussing long or hard enough—so I better redouble my efforts at fussing.*

If they learn that they can wear you down, they will keep doing it. And they won't see anything wrong with their behavior either.

"Well, duh, what am I supposed to do if my mom isn't giving in and it's so completely unfair and she absolutely never listens to me? You tell me I shouldn't stand up for myself?"

If they learn that they can wear you down, you are guaranteed huge quantities of fussing from now until the end of adolescence and perhaps longer. The biggest danger in relenting is that they will be the ones running the show from now on, not you. They will control where the lines are drawn. And that simply is not acceptable.

"How can you let her . . . ?" We can hear the voices of others already. They are shocked at what is going on.

"Well, I didn't exactly let her. You sort of have to go through it to understand."

Fortunately, it is not a lost cause. There are rules that can significantly help with this most difficult of all teenage parenting tasks. But be forewarned, there is nothing I can advise—especially if you are possessed of a particularly willful teenager—that guarantees saying "no" will always be easy.

STATING YOUR CASE

Although your kids may not always act maturely, you still want to deal with them in as adult a fashion as possible. This is not always easy, but remaining respectful of each other is always the goal.

To start, say "no" and state your reason. They will always want to know why, and they deserve an explanation, which should be as short and as honest as possible.

> *"Mom, can I get a new quilt for my bed?"*
> *"No, I'm sorry, Molly. I think the one you have is perfectly good and quilts are not cheap. I'm sorry, no."*

Of course, do not expect that with your "no" and your reason, that will be the end of it.

> *"But, Mom, my old one is all ratty and falling apart. It's the same one I've had since fourth grade."*
> *"No, I'm sorry, Molly, you're just going to have to make do with the one you have. Besides, it's not that bad."*

It is very important that you then listen to what they have to say. You should always give them that respect. It is their right. They experience not listening as a put-down, and that immediately places a great barrier between the two of you. Listening—at least initially—to what they have to say is important. The next step, of course, is to try to determine whether their argument is reasonable.

> *"But I have a really bad headache today! I can't be expected to have to deal with this kind of disappointment on top of my really bad headache. It's so unfair!"*

However one-sided, emotional, or illogical their argument may be, you still want to give them the respect of letting them know that you did hear them. But then you want to move on.

"I'm sorry you have a headache. But, no, we're not getting a new quilt."

"But I have a headache. It's really bad! You can't say no about the quilt! I can feel my headache getting worse!"

"No, I'm sorry, Molly."

But let's say, in this case, Molly presents arguments that do have some merit.

"Mom, you're wrong; the quilt is that bad. Wait a minute. Stay right where you are."

"What? Where are you going?"

"Just stay. I'll be back in a second."

And Molly runs to her room, grabs her quilt off her bed, and returns to her mother.

"Look at it! Look!"

Molly points to a number of holes in the quilt where the stuffing is coming out, and indeed the whole of the quilt's outer fabric has worn down and is now quite thin.

"Mom, Mom. Listen to me. I saw this really nice quilt at For Bed and Bath that was on sale, and was really affordable. I'm not just saying I need a new quilt because I'm a spoiled brat. I really do need a new quilt!"

And let's say in this particular instance Molly's mother, looking at the quilt, is no longer so certain. She thinks, *Molly's right. It does look pretty ratty. I don't know how long it will be before it just falls apart.*

"How much was the quilt at For Bed and Bath?"

"Sixty-nine dollars."

"I guess we can afford it. We could go over there maybe this weekend."

"Thank you, Mom. Thank you. You're the best mom!"

Is it okay that Molly was able to argue with her mother and ultimately change her mother's mind? Absolutely yes. It is excellent to sometimes change your mind in response to what your teenager has to say. It sends two very good messages. First, it says that not only do you listen to your kids, but that you also give genuine weight and consideration to their words. You don't just hear what they are saying, but you think about it too. You are extending genuine respect. And *that* is a very big deal.

Second, you are letting your child know that you can be flexible. You are not someone who, once you get an idea in your head, will refuse to change it. You are not totally rigid. In response, Molly is likely to think, *Mom is flexible. She isn't a total jerk—only about almost everything else. But she's not a complete jerk.*

ENDING THE CONVERSATION

Listening, as we have just seen, is good. In fact, it's not just good, it's essential. Discussion—a true back-and-forth dialogue—is also good. Arguments and counterarguments, however, are only good to a point. Let me ask a question: How many parents of current teenagers have ever experienced a scene similar to the one described below?

Serena did not want to go to her grandparents' home for the weekend while her parents were away. She wanted to be able to stay at home by herself. She argued vehemently with her father, but he was just too uncomfortable with the idea of Serena being alone at the house while they were gone.

> *"But nothing will happen! When have I gotten into big trouble? When have I shown really poor judgment? I can call Grandpa and Nene if there is a problem."*

> Try as she might, Serena was unable to sway her father. And her father was unable to sway her.

> *"It's not you I don't trust. But other kids will know you're home alone, and that is just too much of a temptation."*

They went back and forth for a while, Serena giving her objections, her father responding until gradually, Serena's arguing began to take on a less strident tone. Her father's words were starting to get through. His reasons as to why he was so uncomfortable with Serena staying home alone began to look increasingly hard to refute. From Serena's standpoint, he *was* actually making a lot of sense. Until finally—a good thirty minutes after the argument had begun—Serena relented.

"I guess I see where you're coming from. I understand. I hate to admit it, but like you say, 'You can't always get what you want.' I guess I'll just have to accept it. I don't like it, just for the record. But thanks for at least hearing me. I'll get over it. It's not the end of the world."

It's probably safe to say that none of you have ever had such good luck. It's just not possible. This has to be a pretend story. Nothing like this happens in the real world.

"I see where you're coming from?" I don't think so. The real response would be more like:

"I can't believe this! Dad, I don't want to hurt your feelings, but your parents are the most boring people in the world. I will actually die if I have to spend three days in the house with them. I will actually die!"

"Serena, I am so fed up with your not accepting anything when it's not the way you want it. You have no idea how lucky you are. Your mother and I—for once—just want to go away. But you have to make everything difficult. Maybe you could think of somebody besides yourself for a change. You are impossible. Impossible."

"You're impossible!"

As the *real* example above illustrates, when delivering "no" to a teenager, genuine, respectful listening is required. It is good, useful, and necessary to engage in a true discussion and weigh what a teenager says against your own reasons for saying no. But carrying the conversation past a certain amount of reasonable back-and-forth rapidly diminishes the value of that discussion. Past a certain threshold, I guarantee that meaningful discussion will just turn into unremitting case pleading.

"But, Dad, you aren't getting it. I cannot be there for three days. That is not a viable plan. Grandpa and Nene watch Wheel of Fortune *reruns. It is not an appropriate environment for a teenager."*

The rule is simple. After presenting a "no," listen, discuss, change your mind if you feel so inclined. But if you are not going to change your mind, disengage. End of story. It is the only safe way out.

So how do you know when it is time to end? How can you recognize that point where reasonable discussion has switched over to case pleading, which will only lead to escalating anger on both sides? How can you anticipate that moment when the balance will start to tip? The answer is simple—let your blood pressure be your guide. I say this in all seriousness. As you well know if you are the parent of a teenager, pretty early on in any "no" discussion, there is a point where you clearly feel a rush of anger building—a distinct increase in stress inside your body. You may not immediately notice it because you are immersed in the interaction with your child. But if you train yourself to be on the lookout for it, it is not very hard to recognize that point at which the discussion enters a clearly combative stage. That is when to disengage—and do so as swiftly as you can.

> *"No. I'm sorry, Serena, you are going to have to stay at Grandpa and Nene's."*
> *"But I can't! It's not fair! I will die! You have to trust me! You don't listen to a word I say. . . ."*

An important benefit of learning to disengage early is that you avoid the vicious cycle that ensues when you stay in an argument too long and both you and your teenager have built up a head of steam. The longer the back-and-forth goes on, the more difficult it becomes to disengage—and the more likely that what began as a discussion and progressed to an argument will become a full-scale blowup.

> *"Screw you! I'll run away for the weekend. Screw you! That's what I'll do. Screw you!"*
> *"You just better watch it, Serena."*
> *"No, you watch it! Screw you! I'm going to run away! Screw you!"*

DISENGAGING AND THE IMPORTANCE OF THE SOONER-RATHER-THAN-LATER RULE

So how exactly do you disengage? What are the techniques to best achieve safe disentanglement? They are very simple. Just shut up. Stop talking. Do not say anything else. Once Serena's father has decided that the discussion has entered the no-longer-useful zone, whatever Serena might then say— and Serena will say more—Serena's father should say nothing.

"Tell me just one time when you have ever trusted me to do anything! You never trust me! Never! Just tell me one time that you did!" she'll continue.

But no matter how hard she tries to bait him, Serena's father must not bite. The discussion is over.

If Serena's father wants, he may say one more time:

"I'm sorry, Serena, but you will have to go to your grandparents."

But that is it. The one big trap to avoid at this point is telling your child the conversation is over. Serena's father shouldn't tell Serena not to talk anymore.

"Serena, I do not want to hear any more about it."

The only thing that this statement is sure to accomplish is that Serena will say more—and will be a little angrier at her father for having told her to shut up. *Who the hell does he think he is telling me to shut up?*

"You don't want to hear any more about it because you know that you are being unfair and unreasonable!"

Serena's father needs to go. He needs to separate himself from his daughter.

"What are you doing? Where are you going? You still haven't given me a good reason! You can't make me stay at Grandpa and Nene's! Dad!"

No words exist to get Serena to be the one to back off. There are no words to make her stop pleading. Trust me when I tell you there are no words to make her disengage.

"That's it, Serena. I have had it. You just better watch it, young lady. You are starting to go too far. Not one more word. Do you hear me? Not one more word!"

The above would be a *big* mistake. It is Serena's father who has to be the one to stop. Once Serena's father has truly made up his mind, he needs to separate and exit. As fast as he can.

Bear in mind that even if he does disengage, Serena may well persist. She may be one of those tough ones whose baby selves just keep going and going like the Energizer bunny.

"Dad, you don't understand! Dad. Dad. You're not listening. Dad!"

Teens can get desperate in their persistence. So what do you do then? What if Serena keeps it up for half an hour? An hour? Many kids truly can go on for that long. Some parents have left the house just to get away from their unrelenting child. Threats of punishment—even when the threats are followed through—are surprisingly useless. As many parents discover, once teenagers get riled up and are deep into their baby selves, they could care less about consequences. The threats, if anything, only increase their raging.

The best advice I can offer for situations that seem unstoppable is: don't get back into the fray. Ride it out, as difficult as that may be. Ultimately your child will power down. But it can be a long and unpleasant experience. The reason that this is the best advice I can offer is simple: all other alternatives involve reengaging in some manner, which will only make matters worse. When teens are going at you, and at you, and at you like that, anything you do that might involve reengaging with them will only feed the flames. Also, standing firm instead of engaging—even under such relentless attack—sends the best message of all: *no matter how much fussing you do, I will not change my mind. Regardless of how long you go on, you will not be able to get me to reengage. It will not happen.*

Of course, the inevitable question parents have is: *What if they start making sense? What if you had initially said no, but then your child's persuasive arguments have caused you to be less certain, have caused you to question whether maybe they're right?* I assure you, this is not a problem. You always have an acceptable option.

> "I will think about it."
> "You will think about it? What's that supposed to mean? How long is that going to take? What am I supposed to do while you think about it? Am I just supposed to stand here and wait?"
> "I said I would think about it."
> It is a perfectly good response. It's the truth—you're not sure. It gives you time to give it more thought. But, most important, it lets them know that you are now ending the discussion.
> "I will think about it."
> For now, that's it.
> "I'm standing here. Have you decided yet?"
> "I said I would think about it."

REMAINING CONSISTENT

As I have said before, the biggest single day-to-day challenge in parenting a teenager is dealing with their ongoing attempts to wear you down, to bully you into changing your mind, to reverse your "nos." Sometimes they will succeed. Despite your best efforts you will occasionally cave in and allow something completely opposite to your intentions. But a single occurrence is not a disaster. It only becomes one if relenting happens too regularly. Then it is definitely a problem. A big problem. So if you are going to have a "no" that consistently works, you need to stand by your "nos." You have to be willing to see them through to the end.

While some teenagers are easier than others, there are those out there who need to hear tons of "nos" and who still launch a major battle with each one. If yours is such a child, you will have to pick and choose your battles carefully, so that the great majority of the time you will be able to see them through. There are, of course, teens for whom constantly saying "no" and battling over everything just does not work. When dealing with those teens, there are two basic rules that will help your "nos" remain effective over the long haul.

I should mention here that I have a little bit of a different take on that most revered bastion of good child rearing: consistency. My recommendation is that if, on a given day, you are not up to standing behind a particular "no," and you sense that in this particular instance your "no" is going to produce a protracted struggle, and if it is not about something really serious, you *can* choose to back off.

> *I've just had a really hard day. It doesn't have anything to do with Cameron, but I am stretched very thin. I am feeling totally frazzled, and I think that if anything else, even the slightest problem, comes along, I am going to totally lose it. I am just not up for a fight. Not today. I am just not up for it.*
>
> *"Mom, can I eat your special yogurt?" asks Cameron. "I'm really hungry."*
>
> *Of course he can't eat my special yogurt. This is the last one. I want to take it to work tomorrow—which he knows. I can get yogurt at work, but not this kind, which I like so much. But do you know what? If I say "no," he's going to start his pestering. I can tell.*

And I'm really not in the mood for it. I'm really, really not in the mood for it.

My advice under those circumstances is to let him have the yogurt.

After years of being told the exact opposite, I can just imagine your thoughts: *But doesn't that break all the rules of good child rearing? Everybody knows that children won't respect rules unless you're going to be consistent about sticking to them. Isn't Cameron's mother undermining her own rule about her son's not eating her special yogurt? Don't rules have to be consistent? You can't just back down on a rule because you don't feel up for a fight. Doesn't that mean that Cameron now knows that it's open game on yogurt, that the "Do-not-eat-Mother's-special-yogurt" rule no longer stands?* My answer to all those questions is: not really.

Parents hear about the importance of consistency all the time. I understand. But I believe that consistency needs to be in the firmness of your "nos" rather than in the absoluteness of any given rule. What needs to remain consistent is not the notion that rules are unbreakable but that if you say "no"—and really mean it—"no" is consistently going to mean "no."

> *"You know what, Cameron? Today, for a special treat, yes, you can have my yogurt."*
>
> *"Gosh, thanks, Mom. Are you feeling okay? This is so weird."*

If his mother is someone who, most of the time, really means it when she says "no" and stands firm on that "no," then this one-time reversal of the rule will do absolutely no damage. Because her "no" really means "no" 99 percent of the time, the "Do-not-eat-Mother's-special-yogurt" rule will snap back into place the next time she's asked.

> *"Mom, can I eat your special yogurt?"*
>
> *"No, Cameron. You know I don't want you eating my special yogurt."*
>
> *"But you let me last time."*
>
> *"That was a one-time deal as a special treat. No, I don't want you eating my special yogurt."*
>
> *"Please, Mom."*
>
> *"No, Cameron."*

And if his mother says "no" in a way that Cameron recognizes from past experience really means "no," there will not be a problem.

"I still don't see why I can't eat the special yogurt."

But at that point Cameron, still grumbling, will leave.

PICKING YOUR BATTLES WITH EASY KIDS

Thankfully, seeing "no" through to the end is not so difficult with some kids. Such is the case with Leanna.

"No, Leanna, eleven P.M. is your curfew; after midnight is just too late."

"But, Mom, the movie that we're going to really doesn't get out until eleven-thirty. And I won't get dropped off until after midnight because that's how late it will be by the time Roxanne's mother will get me home. It's not my fault that the movie ends so late."

"No, I'm sorry, Leanna; my answer is still 'no.'"

In this case, Leanna might fuss for a while, there might be some continued back-and-forth, but Leanna's mother remains unwavering.

"No, Leanna, midnight is just too late."

Given her mother's consistent and firm nos, Leanna is feeling that she will get nowhere, gives up, and goes off to her room, mumbling to herself as she exits: *"Mom never lets me do anything that I want. This is so stupid. Other kids don't have to deal with anything like this. Why did I have to get stuck with a mother like her?"*

Maybe Leanna calls a friend or goes online and complains further about her miserable lot in life. Maybe she gets some sympathy too.

"I hate to say it, Leanna," writes her friend Jeanine, *"but I'm lucky to have my mom. You do have it tough. I would go crazy."*

"I do go crazy."

But gradually Leanna becomes less upset. Gradually she resigns herself to her bad deal, gets past it, and does not bring it up again. Her mother's "no" held up and without any protracted fussing from Leanna.

Really, from Leanna's mother's standpoint, her daughter was pretty easy.

It's true. She'll fuss some, but once I take a firm stand, Leanna usually doesn't give me too much trouble.

Not a big problem. Most of the time, if you truly stand behind your "nos," this is what will happen.

PICKING YOUR BATTLES WITH DIFFICULT KIDS

But let me change the story somewhat to illustrate the actions of a different type of child. Let's say Leanna isn't so easy at all. Let's say she's just the opposite. She has a temperament that varies significantly from my first version of Leanna. She's a real pistol. She always has lots of stuff going on. She breaks lots of rules. Or bends them when she's not breaking them. She's tough to deal with. She goes against whatever her mother wants, and she does not resign herself to the "nos" nearly as easily as the other version of Leanna did.

Let's say Leanna doesn't just want to extend her curfew so she can go out to a particular movie; let's say she wants to change the whole deal on curfews. She wants to extend her curfew for all Friday and Saturday nights from 11 P.M. to midnight. And let's say that at Leanna's current age—fifteen—her mother is just not comfortable with that. Leanna's mother absolutely does not want her daughter staying out past 11 P.M. on a regular basis. She just feels that staying out that late leaves her daughter far too vulnerable to getting into trouble.

> *"Mom."*
> *"What?"*
> *"I want to change my weekend curfew to midnight. Eleven P.M. sucks. I totally miss out on all the fun. You have to change my curfew."*

But let's also say that, within the same week that Leanna started her campaign to permanently change her weekend curfew, she also decided that she wanted to dye the front of her hair bright red. Her mother thought this would look ridiculous, make Leanna less attractive, and mark her as a weirdo at school—more than maybe she already is. Leanna's mother did not want her daughter to dye the front of her hair bright red.

Therein lies the real problem: when you have a child who is not so easy, you are forced to make difficult choices almost daily. If you have a teenager who constantly pushes limits, who constantly gets into battles with you, and who constantly brings considerable energy and persistence into each battle, you cannot possibly take each battle all the way to its end. It does not work because you simply do not have the strength or the energy to see each battle to its conclusion. Too often you will get worn down and end up giving in. Too often you will blow up, which can result in some really bad scenes. But worse, the constant battles will color your relationship with your child. It will make their teenage years a constant struggle. It will lead to massive ill will between you and your child. It is not good for her. It is not good for you.

Leanna will think, *I hate my mom. It would be really nice if she were just friendly to me some of the time. But all we do is fight.*

Leanna's mother will secretly confess, "*I cringe when I come home and Leanna is there. What's it going to be this time? I never enjoy being with her because there is always some point of contention. It's always something. You cannot know how draining it is.*"

Leanna's mother has to make some choices. I would ask a parent in such a tough spot,

> "*How about her curfew? Would you consider letting her stay out later on weekends?*"
>
> "*No, absolutely not. I don't trust her. You don't know how much I worry just knowing she's out there. Even eleven P.M. is pushing it.*"
>
> "*How about dyeing the front of her hair red?*"
>
> "*No, she'll look like some kind of hippie tramp.*"
>
> "*Do you really feel that it's a serious problem if she were to dye the front of her hair red?*"
>
> "*Well, it's not exactly a gigantic problem. But, no, it makes her look too freaky—which is exactly what she wants. She'll be more isolated than she already is.*"

Parents of most teens—not just the wild ones—at different times during their child's adolescence do need to make some hard choices regarding what is important and what is *really* important.

A good working rule is to have two categories:

1. Those issues that I care about.

2. Those issues that I *really* care about.

Ask yourself: *Is this "no" really so important that I am willing to put considerable amounts of unpleasant time and effort into standing behind it—given that there are many other "nos" that I am also going to have to stand behind? Is this so important that I'd categorize it as a top priority?*

If the answer is yes, then you do want to see it through. If you are not so sure, then you have to think about whether it is worth the battle.

Some examples of "nos" that a parent might feel strongly about include:

"Can Dave (her boyfriend) *come over after school?"* (They will be alone in the house and her mother is certain they will have sex—which they will—and her mother is just not comfortable with that.)

"Can I buy that Bowie knife?" (During the previous year this boy had gotten into serious trouble bringing a small knife to school.)

"Can I go to Erin's? I can get a ride from Elisa's brother." (This is the same boy who, she mentioned just last week, has a drinking problem.)

Some examples of "nos" that parents might feel somewhat less strongly about include:

"Can I dye the front of my hair red?"

"Can we rent Zombie Death Party?"

"Can I move my bedtime back half an hour on weeknights?"

Again, if your "nos" are going to stand up, you need to be willing to see them through to the end. And for the "nos" you really care about to stick, you have to be careful that you don't have too many other "nos."

WHEN DEFEAT IS SNATCHED FROM THE JAWS OF VICTORY

Whenever you are saying "no" to your teen, it is crucial to remember that you are dealing with their baby self. And it is in the nature of baby selves—*all* baby selves—to hang on when not getting their way (consequences be damned). And not only do they hang on, but they also learn—by trial and error—the most effective techniques to invariably suck you back into the debate, even when you have successfully sought to disengage. In other words, they've discovered over time exactly how to push your buttons.

Emma and her mother were shopping at the mall. They were in JLaFlamme's, a trendy but expensive women's clothing store. Emma had seen a winter coat that she really liked, but it was very expensive. Too expensive. No way was her mother going to let Emma buy that coat. But Emma really liked the coat. After seeing the coat, she had fallen in love with it; her heart was set on getting it. And so she argued passionately, using every ploy, every entreaty that she could come up with. But to no avail. After she and her mother had gone on for quite a while, finally Emma's mother said,

"No, Emma, I am sorry. I know you really like that coat, but you can't get it. It is just too expensive."

Emma's mother said this in a tone that Emma well recognized. She knew from previous experience that this meant that no matter how much further Emma pushed, her mother would not relent. It was now, truly, the *end of discussion*. Nothing further that Emma could say was going to change that fact. And so Emma, both disheartened about not getting the coat that she deeply desired, and quite angry at her mother for refusing to allow her to get it, said in the most bitter tone she could muster,

"Forget it. Finish your shopping by yourself (her mother had one more store that she had planned to visit to look at curtain fabric). *I'll be at the coffee shop. Get me when you're done. I never get anything I want, do I? Not once!"*

Then Emma turned with the intention of walking over to the benches outside a coffee shop a little ways up the mall.

Let me say right here that, up until this point, Emma's mother had clearly achieved a brilliant victory. Since the last thing that a baby self ever wants to do is to separate, Emma's turning was an absolute indication that her mother had been a firm, strong parent. On the Olympic Parenting scale it was a perfect ten. A brilliant victory for Mom. But baby selves do not go down easily, as we all know by now—at least not without one last gasp. And so Emma, even as she turned to leave, in one last desperate attempt to reengage her mother, mumbled, *"Bitch."*

The best rule, should your child say something that you feel really does need to be addressed, is to wait until a later, neutral time. If Emma's mother still cares so much about what was said and still wants to deal with it, then at a later time she can say, *"I heard what you said this afternoon and I do not want you to talk to me again that way, ever."*

This is far better than picking up on it at the time, because to do so would almost certainly make things worse, not better.

But let us say that, in this particular instance, Emma's mother did not want to let it pass, did not want to wait until later, and so she said to her daughter, *"What did you say?"*

And—this is my whole point—Emma, even as she had turned to go, even as she was about to walk away, immediately upon hearing her mother's words, turned back toward her mother and said, still mumbling, *"I didn't say anything."*

But the baby self inside of her chortled with joy. *Yes!*

Emma's mother then said, *"Do not use that kind of language with me."*

But now, her baby self reengaged, Emma responded, *"I'll use any kind of language I want. In case you hadn't noticed, this is a free country."*

Now Emma's mother was lost. Emma had her. But Emma's mother plunged on. *"No, as long as you live in our house, under our roof, you will act and talk as we say."*

But of course teens have an answer for everything. *"Fine, I'll call Kendra on my cell. Her mother said I could live at their house. She can come over to our house to get me by the time we get home. Oh, by the way, is it okay if I come over tomorrow to get my stuff?"*

Like I said, they will have an answer for everything.

My point—and I do not back down from it—is that if your aim when you are saying "no" is to get the least possible fussing and back talk both at the time and overall, there is nothing—other than returning to the old days of fear and harsh punishment—that will come as close to being effective as what I am recommending. That is: swift disengagement.

To swiftly disengage is the parenting skill that can make the greatest single difference in dealing with a teenager.

It is a skill that must be learned, for it goes against our natural instinct not to respond to each new piece of obnoxiousness that screams to be responded to. But to do so is a mistake. These are skills that, if learned, reinforce themselves because they work. And it feels very adult. Far more so than the usual,

> *"Don't you dare talk to me that way!"*
> *"I will too!"*
> *"Oh, no you won't!"*
> *"Oh, yes I will!"*
> *"Oh, no you won't!"*
> *"Oh, yes I will!"*
> *"You're treading on dangerous territory."*
> *"You're treading on dangerous territory."*

What usually follows are threats of punishment that will or won't be followed up on. But either way, the parent comes away from the experience feeling as if they lost control, feeling badly about how they handled the situation, and feeling badly about themselves, having been through the wringer once again.

The main question I hear in response to what I am recommending—understandably—is, *"If I do not immediately respond to a particular shard of teenage disrespectfulness, won't my child feel as if they are getting away with it?"*

The answer is: absolutely not. The proof? Just try my approach and see how much they hate for the power to rest in your hands.

"You're not listening to me! You have to listen to me!"

You can actually feel their desperation. They will pursue you, trying to get you to respond.

When you don't respond, the message they get, which is precisely the message that you want them to get, is:

"If you choose to act in an unacceptable and unpleasant manner toward me, what you will get, what you will always get, is my swift absence. I will not choose to reengage in your life until you choose to once again act in an acceptable manner."

That is truly the message you want to send.

If we had transcripts of the hundred worst teen-parent arguments ever, I am sure we would see that all of the really bad arguments could have been avoided had the parent just disengaged earlier . . . or never reengaged. Once you have truly decided on a "no," anything further that you say only works against you. I cannot say this often enough, as it is a very important and learnable skill. Moreover, it reinforces itself because it works.

DEALING WITH BACK TALK

The challenge most parents have with the advice I've just offered is this: independent of the subjects that parents and kids fight about, parents have a hard time with the whole concept of back talk in general. To not lecture their teen, not punish their teen, not try very hard to make their teen understand how unacceptable back talk is, frustrates them to no end. Parents are just not comfortable with the idea of saying nothing. They feel that back talk is disrespectful, and that it is not okay to allow any act of disrespect, large or small, to pass unnoticed. They feel that they are required to respond to the back talk in some manner so that their child will know that it is wrong. They simply can't ignore the disrespect.

Marissa's mother had a visitor.

"Who are you?"

"You can't tell?"

"Well, yes, you look exactly like Uncle Sam. But why are you dressed up in that Uncle Sam costume?"

"I am Uncle Sam. I am the United States of America. And I am here because your daughter is acting toward you in a completely disrespectful manner."

"Yes, I know. I'm not proud of it."

"I am here because not only is she acting toward you in a completely disrespectful manner, but you are also letting her get away with it. And, in doing so, you are undermining the very fabric of the USA. You have an obligation to your country and to your fellow citizens to get your child back in line."

"I know. I know."

Then Marissa's mother broke down into tears.

"But what can I do?"

"You have to stand up to your daughter. You cannot let her talk to you in that disrespectful manner and do nothing about it."

And, with that, Uncle Sam vanished.

Sounds silly when you hear it like that, doesn't it? Yes, you have an obligation to raise good citizens, but bear in mind that you are already on your way to doing so. It's important to remember that raising fine, upright kids to adulthood is a *process*.

My recommendation regarding back talk is quite simple. If your aim is to get the least possible back talk from your teenage child both at the time and overall, then—other than returning to the old harsh punishment model— there is nothing that comes as close to being successful as what I recommend here. And isn't that, after all, the aim of any plan for dealing with back talk? To get as little of it as possible?

If your child talks back, you have two options. You can either respond immediately to the back talk, or you can not. I recommend not responding.

There are two basic ways—both unsuccessful—that parents tend to respond to their children's back talk. One is to directly address the fact that their child is talking back and to note that the talking back itself is not okay.

"Lucinda, would you please wipe off the kitchen table?"

"Excuse me, I'm not your slave. What about Andrew? Why do you always ask me and not him to do stuff in the kitchen? It's because I'm a girl, isn't it? It's not fair!"

"Lucinda, do not talk to me in that manner."

Lucinda's mother is criticizing her for talking back. The problem is that the above will invariably cause the back talk to continue.

"What manner? It's the way you talk to me!"

And the back-and-forth will continue as long as Lucinda's mother continues to focus on her daughter's back talk.

"You just better watch it, Lucinda!"

"But you talk to me that way all the time!"

"You heard me, Lucinda!"
"You should hear you!"

Etc.

The other common way that parents respond to back talk—with equal lack of success—is by addressing the content of the back talk.

"Lucinda, would you please wipe off the kitchen table?"
"Excuse me, I'm not your slave. What about Andrew? Why do you always ask me and not him to do stuff in the kitchen? It's because I'm a girl, isn't it? It's not fair!"
"You know that's not true. I ask Andrew to do plenty of stuff around the kitchen."
"Yes, it is true! All you ever ask Andrew to do is to chop wood."

You get the idea. This discussion will also continue ad infinitum, as long as Lucinda's mother wants to discuss gender-role stereotyping and household chores with her daughter.

"That's ridiculous, Lucinda. It has nothing to do with the fact that you're a girl. You just don't like doing household chores."
"You are so wrong! Look at yourself. Watch what you do. You'll see!"

And so on.

If you respond to the back talk, you'll get more back talk. It's that simple. What I recommend instead is handling the situation as follows:

"Lucinda, would you please wipe off the kitchen table?"
"Excuse me, I'm not your slave. What about Andrew? Why do you always ask me and not him to do stuff in the kitchen? It's because I'm a girl isn't it? It's not fair!"
"Lucinda, would you please wipe off the kitchen table?"

Do not respond to the back talk at all. In the above example, Lucinda may well continue her back talk, but if her mother steers clear of it, repeats her request, and then says no more, Lucinda is left with nothing other than two choices: she can comply or not. But the back talk will die down as it has nothing to feed off. And so over time, if Lucinda's mother regularly refrains from responding to her daughter's back talk, Lucinda may continue to talk back, but she will do it far less, knowing that there is no point to it—because her mother never seems to respond. Lucinda may think, *I hate my mother. She never listens to me when I try to tell her something. She is so unfair. And I can't even talk to her. Just yesterday I was trying to get her to see how unreasonable she was being by not letting me stay over at Cassie's for the weekend when her parents aren't going to be there. It's like talking to a wall. What's the point?*

COMBATING DISRESPECT

I believe most parents think, *But you can't just ignore the disrespect that is implied in the back talk. You can't just let it happen without some kind of response. Can you?*

In answer to that I say, yes, you can.

What if a child's back talk did not mean that they act in a similarly disrespectful manner to other adults out in the world? What if back talk to a parent did not portend future back talk once they become an adult—either to parents or to other adults? What if, without your responding every time they act disrespectfully toward you, they learn, nevertheless, that disrespectful behavior is wrong?

What if they think that back talk to you is bad, but not *really* bad? What if, because they are home and feel safe with you—you won't hurt them, you won't kick them out of the house— they don't actually exercise a lot of the same self-control they do elsewhere? Would knowing that make back talk more tolerable?

Let's ask the kids what they think about all this.

> *"Jerome, do you sometimes act disrespectfully toward your parents?"*
> *"Yeah."*
> *"Is being disrespectful to your parents bad?"*
> *"Yeah, I guess. I mean, children shouldn't disrespect their parents."*
> *"So why do you do it?"*
> *"I don't know. Because they piss me off."*

"Do you feel bad about it after you do it?"

"A little. Maybe. No, not really."

"You don't feel bad that you act disrespectfully toward your parents?"

"Well, they can act like real jerks sometimes."

"Would you want to act more respectfully toward them if you could control yourself better?"

"I suppose. I don't know. I mean I know I shouldn't do it. But I don't really see what's so bad about it, particularly when they act like real jerks. Which—trust me—they do. I mean, it's just words."

"Do you think that, overall, they're good parents?"

"Yeah. But, like I said, they can act like real jerks sometimes."

"So do you think it's really bad when you talk back to your parents?"

"No, not really. It's just a little bad. Like I said, it's just words."

"Do you respect your parents?"

"Yeah. They've always taken care of me. I know they love me. They try their best. They've had to put up with a lot of shit. I know that. Yeah, I respect them."

"So why do you talk back?"

"Because, when I do it, I'm mad, and I know that nothing really bad is going to happen to me."

"Do you think you will talk back to your parents when you're an adult?"

"No."

"Why not?"

"Because that would be me as an adult disrespecting them. It's different if you're still a kid."

"Why is it different?"

"Because you're a kid."

"If you were smacked every time that you talked back, would you talk back?"

"No, probably not. But they can't do that, it's child abuse."

"Which do you think is worse: a kid talking back to his parents, or a kid getting smacked in the face by his parents?"

"The kid getting smacked. That's way worse. Back talk is just words. Smacking a kid in the face, that's child abuse."

Are we raising a generation of disrespectful monsters?
No.
Do kids think that talking back is wrong?
Yes.
Do they think that talking back is very wrong?
No.
Why do they talk back?
They talk back because they do not think that it is very wrong, and because they know that nothing really bad will happen to them as a consequence.

Do we want to go back to the old harsh-punishment model of child rearing—which would eliminate back talk?

I don't. And I suspect you don't either.

WHEN DOUBLE STANDARDS ARE GOOD

Let me discuss a way of looking at disrespectful behavior that I think is useful in parenting today's teenagers. It has to do with a double standard. The idea is pretty simple. I think it is useful for parents to have two separate standards for what is acceptable behavior: one standard is relatively lenient, and is for when just immediate family is present and at home; the other, stricter standard is for when your teen is out in the world, and for when they are in the presence of people who are not immediate family members, regardless of where they are. In effect, you are saying that certain behaviors are less bad if they are done in relative privacy, if only immediate family is present.

Some examples of these two different categories follow.

Less bad behavior: Kelsey and her father are in the car.

"What do you think of school so far this year?" asks her dad.
"That's a stupid question. How do you think it is? It sucks like it always does."

More bad behavior: The family is visiting Kelsey's great-aunt.

"Kelsey, dear, how are you liking school this year?" asks her aunt.

"How am I supposed to like it? What do you think? It's stupid."

Less bad behavior: Jason and his father are in the kitchen at home.

"Dad, can I have five dollars to buy a box of charity candy at school?"

"No. I'm sorry, Jason."

"You are such a tightwad. It's for charity."

"No, you can use your own money if you want."

"You're such a jerk."

More bad behavior: Jason and his father are in a checkout line in the supermarket.

"Dad, can I have five dollars to buy a box of charity candy at school?"

"No. I'm sorry, Jason."

"You are such a tightwad. It's for charity."

"No, you can use your own money if you want."

"You're such a jerk."

Everyone in the supermarket line could not help but overhear Jason's words to his father. Jason's father thought he could see them all rolling their eyes.

Less bad behavior:

"Melinda, would you please be a dear and go into the kitchen and get me a soda out of the fridge?"

"Why can't you do it yourself?"

More bad behavior: The Queen of England has come over to visit and is being served tea.

"Yes, I'm particularly fond of tea."

"Would you like some sugar?" asks Melinda's mother.

"Yes, thank you. And I would also enjoy some cream for my tea."

"No problem. Melinda, would you please be a dear and go into the kitchen and get one of the little pitchers and put some cream from the fridge in it so the queen can have some cream for her tea?"

"Why can't you do it yourself?"

"Oh, what a nasty little brat," remarks the Queen of England.

The first category is obviously bad, but since these occurrences involve just family members, they are not such terrible infractions. The second category is considerably worse, as out in the world or with non-family members, things shift quite a bit. The same behavior can be ranked at different levels of badness, depending on the circumstances. What may be acceptable in one instance is completely unacceptable in another. And your reaction should differ accordingly.

Again, with bratty back talk at home, or when it exists just among family members, you would do well not to pick up on it. Or, if you really want to—if their words or attitude have really gotten under your skin—you may later say:

> *"Kelsey, earlier today, when I asked you about school, I really did not like the way you talked to me. It is not okay for you to talk to me in that manner."*

That's a reaction, but not a very big one.

However, for the stricter categories of behavior—the ones where you are out in public or when you have guests over—you do want to let your child know that their behavior carries a different weight or level of acceptability. Then you might want to say:

> *"Kelsey, that was totally inappropriate, the way you answered your great-aunt Vivian's question today at her house. She was trying to be nice. It's one thing to talk that way with us, but you cannot talk that way with other adults, especially someone who's elderly, like your great-aunt. We will not tolerate it. I don't care what your reason is, you have to do better."*

> *"Jason, that was very humiliating to me today in the super-market. It's one thing to talk to me that way when it's just us. But you really embarrassed me in front of all those people*

in the supermarket. You just can't talk to me that way out in public."

"Melinda, don't you ever act that way again when we have the Queen of England over for tea. It was humiliating. When we have guests over, I expect you to act politely, regardless of whether you feel like it or not."

If you really do maintain two different levels of disapproval in your head, your child will hear the difference. And they will feel less pressure to act respectfully at home and with family than they do when they are out in the world and with nonfamily. The major advantage of this policy is that it increases the likelihood that your child will behave more respectfully in nonfamily situations. They will come to feel that bratty is worse when it extends outside the safety zone of home. They themselves will have a stricter standard. I would argue that there is nothing you can do about the lesser standard at home. It is, after all, where the baby self comes out, and you're not going to win that battle anyway. Also, if they are being required to talk respectfully in some situations but not all, it becomes easier for them to comply and their success ratio is apt to rise, making everyone feel good about the extra effort.

Some parents will no doubt ask, "But doesn't this give them tacit permission to act disrespectfully at home?" To some extent it does.

"Oh, so it's okay for me to act that way when it's just us?"

"No, it's not okay for you to talk to me in a disrespectful manner. But, yes, there is a big difference between being at home when it's just us and when we have guests over or out in public. Then it is really not okay. It is definitely not acceptable. I care about it a lot more."

"So you won't be as mad at me when I act like a brat when it is just you and me, as you would when there are other people around?"

"Yes, what you just said is correct."

It is, like I said, a double standard. But I think it is a very useful double standard.

Two

GETTING YOUR TEEN TO DO ANYTHING

Earlier I described how, when I am home with my very nice wife, I am inexplicably seized by an extraordinary exhaustion that makes it virtually impossible for me to perform any tasks that my very nice wife might ask of me. I may also have mentioned how my very nice wife has no sympathy or understanding at all of what clearly is a certifiable medical condition and not immaturity or laziness.

I mention this because, when asking one's teenagers to do something that they do not feel like doing, their invariable response is amazingly similar to what I so regularly experience. As I said, with me it is a certifiable medical condition, but with them, it is clearly the fault of their baby self.

Like magic, when you make any requests of them requiring motion, they are immediately very tired.

> "Madison, would you please take Raja out for his walk?"
> "I'm really tired."
> "You didn't look tired a minute ago."
> "Well, I am. I really don't feel well. I think I have mono."
> "You don't have mono."
> "What, are you suddenly a doctor? I thought you worked in

human resources."

"Don't get fresh with me, Madison."

Teens feel that you are being an incredible nag. They feel that you are constantly at them, always asking them to do something. They feel that the only contact they have with you involves prodding.

"Well, they do! That's all she does! She can't look at me without nagging me about something!"

They see no relationship at all between the frequency of your having to ask them to do tasks and their consistent track record of not following through with previous tasks that they had agreed to do but never did.

"I know what this is about. This is all about the time that I accidentally dropped a couple of raw eggs that broke on the floor and then said I was going to clean them up, but I was interrupted by a phone call. And then I never did get back to the eggs, but meanwhile Mom slipped on the eggs and got really pissed off. It's not like that happens all the time! Besides, it's not my fault I forgot about the eggs! The phone call was really important: Candace had just broken up with Jonah."

They usually say that they will do what is requested. So long as it is not now. Furthermore, they genuinely believe that they will do it later, that their promise is real.

"Yeah, I will clean out the refrigerator. Why are you looking at me like that? I am going to do it."

They can promise and believe the promise because they think that "he" or "she"—the "future them"—will do it. And, in fact, they can continue to make promises on behalf of the "future them" because the "future them" is always and endlessly available and willing to do the task. It is just that, at any given moment, it is the "now them" who happens to be there.

If we were to interview the "future them," this is what might transpire:

"Don't you mind that Madison always puts everything off on you? That you always get stuck with having to do all of the work? That it's never her—the one who's there right then—who has to do anything?"

"No, actually, I don't mind at all. I'm always happy to agree to

do whatever Madison wants me to. It's no problem. I don't mind.
You see, when it's time for me to actually do what I've said I would,
I don't have to do it because I can always get the 'future me' to do
it."

"But that's you."

"No, that will be me."

If teens have an allergy to anything—besides you, of course—it is to doing anything right when you ask them to do it.

"Well, I can't do it now! That is so unreasonable! But, like I said, I will!
What? Why are you still giving me that look? What is your problem? I said
I'm going to do it!"

They believe that you are a lunatic. With regard to neatness and time- liness, they believe that you are a tragic and extreme example of someone suffering from obsessive compulsive disorder (tragic because they are stuck with you as a parent).

"Mom had a full-scale hissy fit about how, when I put the clean glasses
away, I mixed the short glasses in with the tall glasses. Omigod, I have a
mother who is totally anal!"

Above all, teens feel extremely indignant about the demands placed on them. They feel that their parents simply do not understand how extraordinarily hard their life is, that they have no idea how many de- mands are made on them at school and in their social life. That having their parents make demands on them at home is really just pushing it all too far.

> *"That's right: my life is really hard! I have constant pressure!*
> *There are so many demands on me! So much stress! It is all too*
> *much! How can they expect me to do stuff at home all the time on*
> *top of everything else I do?"*
>
> *"But all you do is text your friends, watch TV and YouTube*
> *videos of cows getting their heads stuck in car windows."*
>
> *"See, that is an example of exactly what I am talking about! She*
> *has no idea whatsoever of what goes on in my life! How difficult*
> *and stressful it is!"*

I mention all of this because it is important to understand who you are dealing with. The vast majority of teenagers, the vast majority of the time, are functioning in baby-self mode when they are with you. And all baby selves are the same—if you are asking a baby self to do something that it does not *feel like doing*, just know that it is more than what a baby self will *ever* be willing to do.

WHEN YOUR TEEN DOESN'T FEEL LIKE IT

For those parents who need added assurance, I must reiterate that there is probably nothing more frustrating daily than getting one's teenage child to do something that they do not feel like doing.

> *"Tanya, would you please help me bring in the groceries from the car?"*
> *"I can't."*
> *"What do you mean, you can't?"*
> *"I can't. I'm doing something else."*
> *"You don't look like you're doing something else."*
> *"Well, I was about to. I promised Kendra I would call her."*
> *"You can help me with the groceries and then you can call her."*
> *"No, I promised I would call her. She's already going to be pissed at me because I didn't call her as soon as I said I would."*
> *"Tanya, I need you to help me bring in the groceries—now!"*
> *"You don't have to yell at me! Everything has to be exactly when you want it! You are such a bitch!"*
> *"You just better watch it, Tanya!"*
> *"You better watch it!"*

As this example illustrates, not only do requests often go unheeded by baby selves, but interactions following such requests can frequently end up in a contentious mess. As already mentioned, a teenager's initial response to any request that goes against what he or she wants is almost always some form of objection. Unfortunately, as also discussed, parents frequently respond to that objection. That is, they often question the validity of—or criticize—the objection itself. But to do so, more often than not, leads to a dead end, because any response to their response only prompts another response. And with each of your subsequent responses, you move that much further away from compliance.

"Tanya, I'm not asking you to do anything so difficult. You can do it in two trips."

"But you're going to make me carry the heaviest bags! You always do! You know I had pneumonia and I get tired easily!"

"That was in third grade."

"Well, I still do get very tired sometimes. I just don't tell you about it because I don't want you to worry."

"Tanya, how can you expect me to believe such nonsense?"

"Because it's true! I get tired! Listen to my breathing!"

DEALING WITH RESISTANCE

There is, of course, another option. What I am going to recommend does not produce perfect compliance. But it works most of the time— far better than anything else you might do—and it significantly reduces back-and-forth fussing too.

The rule is straightforward: if you want your teenagers to do something that they do not feel like doing, you have to persist. You have to stay with your initial request, and at all costs you must not pick up on the reasons they offer for not doing whatever it is you want them to do. Nor should you pick up on the disrespectful attitude that will undoubtedly be reflected in their words. Responding to them only moves you further away from getting your request acted upon and toward an unpleasant confrontation. That, I assure you, will be the only outcome.

It is far better to doggedly stay on the subject.

"Tanya, would you please help me bring in the groceries from the car?"

"I can't."

"Tanya, I would appreciate it if you would help me bring in the groceries."

Repeat your request. Nothing more.

I definitely recommend not biting on the *"I can't."* As soon as you challenge them, you are in for it. They would always rather get into a debate than the alternative, which is to perform the requested task.

Your tone should be similar to the tone of your first request—respectful, not challenging, but definitely businesslike. Then—in response to anything else they may say other than *"Sure"*—you may want to repeat your request one more time and then say no more and simply wait.

"But I promised I would call Kendra. I have to do it now."
"Please help me bring in the groceries."

And then you simply wait, not picking up on anything further that she says. And if that is all that you do, what will happen—most of the time—is that, grudgingly, Tanya will comply.

"Everything has to be when you want it. Everything has to be exactly your way. You are a control freak."

But Tanya does head out to the car and starts to bring in the groceries. At that point, you definitely want to say,

"Thank you."

Definitely not: *"You know, it would be nice if, just once, you did something that I ask you to do without giving me such a hard time."*

Because what she then will think is,

See? I do something for her and I get no appreciation!

Which will produce a far poorer response in the future than would *"Thank you."*

Why does Tanya comply?

Since her mother did not pick up on Tanya's objections, and since her mother also chose not to get into a battle of wills that included threats—*"You just better help me when I ask, or you are going to get some unpleasant surprises next time you want anything!"*—all Tanya is left with is a simple request: her mother wants her to help bring in the groceries. Tanya knows the request is reasonable; she just doesn't feel like doing it right then, but she never will feel like doing it. She also knows that her mother will be mad at her if she does not comply. Furthermore—and most important—her mother has not said anything that allows Tanya to twist it around to make her mother into the bad guy. For example, her mother did not say,

"When will you ever stop trying to get out of complying with even the littlest requests?"

And Tanya thinks,

I don't always try to get out of requests! Mom's not being fair! I do stuff! But, see, she just criticizes me all the time! It's not fair!

In fact, that shift into "me-as-victim, parent-as-villain" mode is probably the number one way that teenagers justify their bad behavior to themselves. How else can they earnestly believe their responses are somehow not their own fault? If their parent is mad at them, that wrath must be unjustified.

They thereby circumvent the reality, which would sound something like this:

> *I'm lazy and I just don't feel like it.*
> Instead, if Tanya's mother can be made into the villain, Tanya is no longer morally obligated to comply.
> *She always yells at me! It's not fair! I would do much more stuff for her if she talked to me nicer!*

This *is* the way teens think. Like it or not.

THE POWER OF CONSEQUENCES

But what if Tanya does not comply, does not bring in the groceries.

"No, I have to call Kendra," she insists.

And then Tanya leaves, goes to her room, and gets into a twenty-minute phone conversation with her friend. Meanwhile her mother, wanting to get the groceries inside, empties the car herself.

What do you do then?

My recommendation is that, in this case, Tanya's mother should go to her daughter later and say,

"This afternoon I asked you to help me bring in the groceries and you didn't. Sometimes I need you to help. Leaving me without helping was not okay."

Very short, to the point, and then exit.

You might wonder what good this does so I will tell you: it puts a bad feeling inside of Tanya, and now there is nothing she can do about it. It is too late.

How do I know that such a simple statement by her mother will bother Tanya? Because she will try to defend herself or counterattack.

But she will be doing this to her mother's back, because her mother is already leaving.

"You always ask me stuff at inconvenient times! If it didn't always have to be your way, exactly the way you want it, then maybe I would do more stuff!"

But, like I said, she will be saying this to her mother's back.

What does this accomplish? It leaves Tanya stuck with the bad feeling still inside of her. A little remorse. She knows that she acted poorly and that her mother did not like it. And she will remember this. The memory definitely lingers, and should similar circumstances arise in the future, this particular memory of her acting poorly and her mom being right in recognizing it will exert pressure on Tanya to comply.

Shit. I really don't feel like doing this, but if I don't Mom will be pissed.

Which might not be enough to help Tanya overcome her laziness. But maybe it is.

The next time:

"Oh, all right, but I wish one time that you would ask Jason instead of always asking me."
"Thank you, Tanya."

Will this always work? No. Of course not. But it works as well—probably even better—as anything else, and with considerably less fuss.

Let's look at a slightly different scenario: What if Tanya's mother chooses not to bring in the groceries but decides instead to wait for her daughter to do it? In that case, Tanya's mother needs to go to where her daughter is talking on the phone and say,

"Tanya, do not forget. I need you to bring in the groceries."
"Mother!"
"Do not forget."
Tanya's mother then needs to stay after her daughter in order to make sure that the groceries are brought in.
"Tanya, you need to bring in the groceries."

In similar situations, the vast majority of the time, the Tanyas of the world will—begrudgingly, in order to get her mother off her back—bring in the groceries.

Then if Tanya's mother wishes she may say:

> *"I would have liked it better if you had brought in the groceries when I asked."*
> Though I still prefer the simpler response of,
> *"Thank you, Tanya."*

But regardless of what Tanya's mother says, the message is clear:

There are things that I expect you to do, and those expectations do not go away simply because you've shrugged them off. You may at times ignore what I ask of you, but tomorrow and the next day and the day after that, my requests will always keep coming.

The obvious next question is, *What about rewards and punishments?* To that I say, rewards such as tying cooperation around the house to an allowance or special bonuses for extra tasks could work. Punishments might also include groundings or taking away access to cell phones, favored sites on the Internet, or video games. Rewards and punishment do indeed work, but only temporarily. In the long run, as a means of getting today's teenagers to do what they do not feel like doing, rewards and punishments tend not to be very effective. If they truly worked better than what I propose, then I'd have less of an argument. But I do not believe this to be the case. I should add that escalating punishments for continued lack of cooperation—longer grounding, lengthy restrictions, taking away a long anticipated class trip—is a mistake. The risk is too great that the child is likely to be bitter toward his parents. A strong adversarial relationship does not produce better cooperation. It produces sullen, passive rebellion.

I prefer that tasks are expected as part of living in a household, rather than that they are always tied into a reward or an escape from punishment. If you want to use reward and punishment and they seem effective, then I have no strong complaint. I also have no objection at all to natural consequences. These are where an unpleasant outcome becomes the direct consequence of an action not taken. For example, a teenager not putting her dirty laundry into the hamper next to the washing machine results in those clothes not being washed. These are fine—and often work. But most day-to-day chores do not have such clear or acceptable deprivations. Would a bathroom not cleaned actually result in losing the right to use the bathroom? Would groceries not brought in from the car yield a punishment of no dinner? The truth is that there are no hard-and-fast answers. Getting teens to do what they do not feel like doing takes work. It just does.

THE "I'LL DO IT LATER" SYNDROME

We all have an inner procrastinator who puts off doing the things that we like to do least, but the teenage inner procrastinator is a master, managing to avoid the inevitable far longer than even the craftiest adult. The following may be an extreme example, but it does make my point:

> *"Evan, would you please bring your dirty laundry down to the cellar?"*
> *"I will, later."*

Later:

> *"Evan, I asked you to bring your laundry down to the cellar."*
> *"Yeah, I will. I'm planning to."*
> *"When are you planning to?"*
> *"I said I would do it. I will. Later."*

Still later:

> *"Evan, you still haven't brought down your laundry to the cellar."*
> *"Jesus! I said I would do it! What do you want?"*
> *"I want you to bring your laundry down to the cellar."*
> *"I'm going to!"*
> *"When?"*
> *"Soon. Later. Whatever. I'm going to do it!"*

Many, many years later:
Evan has finally brought the laundry down to the cellar. And now, half an hour later, he is standing by his father's gravestone.

> *"It was what Dad asked me to do. It was his last wish. and I've*

done it for him. That was for you, Dad."

"Your father would be very happy and proud."

The best strategy regarding the "I'll do it later" syndrome is to assume that "later" means "never." Parents who get increasingly angry and frustrated when their teenage child regularly promises that a given task will be done later but keeps putting off that task are making a big mistake. If a child's track record indicates that they frequently do not get around to doing what they promise to do, or if they regularly fail to do anything else in a timely manner, then repeatedly asking them to do this task is a waste of time.

"Evan, how many times do I have to ask you to do something before you'll do it?"

"I dunno."

It is better to stick with "now."

"Evan, would you please bring your dirty laundry down to the cellar."

"I will, later."

"No, Evan, I want you to do it now."

"I said I would do it. I will. Later."

"No, Evan, please do it now."

"Jesus, everything has to be when you want it! Everything has to be now! I have a life. I can't be expected to drop everything just because you snap your fingers!"

Don't expect Evan to be happy with the "now." And certainly do not expect him to come unarmed to the task. He will very likely have a diversion in his back pocket. Evan's father, for instance, is trying desperately not to be pulled off the track by his son's objections. He doesn't really want to get dragged into an argument with his son about the rightness or wrongness of his demands for Evan to do the task immediately.

If I were him, I would *not* say:

"This is not about snapping my fingers. If you regularly did get around to doing what I ask, there wouldn't be a problem. But you don't."

The only thing that accomplishes is more arguing.

*"I would follow up on tasks, but you never give me enough time
to do them! You don't know if I would get around to doing them or
not!"*

Again, it is better for Evan's father to simply stick to his guns.
"Evan, please bring your laundry down to the cellar now."

And, as discussed, what happens the great majority of the time is that
Evan will comply.

*"You know, it's really aggravating how everything has to be your
way. You're a control freak, you know that?"*
But he goes and does it.
And as always,
"Thank you, Evan."

WHEN THEY DON'T DO A GOOD ENOUGH JOB

Surely you will recognize the following example of halfhearted compliance:

"Veronica, would you please come into the kitchen?"
"What?"
*"I asked you to wash off the plates from dinner, and most of
them still have food particles left on them. You need to wash them
again so they're clean."*
*"Omigod, I can't believe you! I did wash them good. I don't see
any food particles. What, did you have a magnifying glass? Anything I do, it's not good enough!"*

Perhaps the single most unpleasant task in child rearing is dealing
with teens when they do what is requested but they do an inadequate job.
This is such an unpleasant experience because they will almost certainly
have a major fit.
*"Omigod, you are such a lunatic! You want me to lick the plates? Will
that work? I hate this house. Omigod."*
Many parents choose to live with partial success because they don't
want to risk pushing their luck or provoking a barrage of teenage abuse.

Well, I mean, she did wash the dishes—sort of. I think I'll go with that. I mean, it's not such a big deal, I can rinse them again right now and be done with it.

Which is fine if that is what you choose to do. But be aware that if you do not pick up on jobs inadequately done (with those few rare exceptions when you give yourself the night off from being the ogre), those jobs will continue to be inadequately done.

> *"Veronica, what is this? Look at it. It looks like a big gob of congealed mashed potatoes still clinging to the plate."*
> *"I don't see it. Maybe it's part of the plate design."*
> It's okay if that's what you choose. But, if not, then you do need to persist.
> *"Veronica, you need to wash the dishes all over again."*

If you do regularly and consistently refuse to accept half-assed jobs, then teens do get the message. They learn that if they do an inadequate job, they will hear about it and will be asked to redo it.

> *"Now, isn't that better? Look at the dishes. They're really clean. Doesn't that make you feel a little bit good about having done a job well?"*
> *"No."*
> But actually, Veronica is lying.

The bottom line about getting today's teenagers to do what they do not feel like doing is that it does take effort and persistence on your part. There is no way around it.

Three

COMMUNICATION

Communication—the words that you say to each other in the course of a day, the back-and-forth dialogue you share—is the foundation, the bricks and mortar of your relationship with your teenage child. Recognize these exchanges?

> *"Hello. How was school?"*
> *"Okay, I guess. I don't know. Why?"*

> *"Would you hand me that vegetable scraper?"*
> *"What's a vegetable scraper?"*

> *"Did you remember to take out the trash?"*
> *"I said I would do it."*

> *"Your hair looks nice."*
> *"Yeah, right."*

> *"Love you."*
> *"Grunt."*

We want to have good communication with our teenage children. We want them to feel comfortable talking to us so that if they have a problem, they will not be afraid to come to us. If there are things that we feel we need to say to them, we want them to listen. And we want the daily back-and-forth between us to be pleasant, even fun, so that the relationship itself is pleasant and fun.

Of course, the problem with communication between parent and teenager is that it has a built-in contradiction.

If you were to ask kids if they wanted to have good communication with their parents, on some occasions they would say,

"Not particularly. Mainly I think I'd like no communication, since it's just them being bossy, trying to pry into my business, or trying to be friendly—which is always stupid and not when I am in the mood for it, which is basically never."

But the above is only part of the truth. Ask them on another occasion and they may feel the complete opposite.

"Yeah, I want to have good communication with my parents. If I have a problem, I want to be able to talk to them and have them understand and help. And sometimes it's nice being with them and talking. Besides, how would I ask for stuff unless I communicate with them?"

Whatever the occasion, the majority of parents would answer consistently. We'd all say that we want good communication with our teenager. But on a day-to-day basis, even with the best of intentions and even having taken the utmost care to do it right, communication with our teens doesn't always go so well.

What follows are some of the issues that can get in the way of smooth communication— or even worse, some of the things that can sabotage it. Also included are valuable tips about how to promote better communication with your teenage child.

THE VALUE OF SHUTTING UP

Sondra enters her mother's bedroom for a chat:

"So then Jolie's mother brought out this weird, mushy-looking stuff and said it was moushala or something like that and—"

"It probably was moussaka. It's a Greek dish. It's made out of eggplant."

"Yeah, whatever. Anyway, I didn't know what to do because I was really hungry, but there didn't seem like there was going to be a whole lot else to the meal and—"

"I hope you didn't say anything rude to Jolie's mother about the meal."

"Jesus Christ, Mom! I can't fucking talk to you! You always interrupt! You always have something to say like I'm a two-year-old!"

Whereupon Sondra walks out of the room angry.

"Jesus Christ," Sondra mutters in a disgusted tone as she exits.

"Sondra . . ." her mother calls after her.

The number one reason—nothing is even a close second—that teenagers give when asked why they do not like talking to their parents is that, when they do talk to their parents, their parents will *not* shut up.

"If I try to talk to them, they can't just shut up. They just can't seem to listen to me. They always have to say something, and usually it's either critical of me, or something that they think is really important that I already know. They can't just let me talk. It's really frustrating. And then I get mad. So most of the time I don't even try. What's their problem?"

Let's ask Sondra's mother.

"Why did you interrupt Sondra's story and tell her that the food was probably moussaka and that it was made from eggplant?"

"I think it's important that she knows things. It's her chance to learn the real name of something that is new in her life. Otherwise, how will she ever even learn about it? And, second, if she comes across it again, isn't it better that she says the right word?"

"And why did you interrupt her the second time?"

"I just wanted to make sure that she knows to be careful about saying things that might put other people off. I know that I sometimes say it too much—but how is she going to learn otherwise? Nobody else cares how she presents herself to the world. Nobody else cares one way or the other whether she learns basic social skills. It's only parents who care."

You can't really argue with what Sondra's mother says. She makes good points. Her reasons are valid. The problem, of course, is the cost: Sondra doesn't want to talk to her.

It is a basic dilemma when parenting teenagers: whenever teens talk to us, there is so much that screams to be pointed out. So much that you can't just let pass because if you do, the moment is gone. But, at the same time, your valuable interventions seem to turn them off.

There are basic rules to follow in such circumstances. When your teenager has initiated a conversation with you and you feel that you need to comment on what they have to say, ask yourself if what you have to say will initiate a whole new agenda. Recognize that if it does, it is your agenda that you are introducing, so you are better off not saying it. It is much better to continue the flow of the conversation by either saying nothing, or by making comments that continue the already established direction of the conversation.

> *"But there didn't seem to be a whole lot else to the meal. . . ."*
> *"You were stuck, huh? Eat the moussaka or go hungry."*
> *"Yeah, I wasn't going to eat the whatever-it-was."*

Second, if there is something they have said that you feel needs to be commented on, wait until later.

For example, if you don't like how they said it:

"Don't use that tone of voice."

Or you think that there is an important piece of information that they should know:

"If you don't show good manners at other people's houses, they are less likely to invite you back."

Or you feel that their comments raise certain questions that need to be asked:

"You knew not to make a face or anything if you did taste the moussaka, right?"

If you really feel the need to comment on what they have said, bring it up later. Not then.

It is a matter of competing priorities. On the one side is all the information that you feel needs to be imparted to them. On the other side is having your teenager feel comfortable talking to you on a regular basis.

It is not wrong to put in your two cents; it is part of a normal parent-and-child interaction. But wait until they have said all that they wanted to say before doing so. Also, because you are human, some words may simply pop out of your mouth unbidden when you are talking with your child. It is inevitable. And this is fine. But it is also true that too many words, too often, especially if those words follow your own separate agenda, do work against your teenager's long-term desire and interest in talking to you.

"I mean, I know it's what parents do. But when I try to talk to my mom, it always ends up being about her stuff. It's very frustrating. I would talk to her more if she could somehow just learn to shut up."

The problem, of course, is that shutting up is not an easy thing for us parents to do. Above all, what makes it so hard is that by not making your usual parental comments, you often feel like you are sending your child off into the world unprotected by your wisdom. Every time you let something go by without making a comment, you fear, to some extent, that your child is one step closer to living a doomed and wrongheaded life.

"Yes, it's really too bad what happened to her. If only her parents had given her more guidance. There was so much that she didn't seem to have learned. Such a shame, really."

But what if because you passed up too many chances to properly guide your child, theirs becomes a life in ruin? Not to put in your two cents does feel very much like a grave loss of control.

"I know it sounds strange. But she still is just a kid, and the world has so much going on that she doesn't know anything about—not that I know everything—and there are so many opportunities for her to make mistakes that can harm her, and to make choices she will absolutely regret, and I know I can't protect her from everything, which is all the more reason why I want to get in as much as I can."

It is how parents feel.

WHEN AND HOW TO SHUT UP

So how do you get yourself to shut up?

First of all—and without this first step nothing else is going to be of any use—you must really buy into the idea that saying something in response to everything your teenage child says is at the cost of their willingness to communicate with you. And without that communication, you lose too much. That is, at least *some* restraint on your talking is a good idea. If you buy into this, then you have put into your head a monitor, a monitor that watches how much you talk, and a voice that says:

I know you feel that this is really important to point out to her, but maybe it would be better for the sake of your overall communication if, just this one time, you shut up.

You may or may not heed the words, but it is a big deal that the words are even there.

Also important is to accept that you cannot control everything. You just cannot. You have to take chances because you don't really have a choice. Having a teenage child exposes you to the absolute probability that some things you really do not want to have happen will happen.

- One Saturday night they get very drunk.

- They lie about their whereabouts in order to hang out at a friend's house where there are other kids you aren't particularly comfortable with.

- They enter into a sexual relationship that is considerably more than what they can handle.

Parenting a teenager means that you have to take the chance that, despite your best efforts to anticipate and instruct your child about everything, much of what they experience is out of your control anyway.

Another attitude that can be useful in restraining yourself is to view their talking with you in an open and spontaneous manner as a treasure—a delicate flame that you do not want to inadvertently blow out. You want to do all you can to fan the flame, not extinguish it.

Let me give another example of an instance when a parent got it, to a point, but then blew it.

Carly comes home from school; her mother greets her.

"How was your day, dear?"
"It was okay."
"You don't sound too happy. Is something wrong? Did anything happen in school?"
"No, not really. It was okay."

"Well, you certainly sound like something went on."

"No, it was no big deal."

"What was no big deal?"

"Do you really want to hear about it?"

"Yeah, that's what mothers are for."

"Well, it was Jeannine again. She's such a bitch. I wish she'd fucking die."

"You don't really wish that. That's just how you feel."

"Yeah, I do! She is so fucking mean! She is, Mom! She is so fucking mean!"

"Try not to use that word. You know how I don't like you to use that word."

"Forget it, Mom. I can't even fucking talk to you!"

"No, I want to hear what you have to say."

"No, you don't! You just want to lecture me. Forget it!"

And Carly leaves.

"I don't just want to lecture you. I want to listen."

But Carly isn't in the room anymore.

"Give me another chance! Please! I'm listening now!"

Carly's mother had been doing well, but then she messed up. She had picked up on her daughter's funky mood and had actually gotten Carly to start talking about what was bothering her. When you can get them to tell you what is going on, maybe even how they actually feel, it's priceless.

Carly's mother was doing fine right up until:

"Yeah, I do! She is so fucking mean! She is, Mom! She is so fucking mean!"

Right there, right then, Carly's mother had a choice. She could shut up or she could editorialize. In this example, she couldn't quite stop herself from doing the latter, and the conversation ended. (As always, if she doesn't like the language she can talk about it later.)

But let's say, instead, Carly's mother bit her tongue and said nothing.

"Yeah, I do! She is so fucking mean! She is, Mom! She is so fucking mean!"

At that point, if Carly's mother says nothing, Carly now completes the story. *"You don't know, Mom! Today at lunch, Jeannine is talking to Greg and we're all at the same table and she goes, 'Greg, did you notice Carly's hickey?' It was from me and Reggie* [her current boyfriend, in whom she is quickly losing interest], *and you couldn't even notice it and you know how I'm interested in Greg, which Jeannine totally knows."*

This really is the way it works the vast majority of the time.

There are always reasons why you can't let something they say pass without a comment. But, so often, you would have done better to just shut up.

What follows are some brief examples of when a parent did not respond as well as he or she could have, and some suggestions as to what could have been said to make things go smoother.

Not such a good way to talk to your teen:

> *"Mom, have you seen my red hairbrush?"*
> *"Stacy, you're going to have to learn to keep better track of your own stuff. You're not going to have me around to help you for the rest of your life. When you put things down, you have to notice where you are putting them. That way you'll remember."*
> *"You know what I just remembered? Fuck you!"*

Better way to talk to your teen:

> *"Mom, have you seen my red hairbrush?"*
> Either *"Yes"* or *"No."*

A not-so-good way to talk to your teen:

> *"I think Jillian's mother dyes her hair."*
> *"Honey, you know not to say anything to her about it, don't you? Many women are sensitive about whether their hair is their natural color or not."*
> *"Gosh, Mom, too bad you didn't tell me earlier, because I started laughing and pointing at her hair."*

Better way to talk to your teen:

> *"I think Jillian's mother dyes her hair."*
> *"Do you think it looks good?"*

A not-so-good way to talk to your teen:

"The stars are really pretty tonight."
"Yeah, when there's a cold snap like we've had, it makes the air really dry and there's no humidity to obscure the stars. Ergo, the stars are brighter."
"That's really interesting, Dad. Remind me to share a moment with you again next year."

Better way to talk to you teen:

"The stars are really pretty tonight."
"Yeah."

A not-so-good way to talk to your teen:

"This is a really crappy program."
"You know not to talk like that if you were watching TV at a friend's and her parents were there. Right?"
"No, I would have said shitty instead of crappy."

A better way to talk to your teen:

"This is a really crappy program."
"Yeah." (Or, if you disagree, *"I like it."*)

Some readers may not agree that what I am suggesting is better. Many may feel that something parental does need to be said in some or most of these situations. Perhaps they are right. My only point is that it is easy to find something to say in response to almost everything a teen says. However, it is up to you to decide, and at what price?

THE SECRET OF GOOD LISTENING

You want to encourage your teenager to open up. You want them to feel listened to. Most important, you want them to think that talking to you is an experience they will want to repeat. I understand that, which is why I will share with you a technique—in addition to saying nothing—that enhances this prospect greatly. It is a strategy that is both very simple and very effective. It is a way of responding that, over the course of human history, has been the number one method of making others feel heard.

Og, returning from an unsuccessful hunting trip, greets his wife, Oglena.

> "Og saw big mammoth."
> "Oh, you saw a big mammoth."
> "Yes, very big. If I kill it, feed many families. Og be hero."
> "If you killed it, it would feed many families, and you would be a hero."
> "Yes, but I not kill it. Stupid spear bounce off."
> "But you didn't kill it because your spear bounced off."
> "Yes, Og very pissed."
> "You were really pissed."

Later Og was talking to his friend Umba.

> "Oglena very good woman. She listens very good. Hears what Og has to say. She is good woman."
> "Yes, but is she a good cook like my Umbalena?"
> "You want I kill you?" said Og.
> Umba was not a good listener.

It is part of being human to want to share our experiences—to tell others what we saw, heard, thought, felt. It is the most basic part of any personal connection. It turns out that when you are in the role of listener, saying exactly what the other person has just said to you is especially effective in making the speaker feel that you heard them—that you are fully sharing their experience. They feel listened to, understood, connected.

Many years ago, at a psychology conference, I saw a video of a famous psychologist named Carl Rogers. Rogers's method was very influential with other therapists. The video showed Rogers practicing his method with a woman client during a psychotherapy session. Rogers didn't just echo the woman's words, he echoed them *exactly*. I was struck by how simplistic this seemed. Wouldn't she catch on?

"Doctor, all you're doing is parroting my words right back at me. How is

this going to be helpful? I'm paying you good money for this?"

But no: she seemed to really like it. In fact, she continued to speak openly and with feeling. Which is to say that people really do like affirmation that you hear what they are saying.

Parents are not supposed to be their teenagers' psychotherapists. But it is useful to know that if your kid is talking to you, there is often nothing better than simply echoing what you think they are saying. Not word for word, but repeating in your own words what you understand to be the gist of the conversation.

Here's how it might go with Kelsey and her mother:

"How was the party?"
"Actually, it was a little depressing."
"You thought it was depressing?"
"Les, that boy I told you about? He didn't even notice me and I kind of came on to him and I kind of made a fool of myself."
"That does sound depressing—and embarrassing."
"You said it! It's going to be embarrassing seeing him in school."
"You worry what it will be like on Monday."
"Yeah, maybe I'll just walk real fast if I see him."

Or with Seth and his father:

"These strawberries don't taste like anything."
"They don't have any flavor?"
"Yeah, they're like zero-flavored."
"Not like the strawberries we get in June."
"Yeah, those are good—from that farm market we go to."
"Yeah, you like those."
"Yeah, those are really good. They taste like strawberries. Maybe I should try to grow strawberries indoors over the winter. I wonder if you can do that."
"I don't know. It's an idea."
"Maybe I'll look it up online. Maybe I could sell them. Make a fortune."
"That would be nice."
"I'd buy you new windshield wipers to replace yours that streak."
"You're very generous."

My point is that the parent is a participant in the conversation, even if they're really not saying a whole lot. The parent's words basically echo what their kid has just said, but they add virtually nothing new. In this way parents avoid being judgmental in any way and thereby allow their child to proceed with his or her own thoughts. You don't always need to do this, but it is good to know that this technique exists and that it can be helpful when you want to encourage your child to talk to you.

DEALING WITH UNCOMMUNICATIVE TEENS

Who hasn't had a one-sided conversation with their child? The ones that go like this?

> *"Hi, Charles."*
> *"What?"*
> *"How was school?"*
> *"Fine."*
> *"Did you have fun when you went out with your friend?"*
> *"Uh. I guess."*

One of the most frequent and perplexing phenomena when it comes to teenagers— especially boys—is how a one-time very chatty little child could grow up to be such an uncommunicative fifteen-year-old. There are teenage boys who talk in nothing but indistinct monosyllables. If they say any words, they are usually, *"I don't know."* And, of course, wherever you are, that's where they don't want to be.

> *Charles used to talk to me a lot. He couldn't wait to tell me about his day. The smallest details. You couldn't shut him up.*
> *"Mom! Mom! Listen! Do you remember how I told you that Robby got in trouble in Mrs. T's class? Well, today he got into really big trouble because he said the S-word! And Mrs. T . . . "*
> *But now, nothing. It's like a wall came down. He shuts me out completely. I'm so lonely.*

Obviously, it is the male form of the teenage allergy to parents. (Girls do this verbal shutting down too, but to a much lesser degree.) To the extent that their words allow you entrance into what is going on in their lives, or what is going on inside of them, conversation is anathema to them. Luckily, the allergy is temporary. They get over it and ultimately go back to talking to you. You just have to wait it out.

But what about now? What can you do in the interim?

First, let me tell you what *not* to do: don't use the direct attack.

> *"Did you like seeing your cousins over Thanksgiving when we went to Grandma Miriam's?"*
>
> *"I don't know."*
>
> *"Why can't you ever answer a question when I ask you? What is so difficult about giving me a simple answer to a simple question?"*
>
> *"I don't know."*
>
> *"Do you understand that it's just common courtesy to answer people when they ask you a question?"*
>
> *"Yeah. I guess. I don't know."*

As anyone who has ever tried knows, the only thing that the direct attack will accomplish is to push them further into their shell. So what should you do—go off into a corner and have nothing to do with them until they rejoin civilization in three or four years? Definitely not. They may want nothing to do with you, but that does not mean that you should simply back off. Just the opposite. They still need the connection with you, even though they do not seem to want it. The trick with uncommunicative teens is that they may not want to talk with you, but you can still keep talking to them. (Yes, this is definitely an instance where I'm suggesting that you *don't* shut up!)

The key is to not get discouraged. Keep trying. Grab what opportunities you can to talk with them. Parents often find that being in the car, just the two of you, yields the best results—your teen doesn't have to look directly at you, which seems to help, and there are fewer distractions than at home. Or try talking whenever it's just the two of you alone in a room together. To get started, just say anything.

> *"How is school? How are you doing in history? How are you liking your new algebra teacher, Mrs. Ehrenfelter? Is there anybody*

new who you've been talking to at school? Who do you sit with at lunch? Is there anything more than the usual day-to-day stuff that's been bothering you?"

Continue trying:

"Tell me one thing that I've been doing lately that ticks you off—not counting sitting here right now asking you questions. What would you like to do next summer? Tell me one t hing that you would like us to have for dinner more often. Do you still think you might like to become an electrician like your uncle?"

Ask any and all questions that come to mind. Just keep them coming. Stupid questions are okay, as are questions that you have asked a million times before. Stay upbeat. The more you do it, the more you get the hang of it. Much of the time they may not respond. That's okay. You're talking to them because you choose to. It may seem like torture to them. But it is not a terrible torture.

"Yes, it is a terrible torture. You don't know."

But most important of all: you must persist. Whether or not you get anything in return, keep coming back for more. Most of the time you may get little or nothing. But sometimes you do. Out of nowhere.

"Mrs. Ehrenfelter? You really want to know? I hate her. I totally hate her."

"You really don't like her, huh?"

"Yeah, can I drop out of school?"

The trick is to keep coming back for more and keep talking.

WHEN YOUR TEEN DOESN'T LISTEN TO A WORD YOU SAY

Hearing them is one issue. But what about them hearing *you*?

"Todd . . . Todd . . . Todd!"

Todd continues watching TV, seemingly oblivious to the fact that his mother is talking to him.

"Todd, please remember to take the cardboard boxes out and

put them with the trash. . . . Todd . . . Todd!"

"What?"

"Did you hear what I just said?"

Todd again gives no answer, still engrossed in the TV and apparently unaware that his mother is speaking to him.

"Todd!"

"What?"

"Please remember to take the cardboard boxes out and put them with the trash. . . . Todd!"

You think:

He doesn't listen to a word I say. Yesterday evening he's playing one of his dopey video games and I ask him to come to the table because supper's ready, and not a grunt, not a nod, not an anything. Or yesterday afternoon as he's leaving the kitchen, "Before you leave the kitchen would you bring me a soda from out of the fridge?" And, not breaking his stride, he just walks right by me.

I don't understand. Does he actually not hear me? Does his brain somehow screen out the sound of my voice? Or is it that he just consciously ignores everything I say?

Teenagers—with acutely good hearing—seem not to hear their parents, to a degree that is beyond maddening.

Maybe it's just that he has a hearing loss limited to the pitch of my voice. That's possible. It could be that.

Or do they simply ignore us? What's going on?

Let's ask Todd.

"I don't know. I'm just doing what I'm doing. I'm paying attention to what I'm paying attention to. It's not that complicated. I'm listening to music or I'm thinking about stuff, or maybe I'm watching TV, or playing a video game. And then Mom says something, and she expects me to drop everything, stop paying attention to what I'm paying attention to and listen to her. And it's always about something she wants me to do. Yes, I hear her. How can I not hear her? She's talking. But she doesn't just want me to listen, she wants me to say stuff like, 'Yes, Mother. What is it that you want? Yes, I certainly will remember to take the cardboard boxes out to the trash. You don't have to worry about it. I'm on the case. But thank you for reminding me.'

"She really expects me to say stuff like that. I mean who, other than my cousin, the incredible suck-up Marcus, would ever say something like that? Give me a break."

They do hear. They hear every word, every time. It is just that their mind correctly registers the fact that answering those words will require something of them that they would rather not do. And, as a defense, they can always plead that they just didn't hear you.

So what should you do? Of course, you can always try to change them.

"Okay, mister, until you start hearing a little better, let's see what your life is like without a cell phone."

But I don't advise the above. You may get some better behavior from them temporarily and begrudgingly, but you will most definitely not get any character changes. What's more, you will also be provoking resentment. Their not hearing you can then result not only from laziness but also from angry defiance. They become more, not less, intractable.

You can talk to them later and try to make them understand.

"Todd, I would really appreciate it, when I talk to you, when I ask you to do something, if you would answer me the first time—and in a reasonably polite manner—rather than simply ignoring me. It is very frustrating for me, and it has to be unpleasant for you, because I so often end up yelling at you. It would be a lot nicer if you would answer the first time, and it really is not good to treat me in what comes across as a disrespectful manner."

The above is actually a good thing to say. It probably will not produce dramatic changes. But if you do not deliver it too angrily, they will hear you and know that what you are saying is true. Maybe they will even feel a little bit guilty. And maybe, just maybe, they will alter their listening behavior, at least a little bit, in the future.

But what should you do right then, when the ignoring is taking place? Here's a suggestion:

> *"Todd."*
>
> And if he does not immediately respond, go over to where he is. You are now there, right next to him.
>
> *"Todd."*
>
> Don't worry about whether he responds or not. You are there, right where he is. He hears you. And he can't really pretend that he doesn't. Now say what you wish to say.

"Please remember to take the cardboard boxes out and put them with the trash."

Do not do this in an angry manner. You are simply making a friendly request. It is just that you are standing rather close to him when you are making it. He will hear you and pay attention to you because you are standing there, right where he is. Again, do not worry about whether he says something in response or not, because he definitely hears you.

He will not like this; in fact, he will feel that it is a big imposition.

"Mom! Why do you have to do this? It is so aggravating! How would you like it if someone stood right in front of you while you were doing something and started talking to you?"

But don't touch it. Definitely do not say:

"I wouldn't have to stand so close to you if you would answer me rather than always ignoring me."

You don't want to go there because it adds an unfriendly note—which can start a battle of wills that will only work against you. Besides, your actions already say the above anyway. The trick is to be unapologetically upbeat.

Also, don't push for some kind of acknowledgment of what you said:

"Okay, I'll remember to take the cardboard boxes out and put them with the trash."

He *has* heard you.

An accompanying suggestion: since you are now in his space and are standing right next to him, it is useful to add:

> *"I would appreciate it if you would do it now."*
> It is best not only to make sure they have heard you but also to get them to do it now.
> *"I can't. I'm busy. I will."*
> *"No, Todd. Please do it now."*
> Of course, you will then get:
> *"Why do you always have to have things exactly when you want them? Can't you see I'm busy?"*
> But stay on course:
> *"No, Todd. Please do it now."*

He hears, and the great majority of the time—to get you off his back, given that you are standing right next to him—he will comply.

DISPENSING ADVICE

As mentioned earlier, I have been married for many years and I believe that I am lucky to have a wonderful wife. There is, however, one problem that does not seem to go away: I am quite a smart person. I know a lot of stuff. But my wife does not seem to understand this, because whenever I give her advice—excellent advice, so excellent, in fact, that I cannot imagine her not following it (did I mention that I'm very smart?)—she often completely ignores my suggestions. I only want to help her!

The same is true of Nadine and her father:

> "The stupid mirror in the bathroom keeps getting steamed up after my shower and I can't see to do my hair. It's really aggravating."
>
> "If you open the bathroom window before you take the shower it won't happen," said her father.
>
> "That's not going to do anything. We should get one of those vent things that people have."
>
> "Maybe someday, but right now we don't have the money for that. But, like I said, if you open the window it will make a difference."
>
> "I highly doubt it. You don't know how aggravating it is not being able to see anything in the mirror."

The next day:

> "That stupid mirror keeps getting steamed up. I hate it."
>
> "Why don't you open the window?"
>
> "Why do you keep saying that? I'm not going to open the window. That's stupid."
>
> "If you open the window it will allow the steam from the shower to escape and it won't fog the mirror."
>
> "I'm not opening the window. You don't know anything."
>
> "Try it one time and see what happens."
>
> "Dad, you don't get it. I'm not opening the window. That's a stupid suggestion."

Nadine's father thinks:

I give her advice and it's like I'm talking to the wall. I tell her something that's going to help her, make her life a little better, and it's as if any advice coming from me is automatically not worth paying attention to. I don't deserve that kind of disrespect. I am not an ignorant person and I do know more than a little bit.

There is a rule about giving advice to teenagers; it is the same rule about giving advice to anybody of any age. If you give good, helpful, it-will-only-make-their-life-a-little-better-if-they-follow-it, 100 percent not-being-a-know-it-all advice, give it with no—zero—strings attached. If you give advice, it should not be with any condition that says they must follow it. It is as if the advice were a little clay statue that you put on a table. It is an offering. They can ignore it. They can call it names. They can stomp on it until it's clay powder. Or they can pick it up and value it. If you give them advice, they have to be able to do whatever they want with it.

It cannot be that if they don't use it—excellent and well meaning as it is—you are hurt. Your feelings cannot be attached to the advice. That does not work.

A better way to give advice can be seen in this interaction between Nadine and her father:

"The stupid mirror in the bathroom keeps getting steamed up after my shower and I can't see to do my hair. It's really aggravating."

"If you open the bathroom window before you take the shower it won't happen," said her father.

"That's not going to do anything. We should get one of those vent things that people have."

"Well, let's try it."

And Dad says no more.

Next day.

"That stupid mirror keeps getting steamed up. I hate it."

"Oh, that must be frustrating."

Nadine's father has already given his suggestion, and his daughter knows it. He has nothing more to say.

Whatever you do, say no more if the following happens. I-told-you-sos will get you nowhere fast:

"Dad, I read an article on this 'Helpful Hints' website, and it said how, for steamed-up bathroom mirrors, all you have to do is get a little air circulating by opening a window. I tried it this morning, and it worked."

Another example:

"Mom, I can't find my sneakers."
"Austin, if you put them in the closet next to the front door as soon as you take them off, this won't happen."
The next day:
"Jesus Christ, I can't find my sneakers."
"How many times do I have to tell you to put them in the closet as soon as you take them off?"
"Yeah. Yeah. Where the hell are my sneakers?"
Next day:
"Where are my sneakers? Where the hell are my sneakers?"
"I don't know why you don't take my advice. We wouldn't have to go through this every time. Do you hear me?"
"Yeah, but where are my sneakers?"
"You know what maybe I'll do? I'll burn your sneakers and then you won't have to look for them because they will be ashes in the trash bin."

A better approach can be seen in this exchange between Austin and his mother, after her initial suggestion and all other comments:

"I can't find my sneakers."
"Gosh, that's a problem."
"But where are my sneakers?"
"It sure is frustrating when you can't find them. Huh?"

Being helpful has, after all, its limits.

RESPECTING THEIR NONSENSE

If teens are going to resort to the most unfair, manipulative, disingenuous means in order to get their way, why can't their parents dish it back a little? If they are going to act like total jerks, why shouldn't we give them a little taste of their own medicine?

> *"No, Pamela, you cannot go to Death Metal Fest VI."*
> *"But, Mom, that is so unfair! I never get to do anything that's fun! It's not my fault you have some kind of problem about it because you had such a sucky adolescence!"*
> *"Oh, right, I should let a fourteen-year-old go to a concert where the police came the last time they performed and a number of kids got injured."*
> *"No, you just don't want me having fun!"*
> *"Pamela, that is such nonsense and you know it."*
> *"No, you're just jealous because you never did anything as a teen, and it makes you sick to see me actually have a good time!"*
> *"I'll tell you what makes me sick. It makes me sick to see my supposedly intelligent daughter saying such total nonsense and thinking I'm going to believe it. I'm not a complete idiot."*

Much of what teenagers say can seem to be—and often is—self-serving nonsense. It's hard to respond without giving it back in kind.

> *"Lawrence, I asked you to empty the dishwasher before I got home and you've done nothing."*
> *"It's not my fault. I was about to do it, but then I wasn't sure if I was going to do it right because I thought you had said that you maybe were going to change where stuff goes. And, anyway, if I did do it you'd probably just change it back because you're such a perfectionist, so what's the point?"*
> *"Lawrence, do you think I'm an idiot? Why do you think that I'm going to believe the stupid crap that you give me all the time?"*

Many teenage responses scream for some kind of comeback with at least a bit of an edge. If they are going to talk like an idiot—especially if it is purely in the service of trying to get their own way or to avoid responsibility—doesn't their nonsense deserve some kind of retort? Are you supposed to reply to everything they say with complete respect?

"You make an interesting point, Pamela. I have to look into myself a little more. My adolescence actually wasn't so bad. But maybe I am bitter without realizing it."

"Yeah, you're bitter and jealous! So does that mean I can go to the concert?"

Absurd as her response may be, your teen probably doesn't see it that way. If we were to ask Pamela if she really believes that her mother doesn't want her to have a good time, she'd probably say,

"Yeah, she hates it if I'm going to have a good time. She gets jealous."

"You really don't believe that your mother thinks an all-night rock fest that ended last time with real violence is too dangerous and inappropriate a place for a fourteen-year-old girl?"

"No, she's jealous, that's why."

And were we to hook Pamela up to a lie detector, it would show that she's telling the truth. I kid you not, when teens are dispensing manipulative nonsense, they really believe their own words. At least at the moment they are arguing.

But if I give a little of it back to her, then she gets to hear what it's like being on the receiving end for a change. Maybe she'll learn that way, right?

Unfortunately, that's not how it works.

"Listen to how my mother talks to me! That's not the way a parent should speak to their child! How can she expect me to talk nicely to her if she talks so rudely to me?"

"That's the way you talk to her."

"Yeah, but I'm a kid. Besides, what am I supposed to do if she is being so unreasonable and unfair?"

This is how teens think. As hard as it may be to stomach, it really is better to deal with your kids in as mature a manner as you can. It sets a good example in the same way that doing the opposite sets a bad example. Pamela's mom can remain firm and not let her go to the show. But she can do so in a way that doesn't belittle her daughter. She can listen to her—she just doesn't have to buy into what Pamela's saying.

"No, I am sorry, Pamela, but I just am not comfortable with it. No, you cannot go to the rock fest."

"You're not comfortable with it? Why is that my problem? You're not comfortable with it? I'm not comfortable with not going!"

And at this point, because Pamela will always have more to say, Pamela's mother, having stated her position, should disengage.

"You're not listening to anything I say! Mom!"

What does Pamela learn? She learns that her mother is not going to be swayed by her ranting. But she also learns that her mother will not attack her for saying her piece—no matter how silly that piece may be.

The same would be true for Lawrence's father. Rather than his picking up on how ludicrous his son's excuses are, it is much better for him to respond in a very straightforward manner.

"It's not my fault. I was about to do it, but then I wasn't sure if I was going to do it right because I thought you had said that you maybe were going to change where stuff goes. And, anyway, if I did do it you'd probably just change it back because you're such a perfectionist, so what's the point?"

"Lawrence, please empty the dishwasher." Finis.

Just remember that you're not a bad parent if you happen to slip and respond at their level. If you are the parent of a teenager and you're also human, this is going to happen from time to time. But there is another way that is far better. That other way should always be your aim.

GETTING BACK CONTROL OF THE CONVERSATION

A common phenomenon between parent and teenager occurs when a completely innocuous verbal exchange somehow digresses into an angry argument. Seemingly out of nowhere there comes a sustained period of ill will. Thinking back, it can be virtually impossible to discern how this switch from harmless conversation transpired into full warfare.

It happens all the time with my Alyssa. I'm in an argument even before I know I'm in it. We're talking, and without my even seeing it coming, I'm already six back-and-forths into a fight. It just happens. I say something. She says something. I answer. And, before I know it, we're at each other's throats. And I have no idea where it came from.

Alyssa and her mother are driving back from the mall.

Alyssa's mother remarks:

> *"There's a lot of traffic."*
> *"So? What am I supposed to do about it?"*
> *"Nothing, honey. I was just commenting that there was a lot of traffic."*
> *"No, you weren't. You were complaining."*
> *"I wasn't complaining, I was just commenting."*
> *"No you weren't. You were complaining. You always complain."*
> *"When I make a comment, it's not always a complaint."*
> *"Yes, it is. You don't hear your own voice. It's like whining all the time."*
> *"Alyssa, that's just not true. I don't whine all the time."*
> *"See, you don't take anything I say seriously, you just get all defensive."*
> *"Actually, Alyssa, if anybody has a negative tone, it's you."*
> *"See, that's just what I mean. You complain about everything! Especially me!"*
> *"Alyssa, I was not complaining about you!"*
> *"Yes, you were! You're lying! You're doing it right now—complaining!"*

Mother and daughter spend the rest of the drive home in a snit.

How does it happen? Who knows? It comes out of normal conversations where one says something that is taken by the other in a negative way—even though there was no conscious negative intention on the part of the first speaker. It's easy to see how it can spark with teenagers— thin-skinned as they often are, and also very quick to see any parental comment as criticism.

"Well, they do criticize me all the time."

But it can also be readily sparked by parents' hypersensitivity to their teenager's disrespectful tones of voice or phraseology.

"Well, it's true. Just about everything out of her mouth has that disrespectful tone that I hate so much."

But the point here is not about what causes it to happen. The point is that it *does* happen. And that it happens often.

Furthermore, it is important to note that you can't prevent these misunderstandings from ever occurring. No one can so carefully monitor everything that they say. It's impossible to always know how what you say will be received. It just cannot be done. There is no way to head off these out-of-nowhere confrontations before they happen.

You simply cannot predict if, when, and why conversations will go awry. Alyssa's mother's initial words could just have easily ended up as a passing comment—no more. You can never know with certainty how your words will be taken.

> "There's a lot of traffic."
> "Yeah."

End of conversation.
Or perhaps even a positive outcome:

> "There's a lot of traffic."
> "Yeah, it always seems like that whenever we go to the mall, no matter what time we go. Doesn't it? Maybe there's a curse on our shopping trips."
> Alyssa's mother laughs.
> "Yes, we don't ever seem to have good luck."

One thing that you do not want to do is to go back and try to untangle where the exchange went so off course in an effort to somehow resolve the disagreement. To do so is a mistake, especially since it is so unclear what the disagreement was really about. It is too hard to go back and figure out who said what and what they meant by it.

> "Wait a minute. Time-out. It all started with me saying there was a lot of traffic. I was only making an observation, that's all. I didn't mean anything more than that. Just my stating the fact that I noticed there was a lot of traffic."
> "No. That's not how it was. You're not counting how you said it.

Your tone of voice. You have that complaining tone of voice. You maybe don't even recognize that you're doing it because you do it all the time."

"Oh, come on now, Alyssa. I was just talking."

"No. You were using that tone of voice."

Reconstruction with the purpose of untangling and making it right just is not the productive way to go.

So what do you do? Again, you want to disengage. But this is a lot easier said than done. First off, you are already well into the disagreement—having been so caught off guard because you didn't even understand that you were headed there until it was too late.

What is going on? How did I get into this?

And, of course, since you are already well into the argument, you now have angry feelings coursing through your body. You are no longer the calm, reasonable, dispassionate person you were just a few minutes before. You are now an angry you.

She's doing it again! Can't I get through one single day without Alyssa giving me a hard time? When is she ever going to grow up? I'm paying for all the years that I was too nice to her, and now I've created a little monster!

The key is in recognizing that you are in the midst of a senseless, going-absolutely-nowhere argument. The voice of reason needs to shout in your head—even as you are continuing the heated back-and-forth:

I am in the middle of a completely ridiculous, going-nowhere-except-to-bad-places argument.

And, hopefully, those words trigger the next:

I have to get out of here!

Here is where it gets tricky. You may want to disengage—end it—but because your child is also now well into the argument, and they have gotten up a full head of steam, they are just as angry and emotional as you. It is possible to shut it off from your end, but now you have to somehow shut them off as well. Not so easy.

You can always simply stop talking. Or, better, say something like:

"This is going nowhere. Let's just stop it, okay? We'll just take a time-out."

This may work and is a good thing to say but, unfortunately, more often than not, they will not be deterred. They are now angry and they do not simply want to stop; they are not satisfied with that. They want something more.

"Yeah, you want to stop it because you've acted like a bitch to me and you think that's okay and you can just pretend like none of this ever happened!"

This is where it gets difficult because what I am about to recommend, what I really believe is the best option, the best way to respond, may be hard to stomach for many parents. They may feel that it too generously absolves their child from any responsibility in causing the unpleasantness. It is what may be described as a partial apology.

Why should I apologize if I did nothing wrong? She should apologize to me for acting like a little brat! If I apologize, she wins. I'm not going to let that happen!

Let me describe how this partial apology plays out. Let's pick up the argument in midstream, where maybe Alyssa's mother has begun to realize that she is in an argument and that it is bound for nowhere good.

"Actually, Alyssa, if anybody has a negative tone it's you."

"See, that's just what I mean: you complain about everything, especially me!"

"Alyssa, I was not complaining about you."

"Yes, you were! You're lying! You're doing it right now—complaining!"

Now the partial apology:

"I'm sorry you thought I was complaining."

"You were complaining! You always complain!"

Here Alyssa's mother does not concede Alyssa's assertion that she was complaining. But neither does she argue the point with Alyssa. She does not say,

"No. I wasn't complaining. You misheard me."

All that would do is continue the argument. It's definitely not an exit line.

"I didn't mishear you! You misheard yourself!"

Instead Alyssa's mother concedes that Alyssa's view of what went on may well have been different from her own view. And that's okay. Alyssa heard her mother's words as a criticism. Alyssa's mother accepts that, inadvertently, her words may indeed have started it all. In effect, she is saying to Alyssa,

"You were not wrong to see it the way you did."

The particular benefit of the above kinds of apologies is that they give Alyssa very little further to fuss about. In no way is her mother challenging Alyssa. She accepts the validity of what Alyssa has said. Immediately, the argument now has a chance to wind down.

Here, and in the examples that follow, the parent does not challenge their child. They do not pick up on each statement by their child to show that what they are saying is incorrect and/or maybe disrespectful. The parent does not keep trying to set the record straight or point out to their child how what they are saying is wrong. It is the parenting approach where you do not always have to be right, teaching a lesson, standing up for yourself, trying to make sure that they understand their responsibility for their own actions, or anything else for that matter. It is the parenting approach that says, in this particular instance, your greatest wisdom is leading you to take responsibility for ending a discussion that is going nowhere.

Here's another example:

Alexander comes into the kitchen.

"Alexander, guess who I saw today?"

"I don't know."

"I saw Mrs. Ambidecker. Remember? Your first grade teacher."

"You think I don't remember who my first grade teacher was?"

"No, of course I know you know who your first grade teacher was."

"Then why did you say, 'Do you remember?' if you knew that I knew."

"I didn't mean anything. It's just a way of speaking."

"A way of speaking where you don't think that I remember anything about my own life?"

"No, of course not. That's not what I meant. That's what I'm trying to explain. It's just a way of speaking."

"I still don't get it."

"Alexander, are you being dense on purpose, just to aggravate me?"

"No, I just don't know what you're talking about! You think I don't even know who my first grade teacher was!"

"Alexander, that's not what I was saying."

"Well, that's what you said!"

At this point, the normal-but-fruitless parenting response would be to push ahead in an attempt to get through to her son—to resolve the apparent confusion. But it's a mistake.

"Alexander, I don't think you don't remember who your first grade teacher was. I don't think that. Got it? No, that's not what I was saying."

"Then why did you say it?"

Now, the much better, simpler approach:

"I'm sorry I made you think that I didn't trust your memory. It's not what I intended."

"So then why did you say it?"

"I'm sorry for the confusion."

And, again, the partial apology gives little for Alexander to keep railing against. It will be an effective exit. A way to move on.

"You shouldn't say stuff if you don't mean it."

But Alexander's mother need say no more.
And here's one last example:

"Nelda, look at all the scratches on the countertop."

"Well, I didn't make them! Don't accuse me!"

"I wasn't accusing you, dear. I just hadn't noticed that the countertop had so many scratches."

"Maybe it was Justin!"

"I'm not accusing anyone."

"Why do you always defend Justin?"

"I'm not defending Justin."

"Yes you are! I do anything and you have a fit! Even stuff like this that I didn't do!"

"Nelda, you know what? For once it would be nice if you didn't turn everything into an argument."

"I'm not the one who accused me of scratching your precious countertop!"
"I didn't accuse you."

Better, once Nelda's mother recognizes that she is in a conversation going nowhere:

"Nelda, I'm sorry I made you think that I was accusing you."
"Well, you did!"
"I'm sorry I made you feel I was complaining."
"Yeah, well, you complain too much." (Nelda's parting shot.)

Here, Nelda's mother need say no more. And usually neither will Nelda. They can now move on. We don't always have to get in the last word.

WHAT TO DO WHEN YOUR TEEN THROWS YOU A CURVE

Who among us hasn't fielded an unexpected fastball?!
Fifteen-year-old Alexis is in the car with her mother:

"Mom, do condoms work?"
"What?"
"Do condoms work?"
"Why do you ask?"
"Mom, I'm just asking a question. Do condoms work?"
"Well, yes. No. I guess so. Sort of. I don't know. Usually. Work against what? Why are you asking?"
Is she having sex? Did something happen? Is she planning to have sex? Omigod, did she have sex and use a condom, but now she thinks she might be pregnant? Is she playing games with me to see how I'll answer? Trying to shock me? If I give her a simple answer will she think I'm being casual and giving her permission to have sex?

Sometimes, out of nowhere, in the course of a normal day—in a seemingly innocent manner—teens will ask a question that is so loaded, so fraught with implications, that it seems impossible to answer. You find yourself in an instant predicament. Their question demands an answer, yet any response you can think of seems either insufficient or potentially sends messages that you don't want to send. Nothing seems even slightly adequate—you are suddenly at a total loss for words. What do you do? You have to say something.

Let's begin with what not to do:

Never counter with a question.

> "Alexis, is there something I should be worried about?"
> "I'm not having sex with Austin if that's what you mean."
> (Which is a lie.)
> "No, no, I wasn't asking you that. I was just wondering if there was something I should know."
> "I just wanted your opinion. Is that so difficult?"

The problem with a question is that it is evasive and will be taken as a counterattack—setting a negative tone to the conversation. And that is not at all what you want.

Don't give too much of an answer either:

> "Alexis, as you know, condoms are used as protection against pregnancy and STDs. You have to understand that this is a serious subject and that whatever I'm going to say to you about condoms—not that I claim to know everything about condoms because I don't—does not mean that I am saying that having sex at your age is in any way okay. But I do think it is important that . . ."
> "Nice talking with you, Mom, but I've really got to get to my homework. Call me when supper's ready. Love you."

Alexis wanted an answer, not a lecture. This is a frequent teen complaint with their parents, a significant impediment to future discussion.

Not answering the question, and offering an opinion instead, is also not a good way to go.

> "It's not a question of whether condoms work or not. You're too young to have sex. What happens with condoms shouldn't have anything to do with you."

Alexis's mother misses a chance to convey important information and, again, lessens the chance of future, useful conversations.

Thanks a lot, Mom. I was looking for some information, but all I get instead is a don't-have-sex lecture.

So what should you do? Answer as straightforwardly, simply, and honestly as you can.

Here's an example:

> *"Mom, do condoms work?"*
>
> *"Yes, but they are not always one hundred percent effective. Also they need to be used correctly. I don't know all about condoms. We could try and learn more and get a better answer, maybe check on the Internet."*

This may or may not express what you want to say. The point is that it's straightforward, honest, and brief.

The problem, of course, is that there is so much that is left unsaid. There is also the worry that the brevity of the conversation implies that you're more comfortable with unspoken prospects than you really are.

Am I giving her permission? Am I teaching her to have sex?

You have two, not totally compatible, aims. You want to convey exactly the right information and message, but you also want to establish the best possible format so as to encourage future discussion on all topics. Of the two, I think that keeping good communication is the more important. Also if you feel that there was more that needed to be said, you always have the option of coming back at a later time with additional comments.

The hard part is having to decide your approach right at that moment. You will never feel totally comfortable with what you say. You have to be willing to say what you think is best on very short notice, take your chances that it is good enough, and then—hardest of all—shut up. To keep an ongoing line of communication between you and your teen, there is nothing more important than being as honest as you can be. After you've imparted some wisdom, say no more, just listen, and you will have increased your chances of getting a second shot at the subject on subsequent occasions.

"Thanks for that answer, Mom. That was good. You were straightforward, honest, and brief. I've got another question. Is it true that being high on marijuana increases sexual desire?"

Four

BUILDING A STRONG RELATIONSHIP

More often than not, it is very possible to develop a good relationship with your teenage child. Teens are fun, lively, smart—and even, at times, affectionate. There are, however, three main impediments to having a truly harmonious relationship with them. One is that you cannot have a good relationship with your teenager *all* of the time. There will always be those moments when you are either saying "no" or are making unwelcome demands on them. A harmonious relationship under those circumstances would be totally weird:

> "No, Cody, I am not going to give you forty-two dollars."
> "That's okay, no harm in asking. Dad, you're still the greatest.
> Did I tell you the joke about the three pregnant monkeys?"
> "I hope it's not like the one about the three pregnant ostriches."

> "Lisa, I need you to interrupt your TV show. Rufus just threw
> up on the rug again and I need you to clean it up right away so the
> room doesn't get too smelly."
> "Sure, Mom. That dumb dog can't keep his food down. But
> we're a team in this house and I need to pitch in. Right, Mom?"
> "That's my girl."

Were it only so.

The second main impediment to a truly harmonious relationship is the aforementioned teenage allergy to parents whereby teens find everything about their parents aggravating.

"I find everything about my parents aggravating."

This allergy makes them not want to be wherever their parents are.

"I want to be wherever my parents aren't."

One last impediment to having a good relationship with your teen is that you are human and this is your child. As a result, you will not always act in the most rational, designed-to-have-the-best-possible-effect-on-your-relationship manner.

"I have had it! Had it! You are just too much. Too much!"

Because you are human and this is your child, there are going to be days where you are just not up for it, but you have to be anyway because your child is still there.

"This is it! I mean it this time! Do you hear me? This really is it!"

Also, because this is your child, your feelings are far closer to the surface and you have far less self-control than when you are out in the world or dealing with nonfamily members.

"Over the top! Too much! Way too much!"

Not only do you want your relationship with your teenager to be pleasant, but you also want it to be supportive of them during what is almost certainly a very stressful time in their lives. You want it to be positive enough to serve as the basis for a good relationship with them when they're adults too. That is, you don't want your relationship with them during their teenage years to screw up your relationship with them later on.

So what can you do as a parent during their teenage years that will ensure that your relationship with them as adults will be as good as it can possibly be? What follows are some dos and don'ts that should help you build as strong and rewarding a relationship with your teen as you can.

THE BUSINESS PARENT VS. THE NURTURING PARENT

Interactions between you and your teenager fall into two very different categories, where you are playing two very different roles. One role might best be described as "the Business Parent." The Business Parent makes demands on them and does not agree to do everything they want. The other role is for all of those times when you are not being a Business Parent. It might be called "the Nurturing Parent." Much of this book is devoted to making the Business Parent role as effective, smooth, and efficient as possible so that it won't dominate the time you spend with your teen. If you can reduce the time that you have to spend being the Business Parent, it leaves more time for nurturing. But I would add one more important point to this discussion of roles: the Business Parent and the Nurturing Parent do NOT mix.

"No, my darling daughter, I'm not going to give you a lift to Valerie's. Mommy just doesn't feel like driving her perfect little treasure forty minutes back and forth to Valerie's only to pick her up again later. But, don't forget, Mommy loves you to pieces. Let's see that big smile."

No, the Nurturing Parent and the Business Parent do not go well together. There is a time for business and there is a time for nurturing. But the good news is that there are a lot of times when you are with your teenager and you are not in your Business Parent role. In other words, there are lots of times when you and your teen can simply relax and enjoy each other's company. The problem, of course, is that you may be ready to enjoy your teenager, you may be in the mood to have a nice time with them, but they may be thinking otherwise.

"Excuse me, why would I want to spend time in the company of the one person in the world, more than any other, whom I don't want to spend time with?"

BEING WITH TEENS WHEN THEY DON'T WANT TO BE WITH YOU

Let me describe a parental attitude you can assume to help solve the conundrum we all face when we spend time with our teens: when we want to be with them, but their allergy to us has flared up. Adopting this attitude can really make a significant difference—for the better— in what transpires between you and your teenager every day. It is a way to cut through the grimness that can suck the joy out of parenting a teenager. The gist of it is that they may be allergic to you, but you don't have to be allergic to them.

Billy Ray's father is in the kitchen preparing breakfast. He is in a good mood. Enter his beloved son.

"What's for breakfast?"

"French toast."

"But I hate French toast."

"I thought you liked it."

"Well, I don't. I hate it."

"When did you start hating French toast?"

"I don't know. I've always hated it. You just don't pay attention."

"Well, that's what's for breakfast. If you want something else, you have two perfectly good hands and know where the food is."

"There's never anything I like in this stupid house."

"Nothing is ever good enough for you."

"Nothing is ever good enough because everything in this house sucks."

"Do you know what I should do, Billy Ray? I should make a videotape of a day at home with you. I think I'd call it 'Twenty-four Hours with My Crabby Teen.' Then you'd see how unpleasant you really are to live with."

"No, then you'd see how everything in this house sucks."

It's a problem. You may want to have a good time with your teen, a pleasant family breakfast, but they may not be cooperating.

"Why would I want to have a good time with my dad? I don't like being with him. And besides, everything he says is dumb and irritating."

So where does that leave you? Either you're playing bad-guy Business Parent, in which case they don't like you, or they're in their surly, allergic-to-you role, in which case they don't like you. So when do you get to enjoy each other?

"How about never, which would be fine with me."

Like I said, it's a problem. But take heart—there is a solution.

THE MOOD-ALTERING POWER OF COMPETING MELODIES

I'm not exactly sure when it started or where it came from, but when my kids, Nick and Margaret, were teenagers I developed what turned out to be a particularly useful attitude toward their occasional teenage grumpiness. Since I loved them a lot and I really did enjoy being with them most of the time, I decided I would be damned if I let their grumpiness dominate interactions between us. If they were going to be grumpy, that did not mean that I had to be grumpy in response—which is how most parents innately react to their own teens' sullen behavior. I was determined not to let their grumpy tone overwhelm my upbeat mood.

What follows is what I did. I know that I actually did this, because I remember having a name for my antigrumpy behavior. I thought of it as "competing melodies." If my kids were going to be crabby, I would not respond in sync with their crabbiness. I wanted my good mood to win out. I was going to fight to have it my way.

When a kid says, *"I hate French toast,"* it's natural for a parent to change their tune and say something more in line with their kid's crabby comment such as:

> *"Well, that's what's for breakfast. If you don't like it you don't have to eat it."*
> Or:
> *"Why do you always have to be so negative?"*
> Or, even the sarcastic:
> *"Well, look who's here. It's Mr. Cheerful."*
> Which does not work, by the way, because kids hear it as a put-down. Which it is.
> All of that inevitably leads to:
> *"Screw you, Dad!"*

But if you employ my competing-melodies technique the exchange is more likely to go something like this:

> *"What's for breakfast?"*
> *"French toast."*
> *"I hate French toast."*
> Instead of my responding to their negative tone with more of the same, I'd respond with a very different, opposing melody— one that is friendly and upbeat.
> *"Well, I love French toast. In fact, I'm going to sing the French toast song:*
>
> *"I love French toast, don't you?*
> *I love French toast, don't you?*

I love French toast in the morning.
Oh, please, please, give me two."

And despite their best efforts,
"Dad! Please! I'm so not in the mood for this!"
I would refuse to veer from my upbeat melody. In the end, more often than not, my way would win out.
"Dad, that is so dopey. I can't believe you sang a French toast song. I have the dopiest dad in the world."
"I know."

But now the comments I elicited from them were not angry; they were good-humored.

I have no idea whether the above sequence actually took place; the story may be apocryphal. But I do know that what I describe above was definitely characteristic of the spirit of competing melodies, which I would often use in response to my teenage children's crabbiness. If not the above, there are other examples that are similar and just as ridiculous.

There is a strong argument for not meeting teenage negativity with corresponding negativity. Not only does negativity almost never work, but it also feeds the depressing cycle that, all too often, occurs between parent and grumpy teenager. I like my way better. So did my kids.

Here are some more examples:

"How was school today, dear?"
"Boring and dumb as always. Why do I have to go?"
A response in harmony with the above might be:
"Because it's the law. And if you paid better attention in class and kept up with your work, you'd like it more."
But that would almost certainly result in something like:
"I do keep up with my schoolwork! But you don't understand how boring and dumb it really is! I want to be homeschooled."
Or perhaps:
"You have no idea how lucky you are to be able to go to a school like yours and to have the opportunities that you have."
"No, you have no idea what it's like having to go every day to a prison, where you don't learn anything that you are ever going to use later on in your life!"

Let's now look at the same scenarios using my technique:

"How was school today, dear?"
"Boring and dumb as always. Why do I have to go?"
Not picking up on their negativity but instead plowing ahead with my good mood, I would then say:
"Well, my day was great. I had a really nice talk with your aunt. She's so hard to catch, but we had a good chat."

It doesn't always have to be funny—just upbeat.
Another example:

"Why can't we get new chairs? I hate these chairs."
An in-sync response:
"There's nothing wrong with the chairs. Besides, as you know, we're not made of money and can't always be getting new furniture."
A better response—one that is not apologetic, not defensive, nor offended:
"Well, I love them. They're my favorite furniture in the house. I was thinking of getting more of them. Look at the way their finish catches the light from the window. Don't you just love that?"
Which, more likely than not, might result in something like:
"Dad, you are so weird." But now, he's responding with friendly teasing—he's no longer hostile.
Again, it doesn't have to be funny, just upbeat. For example:
"I'm sorry you don't like the chairs. I like them a lot. I think they're nice."

It isn't always possible to use this strategy. If you're just not in an upbeat mood then the best thing is to play it straight—but not critical or challenging.

"I'm sorry you don't like the chairs."
"I don't. We should get new ones."

But here you would want to say no more.
Crabbiness in response to their crabbiness is just not the way to go.

It is far better—when you're in the mood— to counter their unpleasant-ness with happy responses. To do so results in a far more pleasant home.

THE CURE FOR YOUR TEEN'S ALLERGY TO YOU

As I have said before, the vast majority of kids contract a temporary allergy to their parents once they hit their adolescence. This is part of their normal psychological development. The result is very much like a force field pushing you away. Hence, one of the most frequently asked questions is: To what extent should parents respect their kids' need to push them away, their need to establish their own sense of independence?

I think the answer is that you respect it to some degree, but not com-pletely. A good example involves hugs.

I am a strong believer in giving one's teenage children hugs. They hate it. But, at the same time, they like it very much. The hugs should be real hugs, not delicate little polite hugs. And they should also be brief.

Renaldo's father gives his son a big hug.

> *"Now, wasn't that nice?"*
> *"No."*
> *"I know you liked it."*
> *"I didn't."*
> The reality is that Renaldo did not exactly enjoy the hug.
> *"That's what I said."*
> But deep down he did.
> *"No, I didn't."*

Deep down, he very much—though he may not admit it—liked the *idea* of the hug.

What's that supposed to mean?

The hug says—more clearly than any verbal statement:

My dad loves me. Despite everything, my dad loves me.

This is a big deal. I'll say it again: teenagers hate hugs. But, at the same time, they like them very much. They may not actually like the hug itself, but they very much like the message.

I don't know why my dad aggravates me so much. Just having him near me makes my skin crawl and everything he says is so dopey, so totally un-necessary. Every word out of his mouth is so aggravating.

But Dad still loves me. I know I can be pretty nasty to him sometimes, but he loves me anyway. He's still there—the parent who used to love me to pieces, and in whose eyes I always knew I was special. He still loves me—despite all the stuff that goes on.

A hug shows your teen that, for all the negativity that they dish out daily, you are able to rise above it. Your love connection to them is so solid that it transcends everything else.

You're wrong. You don't know what's going on inside of me. I don't like the hug.

But he does.

Warning: don't be too disturbed if your teen grows rigid under the hug. It's natural. Which is also why the hug should not last very long.

THE EFFECTS OF A HELPFUL ATTITUDE

It's not fun to have someone you love be allergic to you. It can hurt your feelings. Fortunately, there is a perspective that you can adopt to make it far easier to sustain the upbeat melody that I describe here.

Many parents run into trouble from the start because they make an understandable, but incorrect, assumption. Let me describe the mistake. Jonathan's mother says to her son:

> *"Jonathan, I just want you to tell me one thing and then I won't bother you anymore. Just answer me this one question: Why do you hate me so much? What is it about me that you can't stand? What is it about me that makes being in the room with me such a torture for you? What is it about me that is so terrible? I just want to know because, if you tell me, I will change."*
>
> *"It's you. Everything about you."*
>
> *"But tell me what exactly. I'll change anything. I just don't want you to hate me so much."*

Jonathan's mother doesn't get it: Jonathan's problem with her is not something that she can change. Jonathan's problem is that she is his mother. It's not personal; it's just the normal teenage allergy—and she's what he's allergic to. Even if you change everything about yourself, you are still his parent and he is still a teenager. They don't hate you. It only seems that way.

> "Look, Jonathan. I've totally changed my hair color. I've gotten all new makeup. I don't even look like me."
> "But you're still you. I don't know; maybe if you got a brain transplant."

As I said, Jonathan's mother doesn't get it.

Let me propose a mantra to help parents survive the grimness that can color so much of having a teenager in the house. This mantra is unspoken, but these words are good to have in your head. These are the words that should underlie your interactions with your teenager. You don't actually say them to your teen. But they are there.

> I know that you can't stand me. I know that you can't stand even being in the same room with me. But I also know that this is a direct result of a process—adolescence—over which you have no control or even awareness of. I understand that this is all part of your normal psychological development. In only a few years, you will like me again and have no trouble being around me. It's not about me. It's just a stage that you are going through. And I know it's not personal.
> No, it is personal! It's you!
> No, it's not personal. And not only is it not personal, but I love you so much, and I am so oblivious to all the negativity that is spewing outward from you to me, that I actually like being with you. Aren't we having a good time?

WHEN YOUR TEEN IS OBLIVIOUS TO YOU

We've already covered the subject of being with your teen when they don't want to be with you, but now we're going to address a subtle but important variation on that theme—*enjoying* your teen even when everything he or she is doing would make even the biggest narcissist feel rejected. The trick in these circumstances is to wear blinders to block out the surface negativity, and to help you focus on the love and attachment that has always been there and still is underneath.

"It's not there! There is nothing underneath! You don't know anything!"

But it *is* there. Let me give an example.

It is a Tuesday evening. Renaldo's father comes to his son's room and knocks on the door.

> *"Can I come in?"*
>
> *"No."*
>
> *"Well, I'm coming in anyway."*
>
> *"I know what this is about! You're not welcome in my room!"*
>
> After a brief pause, Renaldo's father enters his son's room.
>
> *"Here I am again. It's Tuesday night and it's time for our weekly father-and-son chat. Isn't this great?"*
>
> *"Omigod, it's happening again."*
>
> *"Let's see, where should we start? Hmm, let me think. I suppose I should begin because you never do, except asking when the chat will be over. I know what we'll talk about: Do you remember last week I told you about this restaurant I went to for lunch where they had this really good pea soup?"*
>
> *"I can't believe this."*
>
> *"Well, anyway, I went back there for lunch today and I had the pea soup again, and it was disgusting. I can't understand it. Maybe they switched cooks or something. What do you think?"*
>
> *"When will I wake up from this nightmare?"*
>
> It is a very useful approach. They may be crabby, but not only do you not take their crabbiness personally, you are such an idiot, so blind to their apparent dislike of you, and you love them so much, that you enjoy being with them—crabbiness and all.
>
> *"Aren't we having a good time?"*
>
> *"No."*

But they do very much appreciate this approach. For it says—again—that whatever is going on with them, whatever it is that makes them sometimes seriously unpleasant, you are able to rise above it. It says that your love for them trumps all. That is what it feels like to them. You do rise above it. And they like that very much.

I know what you're thinking: *But you can't just ignore their negative behavior; it deserves, and needs, to be responded to. Otherwise, they will feel that they are getting away with it. And won't they feel that they can act that way anytime they want?*

Not really. Certainly, there are times—as I have described and will describe—when you should pick up on specific negative behavior. But, yes, I am saying—and it is the position that I take throughout this book—that for general day-to-day teenage bad attitude, there is nothing that comes close to producing a more pleasant home and a more pleasant relationship than what I am proposing here.

And the lesson that they learn is not:

It's okay if I walk all over my parents.

The lesson that they learn is:

I don't know why, maybe they're idiots, but despite everything my parents seem to love me. They even seem to like being with me.

THE UNCONDITIONAL DEAL

I have just described a way of being with teens that runs counter to their negative daily behavior: they can be unpleasant, but that does not mean you have to be. All of this is based on an underlying assumption about your role as a parent. One that lies at the core of this book. I think of it as the "unconditional deal."

It was the holiday season, a time of goodwill and gift giving. Graham's mother was thinking about her teenage son.

What has Graham done in the past year to deserve anything? I'll tell you what he's done to deserve nothing. For the sake of brevity I'll list just a very few items:

> *1. On numerous occasions—too many to count—when I was in the middle of talking to him, he just left the room.*

> *2. Three weeks ago, when my friend Clarisse was over, he called me "stupid" right in front of her.*

> *3. More than once, he has smoked pot in the house with his buddies and denied it—he even gets mad at me when I confront him.*

4. *Two days ago—and this kind of thing happens regularly—
I asked him if he could bring me a glass of diet root beer with
ice since he was going to the kitchen, and he acted like this
was the biggest imposition in the world.*

5. *He constantly says the meanest things to me and swears at
his younger brother, who gets very upset.*

6. *Over the past year, he has given new meaning to the
word sullen.*

7. *And, oh yeah, he's failing all his classes in school
except cooking.*

And I'm supposed to give him presents? Why would I want to do that?
   In a famous song, Santa Claus advises that kids had better watch
their behavior because he knows if they've been bad or good. Santa implies that if the answer is "bad," he's not going to give them anything,
except maybe a lump of coal, or an overlarge and extremely out-of-date
cell phone that can't do anything except make phone calls.
   I take strong exception to Santa's view. What should you do if, on the
balancing scale of behavior, your child has tipped far down on the negative side? Not just in regard to presents and holiday time, but the larger
question: How much good stuff do they deserve to get from you? How
much—if any—attention, caring, favors, gifts, and money should you
give to a teenage child who regularly acts like a total jerk?
   I am a strong advocate of what I call "the unconditional deal": there
is much that I give you, automatically, just because you are my child.
Though I may, at the time, react negatively in response to unpleasant
things that you do, there is much that you will receive anyway—no
matter what. Automatically, just because you are my child, you get certain things from me—love, attention, caring, favors, presents—in order
to make your life as pleasant as it possibly can be. And you get all of that
with no strings attached—just because you are my child.
   *"Ho! Ho! Ho! You can't do that. Then they won't learn what's naughty
or nice."*
   Santa's point is that if your teen acts like a jerk all year yet still gets
loving attention and nice presents as if he had been an angel, what does

that teach him? Doesn't it tell him he can get away with any kind of behavior?

The unconditional deal says that, completely separate from any consequences for bad behavior, there is something built into your relationship with your child where he automatically gets good stuff from you just because he is your child. Your teen does learn a lesson from this, and that lesson is not that he can get away with bad behavior. He learns that you give to him—whether he has acted well or not—because that is what you, as his parent, do. You try to make him happy.

What your teen will think is not:

My parents are such total wusses that I can do anything and they give me stuff anyway. What naive jerks! How can you respect people who are so dumb?

What he thinks is much more like:

I don't know. They can be jerks, and I totally hate them sometimes. And I know that sometimes I don't exactly act right—they deserve it, mind you, because they acted like jerks to me. Still, they try to be nice to me, and sometimes they even give me nice stuff. And the only reason that I can think of for why they do this is because of some kind of bigger deal that goes on just because I'm their kid. I gotta say I like the deal.

And, having been recipients of the unconditional deal, children are far more—not less—likely to be generous themselves.

Regardless of what people—or even Santa—say, I am a strong believer that this is the deal that all children deserve.

ADULTS AS FLAWED BEINGS

Being the parent of a teenager is a very different experience from that which precedes their adolescence. To get along with a teenager requires certain attitudinal shifts on your part. If you don't make these shifts, then parenting a teenager can be a lot rougher than it needs to be. These shifts are necessitated by real changes in who these kids become once they are adolescents.

One of the most important shifts involves accepting your status as a human being who has flaws.

> *"Dad, why do you always brush your hair like that, trying to cover up your bald spot? Do you know how geeky it looks?"*

"Mom, why do you always talk in that phony voice whenever your boss is on the phone?"

"Dad, you're doing it again: you always line up your silverware before you eat. You have OCD."

Teenagers can be brutal when it comes to pointing out your flaws. They seem to take pleasure in detailing every blemish and failing. Their comments can be very hard to shrug off. They know us well, and what they point out are usually real flaws. Their comments often hit right at our insecurities.

I really hate my bald spot. I had hoped that the way I brushed my hair would cover it, but maybe it doesn't look so good. I'm not sure what to do.

It's true that I talk in a different voice with my boss. I can't help it. I just get very nervous whenever I talk to her. I wish I didn't.

That's wrong. I don't always line up my silverware before eating. Actually, I do. Maybe I do have OCD. I don't know. OCD? Do you think?

And it's such a change from how they used to view you when they were younger.

"Hi, Mommy! Look what I have for the best mommy in the world!"

"Why, isn't that sweet, Samantha. Another 'I Love You, Mommy' card with hearts and smiley faces. Thank you, Samantha."

"Would you like another one, Mommy?"

"Not right now, sweetheart. Mommy has enough for now."

"That's okay, Mommy! I'm going to make some more for you! I'm going to put rainbows on them this time!"

"I really have enough, Samantha."

"Oh, I'll just make another one anyway because I love you so much!"

"I have the smartest dad in the whole world, don't I, Dad?"

"Well, maybe not the smartest in the whole world, Jonathan."

"Yes, you are! You're the smartest dad in the whole world!"

They idolized you, this adult person who was the font of all strength, wisdom, and goodness.

"I really love my mommy!"

When they were little kids they needed to see you as wise and powerful because they depended on you. Their sense of security and well-being was rooted in you. If there was a problem, they could always turn to Mommy or Daddy.

> *"Mommy! I have a problem."*
> *"What is it, dear?"*
> *"I don't know."*
> *"Well, Mommy will figure it out and fix it."*

Parents were all-knowing and all-powerful and could be relied on. Parents could deal with everything that they—as little kids—couldn't. They didn't have to worry about being competent as long as their parents were.

So what happened? The worm turned.

As I described earlier, the hallmark of adolescence is that your now teenage children feel they can no longer be dependent little kids. They have to see themselves as independent, adultlike beings, because they know they'll soon be out on their own. They are painfully aware that they are far from perfect. And if being an adult means that you are supposed to be perfect—if adults are expected to be completely competent, know everything, and have no flaws—then they are in big trouble.

It was okay for me to think that my parents were perfect when it was their job to take care of me. But now it's my job to take care of me. And that scares the shit out of me. I'm supposed to be independent and rely on myself to get through life. Which is fine, except that I can't help but notice that I have lots of things wrong with me. There's all kinds of stuff I don't know and lots of things I'm not good at. Also, I don't seem to have anything near total control of myself. I do stuff that I know is not in my best interest. And there's all kinds of stuff that I know I should do, but I can't make myself do them. How is a big mess like me ever going to manage on my own? How am I supposed to survive in the big world if I have so many things wrong with me? Mom and Dad seem to have been able to do it, but they're not a big mess like me.

No, wait—I just got an idea: maybe they're not so perfect. Maybe they have lots of issues just like I do. If so, that would be great! What a relief!

Maybe you don't have to be that perfect to survive. If that's true, then I have a chance. Excellent!

Which is why it's a big relief to teenagers when they see that adults in their world, especially their parents, have flaws. Lots of them. It's something they want to point out at every opportunity.

"Dad, did you know that your left ear is bigger than your right ear? Why is that?"

So what's a parent to do when faced with ever-more-critical children? This is a big issue in building a good relationship with one's teenage child. It's not only an issue that can be troubling to parents; it is one where many parents frequently err.

A DIFFERENT KIND OF STRONG

There are good *and* bad ways to respond when your flaws are constantly being pointed out to you. One wrong way—which teenagers hate, and subsequently fight against tooth and nail—is when parents defend themselves or, even worse, counterattack. Far better are responses that illustrate an ability to accept your flaws and not be so thrown by having them outed for all the world to see.

To do this one must be strong—and by "strong" I don't mean according to the standard definition. Teenagers are not just older, they are now also smarter and wiser in viewing the ways of the world than they were when they were still little kids. With their new, more adultlike perceptions, they recognize that a more sophisticated definition of "strong" exists. "Strong" is not just knowing everything and having power over people. "Strong" can also mean being comfortable with yourself, feeling that you are—overall—a competent person despite the fact that you—like all other humans—have lots of flaws. In fact, they often perceive people's efforts to hide their flaws as a kind of "weakness." Once kids become smarter and wiser teenagers, such bravado starts looking less like "strong" and more like "insecure." Regardless, teens will continue to fight to keep you flawed.

Let me go back to the examples mentioned above.

Eduardo, to his father:

> *"Dad, you know the way you brush your hair to cover up your bald spot? It really looks geeky."*

"I think it looks fine. There's nothing wrong with the way my hair looks. Nobody has said anything to me."

What his son thinks:

My dad won't admit that he has any flaws. I guess looking geeky is a real problem if you're an adult, and my dad hasn't figured out how to handle it. He just denies it. I guess it really is tough having flaws when you go out into the world.

And in response to his father's defensiveness, Eduardo will probably just attack all the more.

"Well, it does. It makes you look really geeky."

Or, another bad parental response:

"It's really rude to talk to me that way, Eduardo. I hope you know never to say something like that to a teacher or one of our friends. Or, God forbid, to your aunt Rebecca, who has such little hair left since she got sick. How do you like it when people tease you about being short?"

Again, it is not a good response. If Eduardo's father is genuinely concerned that his son might talk that way to others outside the immediate family, then he should bring it up with Eduardo at a later time. Here, the only impact of Eduardo's father's words will be to show his son that he cannot handle being flawed, and his son sees—correctly—that his father's words are a counterpunch designed to fend off embarrassment. Which, again, would elicit a continuing attack.

"It's not rude. I'm stating a fact. It's true. It looks really geeky. Who's going to tell you if not your kid? You should thank me."

A better—nondefensive—response would be as follows:

"Dad, why do you brush your hair like that trying to cover up your bald spot? Do you know how geeky it looks?"

"You think so? Yeah, I guess it sort of does. But it's the best I can do if I want to cover up the bald spot, and I hate the bald spot."

Which might well evoke:

"You don't think there's something else you could do? Maybe you should go to a hairdresser. Guys do, you know."

Now Eduardo is an ally.

How would I describe this approach? Honest. Matter-of-fact. Willing to accept and be comfortable with having flaws. Above all, it is not defensive. It is by far a much better attitude to have and a better way to model behavior to your child.

Now let's revisit the second scenario:

> *"Mom, why do you always use that weird phony voice whenever you talk to your boss on the phone?"*

The not-so-good response would be:

> *"If I speak differently it is because she's my boss and I speak more respectfully toward her because that's how you should address your employer."*

Which is a lie, as she speaks that way because her boss—whom she dislikes—makes her nervous.

Or perhaps:

> *"Why do you always think you have to criticize everything that I do?"*

Again, with both responses, the mother is not able to accept her own flaws and is communicating that fact very clearly to her child.

The much better response would be:

> *"I don't know. She makes me nervous. Whenever I talk to her, it just comes out like that."*

Honest. Not defensive. And the lesson your child hears is:

Mom gets nervous about stuff. Like I do.

These better responses definitely show the parent being more vulnerable in front of their child.

For better or for worse, this is who I am.

Many parents have a lot of trouble tolerating this more vulnerable approach. Which is why they so quickly get defensive and angry.

Some even ask, *"Is it okay for a parent to expose themselves to their child like that? Doesn't that make the parent seem weak? Don't they lose some of their child's respect?*

No. As I described, it comes off as more honest. More adult. More, not less, worthy of respect.

The third example:

"Dad, you know the way you always line up your silverware before you eat—even if it's fine? You have OCD."

The not-so-good reply:

"There is nothing wrong with liking things to be neat. And I certainly don't have OCD."

"No, you have OCD. Maybe you should be on medication."

The better reply:

"Yeah, I guess I am kind of a neatness freak."

"Not kind of."

Yet another example:

"Mom, you are such an idiot. You got all these banana-strawberry yogurts for Carrie [her younger sister], but Carrie never eats the banana-strawberry ones."

"Well, if I wasn't so rushed at the supermarket because I had to get back here so I could get you over to your friend Vanessa's house, I wouldn't have made the mistake. Besides, it's good for Carrie to sometimes have to get used to foods she doesn't like."

The best response of all:

"Yeah, I forgot."

A last example:

Darren's father underestimated the time that it would take to drive from their house to where Darren had his soccer game. As a result, Darren got to the soccer game twenty-five minutes late.

"Dad, you really fucked up! Now I'm really fucked! Coach Daniels is going to be really pissed at me! You know how he feels about kids being late!"

The not-so-good response:

"These directions that they gave you weren't any good. They made it look like it was a much shorter trip than it turned out to be. I'm going to find out who was responsible for the directions."

The better response:

"I'm sorry, Darren. I screwed up."

You may rightfully ask yourself, But how can you admit to flaws one minute, and the next minute boss your kid around?

Doesn't this approach undermine you? Isn't it incompatible with being an authoritative parent?

No. It is, I think, a particularly adult approach. In effect, you're saying, *"Yes, I do have flaws. Lots of them. But I feel okay about myself. I even feel good about myself in the job of being your parent—ignorant as I may be at times."*

It's a more real approach. Instead of being an adult who constantly feels they have to appear flawless, you take on a far less defensive persona. It's also a far more useful model for your kids. You're saying that this is what it is to be an adult: not a know-it-all, not someone who can handle all situations, but someone who is imperfect, yet good enough. It is possible to be an adult and not be perfect.

It's an approach that teenagers like. Teenagers want to feel that their parents are competent. Just not too competent. The main problem with the adult-equals-perfect approach is that teenagers hate it and they will attack. They don't tolerate adults who think they know everything. Those are the adults who regularly have the most difficulty in dealing with teenagers. When you admit flaws, they respect you more, not less.

ENGAGING IN FRIENDLY TEASING—WHEN YOUR TEEN DOES IT TO YOU

Owning up to your own flaws can be really useful in building a relationship with your teenager. It can even have an added bonus beyond their being reassured that you don't have to be perfect to be a competent adult. If you are comfortable with being flawed in front of your teenager, then that comfort can allow them to express very nice feelings of love toward you.

"Dad, you are so clumsy," says Bernie as his father trips on the stairs coming into the house. *"Clumsy Man, that's who you are. Maybe you could have your own TV show, kind of a reverse superhero."*

"Mom, you did it again," Johanna shouts gleefully. *"You made a right turn when the GPS lady said to go left. You're directionally challenged."*

Strange as it may seem, both of the above are examples of loving contact from a teenager toward their parent. It is often the one way that teenagers can circumvent the teen allergy. They may indeed have feelings of love and closeness toward you, but the teenage allergy prevents them from showing these feelings in an overt way. Teasing provides a good cover.

There are, of course, some times when teens are comfortable with direct expressions of love and affection.

"I love you, Dad."

Or with giving a parent a spontaneous hug.

In fact, many teens actually do this. But many don't. Many just are not comfortable with such public or physical displays. Since being close and intimate—loving, openly vulnerable, and friendly—directly runs up against the teen allergy, many teens use gentle teasing as their one acceptable way of maintaining loving contact with their family. It's akin to a friendly punch.

If I can somehow make friendly contact in a way that has some kind of a built-in distancing mechanism, that would work. I could do that. I can actually sometimes feel affection toward my dad, but saying "I love you" or giving him a hug just feels too weird.

The above two examples of friendly teasing are okay from the teen's standpoint.

I'm being intimate and friendly, but it's acceptable to me because it's couched in the form of an insult. (None of these words by the teenagers are in their heads. But they are how the teenagers feel.)

If you saw a video of the above two child-teasing-parent examples, you would actually see that the exchanges are truly good-natured. But for that kind of comfort to exist, for the exchanges to be good-natured, the parent must already have established a sense that they are comfortable being on the receiving end of friendly put-downs.

Again, for teasing to be friendly and good-natured, it requires that the one being teased does not mind the teasing. But if you are comfortable with it, as the butt of ongoing jokes, you can fit in with how teenagers often prefer to view their parents. They want to see you as competent when that is necessary, for their sense of security. But they also very much like the idea of a parent who in some ways is clueless.

Teenagers want to see their parents as people who can handle their own lives, who can deal more or less effectively, who are knowledgeable about the world, whom they can count on to provide them with a secure life. They tend to be proud of parents who do well.

At the same time, they do not want their parents to be knowledgeable in regard to *their* world—the world of friends, school, and, especially, those things that are peculiar to the world of teens: what they like, what's current, what's cool, what's not. They very definitely do not want their parents to be knowledgeable about *those* things.

A significant aspect of teenagers' being able to establish a comfortable distance from their parents is in their knowledge that their parents do not know everything going on in their heads. There is much that teenagers believe that their parents would not understand because their parents are old and very much not with it, so they cannot know about this part of their teens' world. They just aren't hip enough.

It is parent-as-sort-of-bozo.

What they want in a parent:

My dad and mom are nice but they are clueless about a lot of stuff. They think that Frank Sinatra is the best. Mom thinks it's really cool to go around the house wearing bunny slippers, and Dad has this hat with earflaps that he wears sometimes in the house, which he says keeps his neck warm. And his stomach gurgles, and they both snore, which Mom denies that she does, but she does. And if we watch something funny on TV, they laugh at the wrong parts. And they totally do not get Rappin Lennie, who they think should be banned, and they 100 percent do not understand how cool he is. Also, any joke that either of them tells is so totally not funny.

It is all part of the image of a parent that teens are most comfortable with.

It is not necessarily a real flaw. It is more of an assigned fictional caricature.

There is a parental caricature that teens are particularly comfortable with. It is of the good-natured adult who in some areas is competent but otherwise is hopelessly clueless.

"Well, duh, Dad. You just have to do a right click, and then double click on the icon."

ENGAGING IN FRIENDLY TEASING—WHEN YOU DO IT TO YOUR TEEN

Your kids like teasing you. It can be genuinely affectionate. Enjoyed by them. Enjoyed by you. It is not, however, a two-way street.

"We call Travis Mr. Big Ears. He knows we're only teasing. That we don't mean anything by it. That it's all in fun."

"Speaking of vomiting, Renee, do you remember that time at the zoo when you threw up?"

"Carly has a crush on this nice boy in her algebra class. He's your new heartthrob, isn't he, honey?"

Often, as part of our loving relationship with our teenage children, we engage in gentle teasing. It's part of the fun that parents have with their kids. The problem is that our children don't like it.

This is what *we* think they think of our loving teasing:

I don't mind when they call me Mr. Big Ears. I like it. I know they don't mean anything by it. It's a way of us having fun together.

This is what he actually thinks:

It's not funny. I don't like it. Yeah, I know I have big ears. I wish I didn't. I'm embarrassed by my ears. They know that. I don't know why they think it's funny, teasing me about something I'm so uncomfortable with.

The only thing that Travis gets out of the teasing is that he is embarrassed and has an unpleasant feeling.

"Ha, ha, ha," he says good-naturedly. *Fuck you,* he thinks.

No, they do not enjoy your teasing. Teasing makes fun of their flaws. It only makes them more uncomfortable, even ashamed.

"He's our Elbow Boy," teases Clement's father. And for the next year, Clement wears only long-sleeved shirts.

Over time, if the teasing continues, they may get used to it so that it does not bother them quite so much. They become hardened to it. But they never like it.

A good rule with regard to teasing one's teenage children is this: don't do it.

But doesn't occasional good-natured teasing allow children to better deal with teasing out in the world? Not really. That skill comes from a combination of their own self-confidence and verbal facility. (For example, children with language-learning disorders have a particularly hard time dealing with teasing.) Teasing from a parent can and does harden children. But that is not a good thing. If anything, it hardens them so that they begin to believe that demeaning and hurtful behavior really isn't bad.

It's normal and natural to want to tease your teenage children. It's just not a good idea.

The nature of acceptable teasing is *always* that the recipient must be comfortable, must be happy, must be willing to be on the receiving end. What may seem like friendly teasing becomes something very different when the recipient is not 100 percent okay with it.

> *"Allison, it looks like you're developing a mustache. That's funny, right?"*
> *"Yeah, it's real funny."*

Parents teasing their children—even if the teasing seems good-natured—is not a good thing.

THE PARENT AS FRIEND

"The problem with parents today is that they don't want to be parents. They don't like the part where they actually have to say 'no' or make demands on their kids. They don't like it when they have to act like adults and maybe have their kid not like them. All that parents today want is to be their kid's friends. Come down to their kid's level. Be best buddies. And, big surprise: their kids are running around wild, doing anything they feel like with no respect for anything or anybody."

The above is a commonly heard criticism of today's parents. That they don't want to be a parent. They want to be a friend, a buddy. Should a parent be a buddy with their own child? Does being your teenager's friend conflict with proper parenting?

It depends. By being a friend I am referring to how you regularly spend time with your teen, when you are just being together. Driving in the car, doing errands, engaging in a hobby or a sport, drinking coffee in the kitchen together. Above all, the times you spend talking. But the talking is not about the usual parenting issues such as plans, rules, or tasks that need to be done; instead, it is about anything else, it is times when you mainly talk about the sharing of experiences—the same as what you would do with a friend.

Daria's mother to her daughter:

"So I went to High Fashion, Low Price at the mall and they had this incredible top that was really nice and would go perfectly with my gray pants. But there was a really long line at the cash register, and I kind of lost my cool in the line, and I said a couple of swears at the cash register lady, and then I was too embarrassed, so I put the top back and left. But the problem is, I really liked the blouse, and I want it and I kind of screwed myself."

"Mom, you are such a loser."

"I know. But what should I do? I really want the blouse."

The above is an example of an excellent mother-and-daughter exchange. It has only a positive effect on the relationship between parent and child, and a positive effect on the child. It is beneficial because it establishes intimacy with your teen in an adult way, a way that is nurturing and pleasurable.

And not only that, when parent and teenager talk openly and comfortably about their own day-to-day experiences, there is always the possibility that your teen may talk not just about the mundane issues in their lives, but also about the risky behavior areas that we worry about and would like to be able to discuss more openly with our teens—sex, drugs, drinking.

"So, PJ got really drunk and was acting so goofy like he does a lot and, Mom, he was having trouble even walking straight. Mom, he was so totally shit-faced."

When parent and teen talk comfortably about these topics, just the fact that they are talking serves as a significant deterrent to overly risky behavior. It allows you to slip in an opinion or two.

"Did somebody watch him? Make sure he didn't drive? You know never to drink like that, right?"

"Mom, you know I never would do that." (Which actually she has done—twice—but was alarmed seeing how out of control her friend PJ was, and was getting a little nervous about her own drinking.)

But, more important, just the act of talking about these topics puts thoughts about these risky behaviors into your teen's head. Now, when the risky situations arise, they may not just react, they may now have thoughts in their heads causing them to make more responsible decisions—just from having talked with you.

Being in a relationship where you are a friend to your teenager is excellent and very much to your teen's advantage. But there are certain restrictions.

For one, sometimes you have to be a parent. There will be times when you will have to say "no" or make demands on them, and usually at those times they will not be happy with you. If that means, for periods of time, you will not be able to be a "friend," you must be willing to ride out those periods.

One afternoon Daria's mother told her daughter that she did not want Daria's twenty-five-year-old male guitar teacher to give her lessons when it would be just the two of them in the house. Daria was not happy with this decision. She and her mother argued, but Daria's mother held firm. Daria stormed off.

> *"You are such a bitch."*
> An hour later Daria's mother, who had not been out of the house all day, thought it would be nice to go out for coffee. She approached her daughter.
> *"Daria, do you feel like going out for coffee?"*
> *"Why would I want to do that with somebody who is a total bitch?"*

Daria's mother chose to go by herself.

Sometimes, because you act in a parental role, your teen will shut you out. It is something you have to accept and be willing to ride out. It only becomes a problem if, because of your need for their friendship right then, you try too hard to get them not to be mad at you. Which will only make matters worse. For example, had Daria's mother kept pressing her daughter,

"Come on, Daria. Don't be mad at me. You'll see, we can both go out and have a nice time," Daria would likely have seen it as a further opportunity to punish her mother for her edict in regard to her guitar teacher.

"How can I have a nice time with someone who is so unreasonable, who doesn't trust her own daughter to have any sense?"

And they would be thrown back again into their argument.

But the above did not happen, because in this particular case Daria's mother handled it well by choosing to go for coffee without her daughter.

What can also pose problems is when, because you do not want to ruin the "friend" relationship, you hold off on saying "no" or making demands when you should. At those times, if your wish to be a friend is your top priority, that is not good.

One of the not-so-easy but necessary skills of parenting a teenager is the ability to make the shift from friend to parent, sometimes turning on a dime.

Just having had a very pleasant time talking together in the car, Daria and her mother arrive home.

> *"Daria, don't forget that I need you to clean up the family room because Grandma and Papa are coming over for supper."*
>
> *"Mom, I said I would do it; you don't need to nag me."*
>
> *"Fine, but they'll be here by five o'clock, so I need it done by then."*
>
> *"I heard you the first time! I said I would do it! We were having such a good time, and now you had to spoil it by becoming a bitch again!"*

The problem would be if Daria's mother did not mention the room cleanup and suppressed day-to-day business so as not to intrude on her nice time with her daughter.

We were having such a nice time, I don't want to spoil it. No big deal, I can pick up the family room.

Backing off on normal parental demands and prohibitions so as to preserve a relationship as friends is a mistake. But, often, parents can and do move back and forth between these roles, albeit not always so smoothly.

What the hell is Daria's problem? We were having such a nice time. You would think Daria, feeling close and friendly toward me, would not want to give me so much attitude about picking up the family room, which really is not such a big deal. You would think that there would be some kind of carryover of the good feeling between us from the nice time we were just having.

You would think. But don't hold your breath.

Another potential problem arises when a parent's friendship with their teenage child becomes something that the parent depends on too much for their own happiness. Sensing this need—as they usually do—children may put restrictions on their own behavior, which they really shouldn't have to.

Mom doesn't really have a whole lot of friends except for me. I may be her best friend. I mean, I like hanging out with her, but what if I don't want to spend as much time with her as she does with me? Then she'll be alone. I don't want to do anything to hurt her feelings.

A teenager may not feel as free as they should to live their teenage life and make their teenage connections.

"Daria, lets watch a video tonight. I'll make that real buttery popcorn that we shouldn't have. Won't that be fun?"

But, earlier, Daria had talked to her friend Shawna about maybe doing something together that same evening. Daria was to contact Shawna to firm up their plans.

"Yeah, Mom, that sounds like fun."

So Daria calls Shawna, explaining that she's busy.

Maybe that's fine. Maybe there is no problem with Daria's choosing to stay home with her mom. But maybe Daria's mother's needs are getting in the way of her daughter having her own full teenage life.

Last, within the friend relationship there are some places that you do not want to go. Some things are too personal, too raw to fit in with the more comfortable image of parent.

I want to think of my mom as somebody who is there for me if I need her, who I can count on, but who, when I'm away from her, out in my life, I don't have to think about. I know maybe it sounds wrong, but I like to think of her as being in this nice little compartment doing mother things, and then there's my life, which is a whole other, bigger compartment. And the two don't really mix a whole lot, except when I choose. Or when Mom does one of her intruding-on-my-life-but-I-can-live-with-it parenting things, which is to nag me about stuff.

I'm happiest when the walls between the two compartments are pretty solid. There are parts of me that I want to keep private, and there's stuff about herself that she may want to talk about that I wish she would keep private, stuff that makes me really uncomfortable.

Teens need to feel that there are boundaries: not too much of you intruding into parts of them that they want to keep private. And not too much of you opening yourself up and exposing them to parts of you that they would rather you kept private.

We will be friends, buddies, close—but with each of us also keeping a certain distance. Close but not too close.

One example of crossing the boundaries is revealing *anything* about your sex life. What you should share with your teenager about your sex life is *nothing*. Teens are not comfortable with it. They are trying to deal with their own emerging sexuality. Your sexuality is the last thing that they want to hear about.

> *"Your father and I have never had the most thrilling sex life."*
> *"Mom, I really don't want to hear about it."*
> Nor should she have to.

It is okay to talk about your problems with your teenager: *"I think that sometimes I worry too much about my sister. I let her problems get to me, and it affects my mood more than it should. But I just can't help it. Sometimes I think it's not fair to you and James—me being upset about your aunt Elena, and taking it out on you two."*

But an example of inappropriately crossing the line is when you share your feelings with your teen, but those feelings are too raw, too unfiltered. Too strong a dose of your worries, unhappiness, or concerns is just too overwhelming for them.

> *"Sometimes I get so depressed that I just think, what's the point? Why should I even get out of bed? Sometimes I really do hate my life."*

That's okay to talk about with a counselor, but it's too much for a teenage child. The problem with this is that it collapses the difference between child and parent. Instead of the mother being the one who still takes responsibility for her child's well-being, now the teenager has to worry about taking care of her mother.

> *"Mom, don't say that! There's still lots of good stuff! There's always your Thursday book club."*

The better way to handle the discussion of these emotions is as follows:

"Sometimes I can get pretty depressed, but it's something that I have to deal with."

The above says that you get depressed, but you are on the case—trying to manage it. The first way puts too much out there and is asking for help.

What am I supposed to do? I'm just a kid. I wish Mom would get a grip and not dump this shit on me.

Children need to feel that their parents can manage their own lives. That their parents' overall well-being is something that they do not have to worry about. This frees them up to worry about their own problems and even to be able to turn to their parent for help. All of that is undermined if a child feels their parent is too vulnerable.

Mom has enough problems. I don't want to worry her with what's happening to me.

There needs to be a line between the real world of adult concerns and the cleaned-up, for-child-consumption version. Children have the right to have parents who will protect them from the full force of adult suffering. Too much simply overwhelms them. It can make them anxious, stressed, or depressed. And it serves no useful purpose.

One of our jobs is to give our children, as much as we can, the freedom to worry about teenage stuff:

"There's this girl in my biology class who I really like, but she doesn't know I exist, except yesterday I was walking next to her in the hall and I said, 'Don't you think Ms. Pemmelman is really boring?' which I know was a really dopey thing to say, but she laughed and said, 'Yeah.' And then I didn't know what else to say so I didn't say anything, but now I don't know what to do." That kind of stuff.

Teenagers do not need to hear about what goes on in your deepest reaches. They deserve the edited version.

Being a friend to your teenager is good. But you cannot be a friend all of the time. And you cannot bring all of you into the friendship.

SUFFERING AS LEVERAGE

Bruno was supposed to work on the house when he got home from school so that it would be all picked up by the time his mother got home. Bruno's mother arrived home only to find her son sprawled on the couch, watching TV and eating Mi Ranchero Taco Chips, the floor near him covered with crumbs as well as some kind of gooey yellow stuff that might be cheese spread.

"Bruno, you were supposed to pick up the house, but all you've done is make a bigger mess!"

"What? Why are you yelling at me?" said Bruno as he changed his position on the couch, causing him to knock over a can, spilling soda on the rug.

"I can't believe you! Look at this room! You don't give a crap about this house or anything I say! You don't understand how much I sacrifice for you! My life sucks! I get no help from you or your father! I'm under pressure all the time at a job I hate! I constantly have to worry about money! I don't have time for anything! What kind of life do I have? And I come home to this? It is so unfair!"

When they act like jerks and we want them to know how jerky they are acting, sometimes it can be very hard not to bring in our own pain and suffering to make our point, adding some weight to our argument.

"How can you do this to me? You don't know what I have to go through! I try to spare you from knowing how hard it is for me because I want you to be free to lead your own life. But you just don't get it! I don't need this! I really don't need this!"

Teenagers can be so heedless at times. They can sometimes be so cruel and seem to think nothing of it. We want to impress on them what their behavior does to us.

I want Bruno to understand how what he does affects me. I want him to understand that what he does hurts me. If he can truly understand the pain he causes me, then he might think twice before he acts like such a jerk.

The problem is that we all have—not so deep inside of us (just get drunk and watch it come out)—a vast reservoir of hurt and pain that includes all of the wrongs that ever have befallen us that never got resolved, that were just as unfair now as they were then, the cosmic injustice that has made our life so much less than what we had wanted—and none of it is our fault. But most of the time our more rational side keeps this wellspring of bitterness safely out of the way.

Actually, when I think about it, I don't have such a bad life at all. There's no reason for me to dwell on stuff that happened well in the past and is never going to get resolved anyway.

But when we feel wronged, there it all is, lurking not so far beneath the surface, waiting for an excuse to come out.

The challenge is that this part of us, when it speaks, is not so interested in resolving a problem in the here and now—for example, having Bruno act more considerately. It wants something far more. It wants everything—including revenge. It is not a nice part of us. To those on the receiving end, it feels like the other person is using their suffering like a club. Which is precisely what they are doing. And the invariable response from a teenager is not sympathy for our suffering but rather resentment toward us for hitting them with all of this.

What is her problem? I'm sorry she has a shitty life. But that's not my fault. What gives her the right to dump all of that shit on me? Fuck her!

"Fuck you! Why don't you get a life? I'm not the one who makes you miserable!"

And Bruno stomps out of the room, leaving the taco chip crumbs and the spilled soda untouched.

"Bruno, you get back here!"

A far better tactic would be to let him know how you feel about his behavior in no uncertain terms. It's fine to be mad at him. It's fine to let him know *how* mad. It's excellent that you let him know how unacceptable his behavior is.

"Look at this mess! I asked you to clean up and instead, look at this! I can't believe you! You just lie there! You don't care about anything! All you care about is yourself!"

The message is: *Boy, Mom sure is mad. She is really pissed off that I made a big mess.*

It is a natural consequence. You act like a lazy slob and your mother has a fit.

Will it motivate Bruno to clean up next time? Maybe. Maybe not. But he certainly will have in his head: *If I don't clean up, Mom will have a major fit.*

That fact won't always get him to clean up. But sometimes it may. *I guess I should pick up because I'm really not in the mood for one of Mom's tantrums.*

But it is not his mother baring her global suffering. That, as I said, gets a very different response. Anger and great suffering are two very different entities. Kids don't like anger, but they can deal with it. Deep personal suffering as a consequence of not cleaning up is not possible to deal with. It's too much. Too big.

You don't like their behavior. Let them know. But keep your own personal misery out of it. That only tends to backfire.

LOSING IT

Let me again use the Bruno example, but this time to illustrate a different point, this time with Bruno and his father. Bruno's father had a hard day. He was under a lot of pressure at work and just that morning had an unpleasant meeting with his boss, on top of which he'd had a brief but nasty exchange with a coworker with whom he was having continuing problems. Also, he was having one of his bad tension headaches. He was not in a good mood. Arriving home that evening, he was particularly on edge and wanted very much not to be bothered by anyone or anything. At least he wouldn't have to pick up around the house, because Bruno was supposed to have done that when he got home from school, so the house should be neat by the time his father got home.

As in the previous example, that didn't happen. The house was a mess, and there was Bruno on the couch eating his taco chips.

"What the hell is this?"

"What do you mean? I don't know."

"Bruno, you were supposed to pick up the house, but all you've done is make a bigger mess."

"What? Why are you yelling at me? I was going to clean up. I was."

"Bruno, I am so sick and tired of this! I've had a really hard day! I really don't need this!"

"Well, I had a hard day too."

"You had a hard day? You had a hard day? I am so sick and tired of this! You are such a fucking loser! And do you know what? That's all you're ever going to be! Lying on the couch, a big fucking loser! It's what you are! I am so sick of this!"

And Bruno's father stormed out of the room.

"You're a fucking loser," Bruno called out. But his heart wasn't in it, as he had been stung by his father's words.

I'm not a loser. That's not fair. I was going to pick up, but I was tired. I was planning to do it. He has no right to say that to me. Look at him. He shouldn't talk.

Bruno ended up doing a halfhearted job of straightening up, but he spent the rest of the evening in his room, avoiding any contact with his father. He couldn't shake his father's words.

I know I'm not as good as I could be about helping around the house. But that doesn't make me a loser. That's not fair. Does he really think I'm a loser? I'm not a loser. He's a loser.

But if it was his dad who was the loser, not him, Bruno couldn't figure out why he felt like crying.

Sometimes we lose it. They push us so hard that we go past where we wanted to go. We say things that we really did not want to say. Hurtful things. Maybe we had a bad day. Maybe we didn't. But our kids can be so maddening. And we are only human.

Does it hurt them? Does it damage them?

Expressing anger toward a teenage child is not necessarily a bad thing. When they act in an incredibly heedless and jerky manner, and when that behavior has a direct and negative effect on you, not expressing your anger would even seem a little inappropriate. Parental anger, especially in response to something that should make you angry, does not damage a teenager—as long as that expression of anger is within acceptable bounds. But being too angry and too loud for too long, and also using words that are too stinging, can be a problem.

"You're a loser!"
"You're an idiot!"
"I don't understand how you turned out this way!"
"You're a disgrace!"

Children have no defense against this. The words cut too deep. They can't change who they are; they can only change what they do. The words stay in their head but not in a constructive way.

Either they think,

I'm a loser, so what's the point?

Or,

He thinks I'm a loser; fuck him! Why should I try to please him? What's the point? I'll try to find somebody who thinks I'm okay.

So if you think that you went too far, what should you do? Apologize. Apologize sooner rather than later. Wait for things to calm down a little, but don't wait very long. Either that same day or the next. And apologizing in person is best.

What should you say?

A short, unequivocal statement:

"Bruno, I should not have said what I did. There is no excuse. I was wrong. I am sorry."

Also, don't look for a response to the apology.

"Will you accept my apology? Okay?"

You are making a statement. You should require nothing of them.

We tend not to do so well when giving apologies. The most frequent problem is that most of us are not comfortable saying "I'm sorry" and then saying nothing more. We don't like to accept straightforward, unadulterated blame. It leaves us feeling too vulnerable.

We strongly prefer to include qualifiers—something to fend off the full brunt of the blame.

"I'm sorry but . . ."

We tend to give excuses.

"I'm sorry, but I had a really hard and stressful day."

Which was true, but to the extent that you include excuses, you negate most, if not all, of the good that an apology might do. Often such excuses make things worse than if you had offered no apology at all. *See, he can't even apologize!*

Even more frustrating is when we try to put the blame back on them. *"I'm sorry, Bruno, but if you would only take more responsibility for what you do around the house, this would not have happened."*

In this case, your words say that you're unwilling to take responsibility for your unacceptable behavior and are transferring the blame onto your child. Here the effect is definitely worse than no apology at all. *He's a dick! Screw him!*

Also, it is not a good idea to say that you will make sure that you won't do it again. The problem, of course, is that you might do it again. So don't promise something you might not be able to deliver.

The message needs to be that you're sorry, that you believe you crossed the line, and that it wasn't okay to do so. End of story.

It may be hard, but there is a giant upside to flat-out, unqualified, no-excuses apologies. For one, they can go a long way toward taking the sting out of your words. *Dad said he was sorry. It still hurts, what he said, but his saying he was sorry does seem to make me feel better.* That is what happens with apologies.

The other excellent result of unqualified apologies is that they set a very good example. *Dad said he was sorry and he didn't give any kind of bullshit excuses. He just said it. That was good.*

But apologies only work up to a point. If the too-strong responses by you happen too frequently—exactly like the alcoholic who has drunken rages and always apologizes but then always does it again—the apologies become empty.

Last, never hit a teenager. It is a disaster. It makes them crazy. And it often will have bad, even very bad and frequently immediate, consequences. It is never okay. Even when you may feel that there was extreme provocation. It is never okay.

> *"Fuck you, motherfucker! Fuck you! Did you hear me? Fuck you!"*
>
> SMACK!
>
> *"Well, what am I supposed to do? After what he just said? He deserved it!"*

No, he didn't.

LITTLE WORDS OF LOVE

Tonia is lying on the couch, watching television. Her mother comes into the room to look for a pencil, finds one next to the magazines, and leaves.

Adam is in his room with the door closed. His parents are both home. Over the course of the next three hours, there are no verbal exchanges between them.

Morgan's dad drops her off at soccer practice. She mumbles "'Bye" as she darts out the car door.

Lance, on the way to his room, passes his father in the hallway. No words are spoken.

Once they hit their teens—as part of the normal but temporary allergy to parents—a teenager's end of almost any conversation can all but dry up. It can become very easy to go through days with virtually no communication at all, other than exchanging words of a business nature.

"Ryan, don't forget you said you'd take out the recycling."
"Whatever."

Days at a time—maybe more than just days—may pass with no real loving contact between parent and child. Even when the relationship is generally friendly, still not a whole lot that is positive is happening. This is not good.

There are things you can and should do under such circumstances: let's try the above scenes a little differently.

Tonia's mother comes into the room to look for a pencil.
"I love my Tonia."

Tonia grunts. Her mother exits but not before she adds, *"I love my Tonia a lot."*

Adam's mother comes to the door of his room, knocks on the door, and then calls out, *"Hello. I love you."* Silence.

And an hour later she comes back and knocks again. *"Hello. I still love you."*

And maybe an hour after that. *"It's me. I love you."*

"Bye," Morgan says as she rushes by her father out to the soccer field.

"Bye. You're my best girl. I love you. Knock 'em dead. I really love you," her father calls out to his rapidly receding daughter.

"I've got the best guy in the world," says Lance's father to his son as they pass each other in the hallway. (This is said even if Lance is a straight-D student and seems to reserve most of his passion for violent video games.)

The above is particularly useful in those little awkward moments when you and your teenager are together but with really nothing to say. It immediately changes a silent and awkward moment into a swift, friendly one.

My point: it is a really good idea to regularly—every day—make an express point of saying affectionate little things to your teenager. Every day. More than once a day. Engage in brief, frequent, loving contact.

This is not a minor suggestion. Make it a habit. This is definitely one of those deals where a little can go a long way.

Your teen may or may not respond. It doesn't matter. The point is that you are reaching out and regularly making brief but loving contact with your child. It is not conditional. You are not requiring anything of them.

Picture the alternative, and how different it is from what I am suggesting.

"You know what? It would be nice if, one time, when I say something friendly, you might actually say something friendly back."
"How about 'Don't talk to me ever'? Would that be good?"

No. It is not conditional.

Some days this will be easier than others. There will be days when you are tired or not in a good mood, are in a hurry, are not feeling especially loving toward your child because they have been giving you trouble lately, and you forgo the loving little phrases. That would be a mistake. You want to keep doing it regardless. Fortunately, it really takes very little effort. And if you do it regularly it becomes automatic, a habit.

The good news is that not only do they like it—this evidence that you love them, that you are not totally put off by the shell that they have grown around them—but it actually gets you to like them more, to feel closer. You are having conversations with their inner loving child, who often may be invisible but who is still very much there. Imagine that this is to whom you are talking—because you are.

"I know you're in there."

The truth is that they grow to like it. A lot.

"Dad, do you always have to say that stuff? 'You're my best guy. You're my best guy.' It's really lame."

"Yes, I do have to always say that stuff."

"Well, it's really dumb. It doesn't accomplish anything."

But it does.

Five

INTERPRETING THE MOST POPULAR TEENAGE PHRASES

Today's adolescents are very skilled at coming up with certain phrases that they have found particularly useful in dealing with unpleasant communications with their parents. These unpleasant communications tend to be of three types:

1. When they are asked to do something that they don't feel like doing: *"Angie, would you please bring in the trash cans?"*

2. When they are told "no": *"No, Jonathan, I'm sorry. It's too late; you cannot go over to Mitch's house."*

Or,

3. When they are being criticized: *"Valerie, you kept all of us waiting; you knew when we had to leave; now we're going to miss half an hour of the basketball game."*

The point of these teen phrases is to allow the teenager to move away from the unpleasantness now confronting them. They hope to undo your words.

"Oh. I'm sorry. What you just said has caused me to rethink what I just said. It was inconsiderate of me to ask you to bring in the trash cans. I'll do it myself. Again, I'm very sorry for troubling you."

Since the above rarely happens, these very useful phrases serve their true purpose, which is to move their parent off course onto a more pleasing, less stressful—for the teenager—irrelevant side issue.

A problem with these teen favorites is that they are very good. By very good I mean very clever, very effective. Teenagers are very intelligent, and, by trial and error, they are able to come up with the most useful, the most stop-you-in-your-tracks-and-make-you-crazy phrases that could possibly exist. What these statements have in common is that they all hit what are genuinely sensitive areas for parents. By their nature, they immediately make parents question whether they are doing the right thing—where only moments before they were confident in what they had just said. Again, they are very effective.

A useful rule when confronted with many such utterances is to ask yourself, *When am I hearing this?* If it is in response to your saying something that your teenager is not happy with, you will want to think long and hard before you pick up on it. If you are truly concerned by their words, ask at another time. But definitely not when you have just told them "no" or asked them to do some onerous chore, like cleaning the sink.

What follows is a sampling of the tried-and-true teen favorites that have successfully sidetracked parents from simple, purposeful communications into endless bickering. After each teen favorite, I will include some frequent, not-so-good parental responses, and I will present alternate responses that serve parents far better.

"I HATE YOU"

There are three words that when strung together can be hurtful under any circumstances but that sting the most when they are said by your child to you. They fall from your child's mouth when you least expect it:

> *"Cherie, I did not like how you acted when your aunt and uncle were over yesterday. You were rude, and it was embarrassing to me."*

"You're always criticizing me! I hate you! I wish I had any parent but you!"

This is a particularly effective teen response because nobody wants to be hated by their own child.

Well, I don't. It's terrible. After all I've done for her. After I've tried so hard to be a good parent. All I've ever done is try to give her a nice life. And now I get this. It breaks my heart.

This is where the *When am I hearing this?* test is mandatory. How does Cherie truly feel about her mother? Does she really hate her mother, or is she just mad at that moment because she doesn't like being criticized? If Cherie is a typical teen, certainly there are times when she has strong negative feelings toward her mother—mainly when Cherie is not getting her way. But there are also times—when there are no points of contention between the two of them—when Cherie can allow herself to feel the fondness that is part of the still-deep attachment between herself and her mother. That is, Cherie's feelings toward her mother vary from situation to situation. As with all teens. But the strong underlying attachment is still there.

The following is the most likely translation of this particular "I hate you."

> *"It makes me feel really uncomfortable when you criticize me—especially when I know that it's justified. How dare you say something to me that's going to make me feel bad?"*

Hence, a not-so-good parental response might be:

"How can you say that to me? I've always tried to do what's best for you!"

How can Cherie say that to her mother? Obviously, very easily.

The big problem with this response is that it begs a response from Cherie.

> *"No, you haven't! All you care about is having a neat house, and impressing anybody who comes over! I could be dying, for all you care!"*

And Cherie and her mother are then launched into a much more pleasing—for Cherie—discussion about her mother's flaws.

A better response would be:

"I'm sorry you're mad at me. But the way you acted was unacceptable."

The value of this response is that it recognizes, but does not react to, what Cherie has said and stays on the real subject: namely, that Cherie's mother thought Cherie had acted like a jerk and wants to let her know.

"YOU JUST WANT SOMEBODY WHO'S PERFECT"

When your child complains that you make him feel as if he's not good enough for you, it's enough to make *you* feel imperfect!

> *"Collin, I asked you to clean up the TV room, and if you did anything it's certainly impossible to tell. Please go back and do a better job of straightening up your mess."*
> *"I did clean it up! You just want somebody who's perfect!"*

This is a particularly effective lament for a teenager because it immediately puts parents on the defensive. But parents shouldn't touch it. And if they do go against my better judgment, they definitely should not say:

> *"That's not true, Collin. Sometimes you just don't do a good enough job."*
> As that will only provoke:
> *"Yes it is true! I never can do anything good enough for you! For you, everything has to be perfect! I'm sorry I'm just human! Us humans are not always perfect!"*

Unfortunately, as soon as a parent responds to the *"You just want somebody who's perfect"* theme, they are immediately shifting into a discussion about whether they expect too much of their son. This, to the delight of any teen, veers away from the unpleasant request to do an adequate job of cleaning up the TV room. What teen wouldn't rather argue with their parents about their having too many expectations?

> *"No, no, you expect way too much of me! I'm sorry I'm not good enough! Maybe you should adopt somebody my age and see if you can get a trade-in!"*
> It is far better to simply repeat:
> *"Collin, I need you to do a better job of picking up the TV room."*

The rules for these better parental responses are simple:

1. In your initial response, you want to talk to your teen in a respectful manner and recognize that they are not happy with what you just said. You do this no matter how nonsensical and manipulative what they have just said may be.

2. You want to stay on the subject—your subject.

3. If they persist, you want to disengage.

4. If you are truly concerned by what they say, ask them about it later, *not* at the time. Asking at the time only leads to trouble.

The list of favorites continues.

"I DON'T FEEL WELL"

This, of course, is a longtime winner—useful for any request, particularly for those unpleasant situations when kids are asked to do something that involves any mental or physical effort.

> *"Angie, would you please bring your bike inside like I asked you to, so it won't get rained on or stolen?"*
> *"I don't feel well."*
> To which you do not want to respond:
> *"How come I'm just hearing about this when I ask you to do something?"*
> *"But I don't feel well. I'm not lying."*
> Do you really want to get into a discussion with your teenager about whether they are sick or not? That's an argument you will always lose.
> *"But I am. I'm really sick. Maybe I have tuberculosis."*
> *"That's ridiculous; you don't have tuberculosis."*
> *"You're right. It's probably not tuberculosis. I have a headache*

and I have these, like, pains in my back and I feel nauseous and my knee hurts too."

A better response would be:

"I'm sorry you don't feel well, but you still need to bring in your bike."

"You'll be sorry! You'll see! I'm going to throw up all over everything!"

"YOU'RE RUINING MY LIFE"

Recognize this?

> *"No, Alyssa, you may not go to the sleepover."*
> *"Omigod, you're ruining my life!"*

That's a good one.

We don't want to ruin their lives. We want them to have nice lives. We definitely don't want them to feel that we are the main impediment to their having a happy life instead of a life that they hate. No, we don't want them to feel that. We're on their side. We want them to be happy. Who wants to ruin their child's life?

> *"That's not true, Alyssa. I'm sorry, but sometimes I just feel that I have to say no. I really want you to have a nice life. But, as your parent, there are some things that I just am not comfortable with. There are many things that we allow, and I know that you enjoy these things. I think you're not being completely honest with me. I think that most of the time you like your life."*

The above response would be fine—reasonable and compassionate—except that it's a disaster.

> *"No, you are so wrong! You don't know! You don't understand what it's like! Anything that's fun, you're against! I don't know why you're like that! I don't know why you do it! And you're at me about every little thing! You really are ruining my life! I'm not just talking about sleepovers!"*

Maybe we do ruin their lives—at least some of the time. Saying no. Asking them to do so many things that they do not feel like doing. Even criticizing them. But it's what parents do.

> "Alyssa, I'm not ruining your life."
>
> "Yes, you are! If it weren't for you, I would have nothing to complain about! My life would be great! And you would see that nothing bad would happen except that I would be happy! Which—by the way—I'm not! Because of you!"

Again, it is better not to touch it.

> "No, Alyssa, I know you want to go, but I don't want you going on the sleepover."

And if Alyssa's parent does not pick up on the ruining-her-life theme, Alyssa is forced to move on to other tactics.

> "But I promised Lorraine that I would go! I can't back out on a promise! You're the one who always says, 'A person is no better than the strength of their word.' I can't break a promise! I can't! You told me that!"

"YOU NEVER . . ."

Again, as she had done frequently before, at a ridiculously late hour on a school night, Brianna wanted her father to drive her to the 24Mart to buy candy.

> "For the kids at my table for lunch tomorrow. You know how on Thursdays we take turns bringing a special candy treat for each kid at our table."

But on this night her father totally did not feel like it.

> "No, I'm sorry, Brianna. It's too late. I'm not going to do it. You'll just have to say you weren't able to do it. Maybe you can do it on a different day."
>
> "But you never do anything for me! If I ask you for a favor, you never do it! Never!"

"You never" and its twin, "You always," are particularly effective because they are so patently untrue, you feel that you have to say something. You can't just let it pass because it taps into a parent's permanent need to set the record straight.

I mean, I can't just let her say something that is so obviously untrue. And if she says it and I don't say anything in response, then she thinks that, by my not saying anything, I'm conceding that what she's saying is true, which it absolutely is not. So I do have to say something.

However, to touch this one results in a special kind of disaster because all teenagers have TUR—"Total Unfairness Recall"—which you cannot possibly compete with.

> *"No, Brianna. Actually, I usually do stuff when you ask. You know that."*
>
> *"No, you never go out of your way for me! Not once! If it's the least bit inconvenient for you, no matter how important it is to me, you never do it! I'm like Cinderella or somebody! I just get your leftovers!"*
>
> *"You know that's not true, Brianna. Of course I do stuff for you. Especially if you really need something."*
>
> *"Uh-uh! How about the time you wouldn't take me to the store to get highlighters for my history project? What about then? What about when you wouldn't go back to the store when I lost my key chain? I can keep going!"*
>
> As I said, this is a discussion that you do not want to begin.
>
> *"No, I'm sorry. It's too late. You'll just have to figure out something else."*
>
> *"I never did get the key chain, and it was my favorite key chain! I still miss it!"*

"I'M SORRY I'M SUCH A DISAPPOINTMENT TO YOU"

This one gets to parents every time.

> *"Justin, how many times do I have to tell you to make sure the door to the refrigerator is closed all the way? How many times do I have to tell you?"*
>
> *"I'm sorry I'm such a disappointment to you!"*

This, of course, goes along with its close relatives, "I'm sorry I'm a failure," and the beloved, "I'm sorry I'm not like my cousin Steven." (This one, however, does require that there is a cousin Steven who gets better grades and more regularly says "please" and "thank you.") It is a proven winner because it strikes a chord in virtually every parent.

Every child disappoints their parents in some way, so parents feel guilty when they are thus accused. And there is always the fear that perhaps their child may be depressed, in which case their expectations—though legitimate—may be hitting their child where he or she may already be vulnerable.

I don't know. Maybe we do demand too much of him. I haven't thought of him as particularly depressed, but he can be moody. I certainly don't want to do anything that will push him over the edge. He wouldn't think about suicide, would he?

I mention here this darkest of parental worries because it lurks in the minds of most parents of teenagers. You do hear about adolescent suicide. It is a reality. And there are always stories of children where "nobody knew." Elsewhere in this book, I discuss suicide—the risks and what you can do about them. Suffice to say that when teenagers talk about being unhappy, rare is the parent who does not experience that pang of fear for their child.

Fortunately, despite these very real issues, there are some pretty simple solutions for the day-to-day circumstances described above.

Here again you'll want to take the *When am I hearing this?* test. If it is when they are not liking what you are saying, maybe you don't want to take it too seriously. But if you do worry, then you always have the backup, which is to ask your child about it at a later, neutral time.

"Justin, do you really feel that you're a disappointment to us?"

And maybe at that time you'll end up in a real discussion. Justin talks—but more genuinely and not manipulatively—about how sometimes he does feel that he's not living up to the model of a teenager that he thinks you want. Or maybe he'll simply say,

"No, not really. I know you think I'm okay. At least about most stuff. And maybe some stuff you don't know about."

But to pick up on it at the time is almost certainly asking for trouble, as it knocks into oblivion the only real issue of the moment, which is Justin's repeated failure to properly close the refrigerator door.

Hence, what not to say in response to *"I'm sorry I'm a disappointment to you"* would be:

"Do you really feel that we think you're a disappointment?"

That response is a great loser because it will only result in the following comeback, delivered with a glow of triumph:

"Yes, I know I haven't turned out the way you wanted. I know I have a lot of things wrong with me. I'm sorry I didn't turn out good enough for you, but what am I supposed to do about it? I'm just me! And I guess that's just not good enough. I'm sorry!"

What is he supposed to do about it? How about being more careful in the future in closing the refrigerator door?

It would be far better to simply say,

"Justin, would you please try to remember to close the refrigerator properly?"

And then no more.

"IT'S NOT FAIR"

And, of course, the all-time favorite: *"It's not fair!"*

"No, Jonathan, I'm sorry. But you cannot go over to Mitch's house."

"But it's not fair! Anything Anderson wants, it's yes, and with me it's always no! This is so unfair!"

This, of course, is the granddaddy of all child-parent arguments. As any parent knows, the first full sentence that human children learn is: "It's not fair." It is so effective because it challenges us regarding the primary rule of socialization—which all of civilization is built upon. We want very much to be fair.

"You know that's not true, Jonathan. There's plenty we say no to Anderson about."

Uh-oh, now you've done it—you've made a big mistake. As I mentioned earlier, all children have Total Unfairness Recall—and they also make up stuff. What you certainly do not want to do is get into a fair-or-unfair debate with your teen. You will lose.

"Name me one time! Just one time!"

Again, it is better to stay on the subject:

"No, Jonathan. You cannot go over to Mitch's house."

"But when was the last time you said no to anything that Anderson wanted to do? When?"

It is good to listen to your teen. It is excellent, having heard what they have to say, to sometimes change your mind. But engage in a true fairness debate? Avoid that at all costs. As a parent, you need to accept that there will be times when you may be unfair to your child. You do try to be fair. You may not always succeed. But if you can say that, overall, you have been a reasonably nice parent, unfairness parenting errors in the service of brevity and sanity—yours—are not going to destroy your child.

"Yes they will!"

"PLEASE, I'M UNDER A LOT OF STRESS; I REALLY DON'T NEED THIS NOW"

"Kendra, this is the third time that I've had to ask you to bring the dirty glasses out of your room and into the kitchen."

"Dad, I'm really under a lot of stress. I don't need this now."

You have to sympathize. You know what it's like to be under a lot of stress. When you're under a lot of stress, it's hard enough to focus on what you *have* to focus on. It is asking too much to have to stop everything and get completely sidetracked by having to do something that there's absolutely no reason to do because it can wait until another time—like bringing glasses into the kitchen.

This is a particularly effective and oft-used teenage ploy because it carries within it the implied and very real threat that, unless you back off immediately, they'll let you know what stress is, all right.

"No, Kendra, I want you to do it now."

"Didn't you hear me? I'm really under a lot of stress now! I can't deal with this! I can't be in this house! I can't stand it." And with each word the hysteria dial gets turned up another notch. *"I can't stand it! I can't!"*

A not-so-good response might be:

"I'm sorry you're under a lot of stress, but it really isn't asking that much to take the glasses into the kitchen."

"Omigod, that's just it! You totally don't understand! I really, really can't take it! I am so stressed!" And she's just warming up.

The better tactic would be:

"Kendra, please take the glasses into the kitchen."

And then exit.

"Omigod! Omigod!"

But she's not saying this to anybody, because you have left.

"BUT ALL THE OTHER KIDS' PARENTS LET THEM"

I want to know: Who are these other parents anyway?!

> *"No, Garrett, I read a review of* A Thousand Ways to Die. *I do not want you seeing it."*
>
> *"But, Mom, none of my friends' parents have any trouble with it! Everybody else is being allowed to see it! I'll be the only one who didn't! The only one! You want to have a son who's a weird outcast?"*

"All the other kids' parents" is another famous one. And for good reason. We don't want to be so different from other parents. We don't want to be the oddball parent who allows their extreme parenting views to separate their child from the mainstream of kids his age.

What if it's true? I remember how sad he was in second grade when he didn't seem to fit in and didn't have any friends. And I'm so thankful now that things seem to be working out for him with the other kids in his grade. I certainly don't want to do anything to jeopardize that.

If it's really nothing so bad, I don't want him to stand out from his peers, to be on the outside because of me. But maybe he's lying. I'll be damned if I'm going to check with all the other parents. I'm going to stick to my guns.

> *"Garrett, I do not think for a minute that all your friends' parents are letting them see* A Thousand Ways to Die. *I'll bet that at*

least half of them don't even know what it's about."

"You are so wrong! Everybody's parents are letting them see it! Everybody's!"

"You can't possibly know that."

"You don't think so? I've already conducted an Internet poll of parents of kids in my grade at school!"

"That is ridiculous."

"You think so? Come here! Look! The results of my poll: 'Would you allow your teenage child to see A Thousand Ways to Die?' *Seventy-three respondents so far, and all say yes, they would! Not one 'no'! So can I go?"*

You do not want to get into a debate over whether the other parents are allowing it or not. This is where you would really be best sticking with what you think is right. But it can be hard, because teens will do all that they can to make you feel that you are a weird minority of one.

Perhaps a useful mantra for parents might be: *I don't know if I'm right. But I'm his parent. This is what I think. And I'm just going to have to gamble that I'm not ruining his life. Which I don't think I am.*

"No, I'm sorry, Garrett, you're not going to see A Thousand Ways to Die."

"But, Mom, they already think I'm a freak because of you! They feel sorry for me because of you! They're going to stop wanting to hang around with me! You'll see! And then what will I do?"

"No, I'm sorry."

"Mom! You can't do this! I can actually feel them moving away from me!"

"BUT WHY?"

"But why? Why not? Why?"

This is another holdover from earliest childhood. Yet it continues to run strong even into adolescence. This tactic gets its great strength from how easy it is to execute: they just keep saying, *"Why?"* or *"Why not?"* with an occasional, *"But you didn't give me a good reason!"* thrown in. Because this has no basis whatsoever in logic, it is very effective for driving parents really quite crazy. This is the one they say as they follow you around the house and also can be called out from a distance. They know they are acting like a baby, but they don't care.

The big mistake here—which is pretty obvious—is when you try to give answers—any answers—to the *"Why?"* in the hope that one of your answers will work and they will say,

"Oh, that's why. Okay."

The only way to deal with *"Why?"* once they truly start asking it is to put as much distance as you can between you and the *"Why?"* asker.

Six

RULES AND CONTROLS

There is a surefire formula for making rules for teenagers. How about this approach:

"Okay, mister. Here's the deal, and I would not want to be you if you even think about disobeying. Cell phone use: no restrictions. Bedtime is when you fall asleep. Use the Internet, but understand that your Internet use will be completely unmonitored. Illegal substances: use your own judgment. Sex: let us know when you want to do it in the house, so your mother and I can make sure we're gone. And one last thing, young man: you should be home at whatever time you feel like on school nights. You got all that, mister? You just better!"

"Yes, sir!"

SETTING RULES

As the parent of a teenager, you have to make rules. But how can you know what your rules should be? Should you require your fifteen-year-old son to be home for supper every school night? Is it okay for your fourteen-year-old daughter to get a small tattoo on her right ankle? Once they are in high school, should they have a set bedtime? How can you know the right rules for your particular teenage child? And how can you make rules that will protect them, but still be obeyed?

One obvious aid is talking to other parents of teenagers. Hear what they have done. What they think works and doesn't work. But remember, all children are different, and nobody else knows your kid as well as you do. Sometimes what other parents say seems relevant, but sometimes it may not be suitable for you and your teen at all. Still, it is always good to bounce your thoughts off others who are in the same predicament. It can at least give you some perspective.

> *"You what? You'd let your Christina go out with a twenty-three-year-old?"*
>
> *"Well, he seemed very polite. She brought him to the house for us to meet him and he seemed quite nice. Very soft-spoken. Made nice eye contact."*
>
> *"You're crazy! He's twenty-three!"*
>
> *"You think so? I must admit you've given me something to think about."*

The above example may seem far-fetched; but, as any parent of a teen knows, you can get caught up in a situation and lose yourself in a way that, if you could just step outside of it, you would see quite differently.

What was I thinking? Actually, he even looks kind of older than twenty-three.

You can talk to other parents; but, in the end, the decisions are up to you. So how do you decide? How can you know what's right, especially when so many situations warranting decisions arise every day with your teenager?

The answer, of course, is that you can't. But, don't worry—all is not lost. There is a standard you can follow to help determine what is best for you and your particular teenage child. That standard is whatever you are comfortable with. Without the ability to see into the future you can't possibly know what is exactly right for the great majority of the tougher decisions.

Maybe the following should be written on a little plaque somewhere in your house:

I'm the one who's deciding what's best. I can't guarantee that I'm right. Sometimes I'll be wrong. But I am comfortable that I'm the one making the decisions. And though my decisions might not always be right, I certainly am the right person to be making them.

But, of course, there's another person in the equation: your kid. And they may not be certain that you are the right person to be making the decisions. Not certain at all.

> *"No, I'm sorry, Teddy. You can't go to the concert tomorrow night. The rule is, no concerts on school nights."*
>
> *"But, Mom, you can't! It's the only time Blades of Confusion is playing anywhere in the area! It's my only chance to see them— ever! It's not fair!"*
>
> *"No, I am sorry, Teddy."*

It is here, when a rule is under attack, that parents make a major mistake in regard to setting rules. And this mistake gives rise to my number one piece of advice about rule setting: *the basis of your authority is not because you are right, but because you are their parent.*

This is where parents consistently get into big trouble. For, if the basis of your authority is that you are right, they will run you into the ground.

> *"But Mom, you have to let me go to the concert! It is so unfair!"*
>
> *"No, you are not old enough to be allowed out that late on a school night."*
>
> *"I will store an extra hour of sleep each night for the four nights before. I will show you on the Internet how a kid my age needs a certain total number of hours of sleep, so even with the concert I will have gotten the right number of total hours. You are so wrong! It is so unfair!"*
>
> *"No, I am not going to look on the Internet. You are too young. It is too late. You never know what is going to happen at a concert."*
>
> *"Mom, nothing bad is going to happen! I will show you the police records for all the nights that they had concerts at the Blue Onion! You'll see, there were no instances of trouble! None!"*

Can you prove to them that you are right? Can you convince them? I can already hear what you are thinking: *"No, because she's wrong. How is she going to convince me that she's right when she's wrong?"*

What if there were some kind of review board—the Teenage Rule Advisement Board—to whom every contested rule had to be submitted?

"We're sorry, Mrs. Millstrom, but we find your son Teddy's arguments to be the more compelling. Teddy may go the Blades of Confusion concert tomorrow night."

"Yes!" says Teddy.

All that you ever get from trying to show that you are right is more challenges. It's a never-ending court case.

"Mom, look at this! It's an article that I downloaded from the Journal of Adolescent Behavior about a large study that showed that high school children who [are allowed to] go to concerts during the week do twenty-three percent better in school grades! You can't refute the Journal of Adolescent Behavior!"

Again, it is fine if, in any given instance, having listened to what they say, you decide—for whatever reason—to change your mind. That is your prerogative. It in no way diminishes your position as the boss. Again, if you change your mind, it has to be done swiftly and early in any discussion. But should you decide to stay with your original decision, ultimately you have to fall back on your basic position: not that you are right, but that you are their parent. This is what you have decided, and they are stuck with it. Whether they like it or not.

So what should you do? What should you say?

Tell them the rule. Tell them why. When you set rules, give them your reasons—not to convince them that you're right, but to tell them why you have decided on this particular rule. Keep the reasons simple, clear, and as honest as you can.

> "No, I am sorry, Teddy, but the rule is that I do not want you going out that late on a school night. I feel you are too young to be out at such a late hour when you have school the next day."
> "But I'm going to get extra sleep to make up for it!"
> "No, I am sorry, Teddy. This is what I have decided."
> "But you can't just decide like that!"

You do not want to get into a debate as to whether you have the right to set the rules. You just do.

> "I'm sorry, Teddy, but I do not want you out that late on school nights."
> "What gives you the right to make decisions that ruin my life? It is my life—and you are completely wrong!"

But your participation in this discussion is over.

Let me give you some more examples of rules and reasons:

"You have to eat dinner with us because it makes me happy for us to eat together as a family."

"You cannot go to school wearing clothing that I think makes you look like a tramp, because I worry that it can give you a bad reputation."

"No video games or TV on Saturday mornings, because that's when I need you to help me straighten up the house."

Those are your rules, and those are your reasons. Maybe you're right, maybe you're not. Maybe the rules are fair, maybe they're not. But remember, the basis of your rules is not that you are right, but that you believe you are right.

"You've got to be kidding! Are you saying that if I'm right and my dad is wrong, I still lose because he's an idiot and I can't convince him that he's wrong, even though he is wrong?"

Actually, that is the deal.

WHEN RULES ARE BROKEN

Okay, you made the rules. So now what happens?

It was Friday night and sixteen-year-old Aaron was supposed to be in by midnight. He had a midnight curfew on Friday and Saturday nights. Also, if there was going to be a problem with getting home on time, he had to call. Those were the rules.

It was now 12:30 A.M. and there was no Aaron, no call, no nothing. His mother had called him, but all she got was his recorded message:

> *"Hey, this is Aaron; leave a message. You know the drill."*
> She left a message:
> *"Call me. Now."*
> *"Where are you?"* she had texted him a number of times. *"Call me."*
>
> Supposedly, Aaron was out with his usual friends, but his mother didn't have a clue as to where they were.
>
> *"I don't know where we're going to be,"* Aaron had said before he left for the evening. *"Jeff is picking me up in a little while. We'll probably go over to Heidi's, but I don't know what we'll do after that. We might go to a movie. I don't know."*

Aaron's mother was worried, but not very worried. She suspected that her son was not responding because he knew he was out well past his curfew, and also knew what would happen if he did answer his phone, which was that his mother would be very mad, and that she would tell him to come home immediately.

However, by 1:00 A.M., Aaron's mother was getting worried, and by 1:15 she was starting to get seriously worried. She was about to call one of his friend's houses to see if anybody knew where he was when Aaron called from his cell phone.

"Hi, Mom."

"Where the hell are you? Where have you been? I've been calling you for the last hour! You get home right away!"

"Oh, sorry, Mom. I was trying to call you, but something has been wrong with my cell phone. It's been doing this for a couple of weeks. Maybe I need to get it fixed, or maybe I need to get a new one. Anyway, I'm at JJ's. Jeff's car isn't working good so we decided to stay here and try in the morning."

"Who the hell is JJ?"

"You know, JJ."

"I don't know any JJ!"

"Anyway, me and Jeff are sleeping over here, but I'll be back in the morning. I'm fine. It wasn't my fault about the cell phone. I tried to call."

"Other kids have cell phones too! You could have used one of theirs!"

"Mom, I tried to call. I finally got through to you. I'm sorry if you were worried, but it wasn't my fault."

It was now 1:15 in the morning, and the last thing that Aaron's mother wanted to do was to get into her car, drive to some kid's house—the location of which she didn't even know—pick up her son, and come home. What she wanted to do was go to bed. She was relieved that Aaron was safe, but at the same time quite angry with him. Nevertheless, Aaron's mother was not interested in an angry confrontation with her son at this late hour.

"All right. Stay there, but you had better be home in the morning."

"Yeah, of course I will, Mom."
"You better!"

What, in fact, had happened was that Aaron had been out with his friends and had gone over to JJ's house, where a number of kids were hanging out. JJ was a kid whom Aaron barely knew but was a friend of his friend Kelly. Aaron had been drinking some, had lost track of time, but was having fun and did not want to leave in order to get home by midnight. Also, he didn't want his mother to think he had been drinking— though not heavily—which he could probably cover up (he had in the past), but he didn't want to take the chance. There was nothing wrong with his phone—though actually he did like the idea of getting a new one, as his was getting a little out-of-date. Maybe he would play that up at a later time.

The next day Aaron arrived home a little before noon. His mother immediately started in on him.

> *"You're supposed to be in at midnight! I don't want any of your crap about what happened, because I won't believe a word of it!"*
> *"But, Mom, it was true! Everything I said! It was not my fault! I was going to be home at midnight, but then, like I said, Jeff's car started acting up and so we decided to stay put. I did call you, and I don't know what the problem was earlier with my phone. You have to believe me, because it's true!"*

Teenagers break rules. Not only do they break rules, but if they do break a rule and are found out, they, to the best of their ability, try to slime their way out of any guilt. They also sneak and lie to the point that often you do not even know they have broken a rule. That is what they do.

WHY KIDS BREAK RULES

Why do they break rules? Many people attribute rule breaking to outright teenage rebellion:

Screw them! I'm going to do what I want to do. In fact, I'm going to break their fucking rules just to show them that they can't run my life. I'm the boss of me, not them. Fuck them!

They believe teens break rules intentionally, simply for the sake of breaking rules, to show you that you can't boss them around.

However, I believe that teenage rebellion as a motivator of teenage behavior is very much overstated. In my experience, that is not why teenagers break rules. The reasons why teenagers break rules are rather simple and straightforward.

1. Teenagers break rules because—first and foremost— they believe that any given rule in some way will make their life less pleasant than they wish it to be.

Their stupid rule is making me come home earlier than most of my friends, and I'm going to miss out on fun.

Or perhaps,

They want me to put my dirty clothes in the hamper—every day. That may not seem like it would take a lot of energy. But they don't understand how tired I get.

2. Teenagers break rules because they think they'll prob- ably be able to get away with it.

I'm sure I'll be able to think of some excuse. I always do.

3. Teenagers break rules because they believe that breaking the rule is not in any way potentially dangerous or harmful to them.

It's not like smoking marijuana is going to turn me into a drug addict.

4. Teenagers break rules because breaking a rule is about *now*—when they are breaking the rule—and whatever negative consequences might ensue are about *later*.

I'm having a really good time now. Yeah, I know I'll probably end up getting in trouble with my parents at some point. But I'm really not going to worry about that now.

HANDLING CONFRONTATION

So what should you do if they break a rule? First, remember that they will always have excuses. They will *always* have a story. And not only do they always have a story, but in their stories, nothing is ever their fault; they are always victims. What's more, if they can possibly spin it that way, things in their story will be all your fault. Even Aaron could spin his story that way. I know what you're thinking: *How could his not coming home have been his mother's fault?* But let's see what he says.

"If you had let me use your car last night—I mean, you didn't go anywhere—then none of this would have happened. I wouldn't have had to get a ride from Jeff. And then we wouldn't have had to rely on his car, which got all screwed up. You yelled at me for something that could have completely been avoided if you had been more generous about the car."

It's your fault, and they get particularly mad when you don't believe everything they're saying. How dare you?

First off, do not waste a lot of effort establishing what really did or did not go on that night.

You would definitely not want to say:

> *"How come Jeff's car is conveniently fine this morning and not okay last night? And how come your phone conveniently fixed itself? And how come, if your phone's not working, you didn't ask to use somebody else's phone?"*
>
> *"But, Mom, it is true! Jeff's car was acting funny. It still is. If you don't believe me, I'll have him take you for a ride in it.* (Jeff's car is fine, but Aaron thinks it's a good bet—which it is—that his mother will hardly take him up on the ride-in-Jeff's-car offer.)
>
> *"I don't know why my phone didn't work, but it didn't. That's all I know. It's working now, but I guess it could go out again. I don't know. And the reason I didn't ask anybody to use their phone? I was embarrassed to. You don't know how really uptight kids get about having other kids use their phones. So it would have been really awkward."* (This he is making up on the spot.)

They will always have an answer for everything. It might not be logical. It may be absurd. But they will keep defending it, with great righteous passion, regardless.

Never will you hear, *"Boy, got me on that one, Mom! You have to get up really early in the morning to sneak one past you!"* Never.

It's far better not to get caught up in the story at all, but to simply say:

"Aaron, you were supposed to be in at midnight. You weren't. If you can't get home when you're supposed to, I expect you to call."
"But, Mom—"
"I don't want it to happen again."
"But, Mom—"
And Aaron's mother exits, having said what she needed to.

But doesn't Aaron's mother have to do something? She already did. She made it clear to her son that he broke a rule, and that this was not okay. And, most important, that the rule was still in place. What most parents do not understand is that their rules—just because of their very existence—have power. Considerably more than they realize. Let me explain.

SEEING RESULTS

The number one fact about rules with teenagers is that they work. Just because you made a rule and made clear to your teenager exactly what that rule is, the rule now exists; and that rule does have a considerable effect on your child's behavior.

Jamal's mother to her son: *"I don't want you having more than one kid over after school when I'm not there."*

That rule, now having been established, enters Jamal's head. *I'm not supposed to have more than one kid over in the afternoon if Mom isn't there.*

How does that rule play out?

Tuesday afternoon, Jamal makes plans with Brant to have Brant come over to his house after school. But then Dewayne hears about it and says he wants to come over too.

That would be cool, thinks Jamal. But then, *Shit. Mom will get pissed if she finds out I had both of them over.*

The rule does enter his head. It does exert pressure on him to obey the rule.

Maybe, heeding the rule's influence, Jamal will comply.

"No, Dewayne, it's not cool. My mom gets all ripshit if she finds out I have more than one kid over when she's not there."

Maybe Jamal will choose to break the rule.

Screw it. Mom won't know, and I'll just make sure one of them leaves before the time that she gets home.

"Yeah, Dewayne. Me and Brant can meet you right after school and we can go straight to my house."

Either way, just because Jamal's mother made the rule and made sure Jamal knows about it, he is far more likely not to have more than one friend over than if his mother had made no rule at all. As I will discuss, rules do not work perfectly. But they work far better than no rules at all.

But what if they break the rule and you find out? What if Jamal did have his two friends over at the house? And what if his mother found out, because later that day she happened to talk with a neighbor who mentioned that she had seen the three boys at the house? What should Jamal's mother do then?

She should confront him. This means that she lets him know that he has broken a rule, and that is not okay.

"Jamal, I told you not to have more than one friend over when I'm not home and you went ahead and did it anyway. I told you and I expect you to obey me."

And you keep the rule in place.

"I do not want it to happen again."

What's that going to accomplish?

Just by Jamal's mother finding out, confronting him, being displeased, and letting her son know that the rule still stands, the rule maintains its power. Just as before, when the opportunity to have multiple friends over at the house after school comes up, the rule will enter his head.

Shit, Mom's going to have a fit if she finds out I have a bunch of kids over.

As before, it will have power. And—as before—maybe he will abide by the rule and maybe he will not. But the existence of the rule still decreases the chances that Jamal will have more than one friend over after school.

You may, if you choose, add a consequence—usually some form of grounding or the loss of a privilege. But with or without the threat of a penalty, rules still have their sway. Rules have impact because the vast majority of teenagers do buy into their parents' right to have rules. And it is they, the teenagers themselves, who are the ones who give the rules their power.

Most teenagers do not want to be an outlaw within their own home. They will rail against rules—how unfair, how unreasonable they are—but most teens strongly prefer to stay within the family system. They do not want to rock the boat too much. There definitely is a sense of peace and security that comes from living within the overall system at home. Teenagers want to be able to do what they want to do, but they don't want to be estranged from their own family. They have enough anxiety to deal with.

Yeah, I'm not looking for hassles. I have enough going on in my life. I don't want them to be permanently pissed off at me. It is much easier if I can usually stay on their good side.

Teenagers do not look to destroy their parents' authority. They do accept their parents' right to make rules for them. Which does not mean that they like the rules. Consequences add little because their power comes only from the child's choice to buy into the system in the first place.

In truth, if teenagers truly wish to defy a rule, they will do so, consequences or no consequences—as parents, much to their frustration, often find out. If teenagers truly wish to defy a particular rule, they will—and there is nothing their parents can do to stop them, other than kicking their child out of the house. Consequences only have an effect because teenagers choose to let them.

How can you know whether your rules have power with your teenager—with or without threatened punishments? If they argue. Teens who truly reject their parents' rules, who truly are not bound by them, don't argue. Since they are going to disobey the rule anyway, what's the point?

> *"Victoria, you just better be home by midnight!"*
> But Victoria doesn't stay to argue. She just shrugs and heads out the door.
> *What do I care about their rules? I'm not going to follow them. I'm going to do what I want to do. I really don't care what their fucking rules are. They really have nothing to do with me.*

"You come back here, young lady! Did you hear what I just said?"

But Victoria is already out of earshot.

As I said, though, most teenagers do care.

I mean, they're my parents. That's what parents are supposed to do. Boss their kids around.

They just don't like any of the rules.

Because these rules are all crazy and ruin my life! If they were good rules, that would be okay. But they're not! So what am I supposed to do?

Most teenagers do their best to get around the rules—which is to say, sneak, lie, and above all obfuscate: twist your rules around so that you don't even know where you're coming from.

"I know you said I was to come right home but I had already told Steven that we would go to the hockey store together and I wasn't comfortable just turning him down like that, and you have always said for me to be considerate, and I didn't have time to call you and get in a whole long discussion about what I should do. So I took independent action—which is what you are always telling me I need to do and not be such a wuss. So I actually did the right thing. Huh?"

Obfuscating. This is something they are very good at.

SETTLING FOR IMPERFECT CONTROL

Earlier I said that the nature of control with teenagers is imperfect. Let me elaborate. Again, rules work. But the way that rules work with teenagers is that they only sort of obey them. Usually. Not quite how you meant the rules to be obeyed.

"Jackie, do you know what time it is?" asked her father as his daughter came in the door.

"No."

"It's eleven-forty-seven. What time were you supposed to be in?"

"Uh, I'm not sure."

"You know perfectly well. Your curfew is eleven-thirty."

"Well, one of my contacts fell out. I couldn't find it."

The following Saturday:

> *"It's eleven-fifty-six."*
> *"It's not my fault. Gregory had to get gas."*
> *"Getting gas took twenty-six extra minutes?"*
> *"I don't know."*

The next Saturday:

> *"Okay, young lady, this better be good! Three times in a row!*
> *It's eleven-fifty-five. Twenty-five minutes late for your curfew! This*
> *better be good!"*
> *"I lost one of my contacts again."*
> *"No, ma'am! That one's only going to work once, and you*
> *already used it up."*
> *"But it's true! I lost one of my contacts again! And it took a long*
> *time to find it! It's not my fault!"*
> *"You know what, Jackie? Let's see how you do with a ten-thirty*
> *curfew next week."*
> *"But that's not fair! It wasn't my fault!"*

There is an important point embedded in the above example. To all appearances, it looks like the eleven-thirty curfew was not working. Three consecutive Fridays, Jackie missed the curfew. But I would argue that the curfew *was* working. It was pulling Jackie in—just not as promptly as her father wanted. But she wasn't coming in at midnight, or 1:00 A.M. The eleven-thirty curfew was pulling her home. It is the way of teenagers and rules. They bend them. It is what you get. It is not totally disregarding a rule; it is just not following it exactly as you would want them to. The rule is still there and it is working. Just not perfectly.

Jackie's father's response was fine. But many parents make a serious mistake, which is that they believe any deviance from perfect compliance means that a rule has failed. Most parents feel that one tear in the fabric of control means that the whole cloth has fallen apart. And so they try harder and harder to hold up what they see as a failed rule. They feel they must maintain the letter of the law. Feeling they are losing the war, they may begin a series of progressively harsher punishments to regain full control.

"Two weeks' grounding didn't work? Let's see what you think about a month!"

This doesn't work. Parents never regain perfect control (if they ever had it in the first place). But, most seriously, they risk alienating their teenagers, becoming permanently perceived as the enemy. It's fine to have your child hate you some of the time because of a rule they don't like. But all of the time, over the course of their adolescence? That only invites worse trouble. You risk losing a battle that you may have been winning.

What you get with teenagers is imperfect control. But—as long as you confront them when they disobey and, above all, keep the rule in place— rules, though tattered, will almost always hold. The secret of rules with teenagers is in understanding that this is what you get—imperfect control—and then hanging in there with what you do have. Never feeling totally in control of your teenage child is not exactly comfortable, but it is control nevertheless. And to exercise this control—which doesn't always exactly feel like control—is very important in the life of your teenager.

> *"YOU WILL OBEY ME!"*
> *"NO, I WON'T!"*

But then they do. Sort of.

For the majority of teens, rules work most of the time, as long as you keep them in place. That is, they work imperfectly. But that's the deal you get if you have a teenager. With most teens it is enough.

DEALING WITH OUT-OF-CONTROL TEENS

Out-of-control teens are a whole different story. These are the ones who regularly stay out all night, have major problems with substance use, or are regularly in trouble with the law. These are the ones who are clearly putting themselves at significant risk.

In those cases, what I just recommended will *not* work. Dealing with truly out-of-control teens is very tough. Here is where parents need to employ all the help they can get—from professionals and sometimes through the courts. With truly out-of-control teens, parents often err by trying too long to do it all themselves. Feeling that they should be able to control a child whom they cannot control, they are reluctant to turn to the world outside of the home to take over a task that they are unable to do. The world says that you are supposed to be able to deal with your own kid. And if you can't, then it is your fault. But very difficult teens can be very difficult to deal with, and even the best parenting efforts often cannot head off serious problems. With out-of-control teens, the wisest parenting is to get all the help that you can.

Obviously the above means that you—in varying degrees—are relinquishing the control of your child to others. And that can be a hard step to take. But you are still their parent. You have not given that up. The connection is still there. What is happening is that you are saying that for now, you, as their parent, cannot do the job that you need to do. For now, you are unable to keep them reasonably under control. For now, you cannot well enough prevent them from harm to themselves or to others. As I said, it is a hard step to take, but sometimes it is necessary.

THE TRUTH ABOUT LYING

Teenagers do not like to openly defy their parents' rules. What they strongly prefer to do is to sneak around and lie. Teenagers lie. Good teenagers. Not-so-good teenagers. Short teenagers. Tall teenagers. They lie.

The plan was for Lila to stay over Friday night at her friend Trudy's house, and go directly from Trudy's to her soccer game the next morning (Saturday).

> "Bye, Mom. I'll be home tomorrow after my soccer game."
> "Have fun at Trudy's, dear."
> "I will. Love you."

A week later, Lila's mother happened to run into Trudy's mother in the supermarket.

> "Thank you for having Lila over last Friday night. I hope she wasn't much trouble."
> "No, she wasn't any trouble—because they slept over at Gabriela's house. Didn't she tell you? There was a party. It turns out that Gabriela's parents weren't there. Apparently, it kind of got out of hand. You didn't hear about it?"

Later that night:

> *"You lied to me."*
> *"I didn't lie to you."*
> *"How could you lie to me like that?"*
> *"I wasn't lying! You never believe anything I say! You never do!"*
> *"You're still lying!"*

Teenagers lie. They lie a lot. They lie because they don't want to get into trouble.

> *"I could have sworn I had five twenties in my wallet. Garrison, did you take twenty dollars out of my wallet?"*
> *"No, Dad."*

They lie because they want to do what we forbid them to do.

> *"Jared, were you just smoking marijuana? Your eyes look a little red."*
> *"No. Of course not. How could you think that?"*

They lie because they don't want to do what they are supposed to do.

> *"Lisa, shouldn't you be doing your homework?"*
> *"I don't have any."*

They lie on general principle just to keep us out of their lives.

> *"Reggie, what were you just doing?"*
> *"Nothing."*

Teenagers say how important it is that their parents trust them.
> *"Yeah. It's important to me that my parents trust me. It shows that they have faith in me and that they recognize that I'm getting to be a mature adult being. Not just a little kid."*
Lying, to them, is beside the point.

"But you lie all the time."

*"Yeah, what am I supposed to do—tell the truth? 'Well actu-
ally, Mom, I'm not going to be at Trudy's. We're all going over to
Gabriela's, who you don't know and her parents are away and I'm
probably going to get drunk and, if Jeannine is there, maybe smoke
some marijuana, and I may end up having sex with this junior,
Dan somebody, who's really hot.'"*

"YOU'RE WHAT?"

"See? That's what I mean."

As I said, teenagers lie. That's what they do.

But here's the good news: the vast majority of them grow up to be
pretty good, honest, adult citizens—just like us.

Lying to one's parents during one's teenage years is not an especially
reliable indicator of whether or not a child is going to grow up to be a
dishonest adult.

And it is in regard to lying that parents repeatedly go astray. They get
far too caught up in the issue of their teenager's lying and lose the focus
on what their teenager is lying about. They lose sight of what should be
the main issue at hand.

"How dare you lie to us?"

"I'm not lying!"

*"Not only are you lying but you're keeping it up! You just keep
lying!"*

"I'M NOT LYING!"

Or, making it even worse—and further off the real subject—
a parent takes it personally.

*"How can you lie to me? I thought I could trust you! I thought
our relationship meant more to you than this! How can you do this
to me?"*

Rather easily.

*This has nothing to do with my mother and me. I still love her—most
of the time. And I know she loves me. I would like it if I didn't have to
lie to her. But I do. There's just lots of stuff I have to lie about, because
if I didn't I wouldn't have a life. At least not the life that I want to have
right now.*

As I said, parents all too easily lose sight of what they really should be focusing on.

That Lila was at an unsupervised party, where trouble did happen.

That Garrison took twenty dollars out of his father's wallet. (Perhaps his father should not leave his wallet lying around.)

That Jared has been smoking marijuana.

That Lisa was not doing homework that she was supposed to be doing. So what do you do? Stay with the real problem at hand.

> *"Lila, I ran into Trudy's mother and I heard what really went on last Friday night."*
>
> *"Nothing went on. I didn't know Gabriela's parents weren't going to be there, and I just forgot to tell you that we were going over there. And I didn't do anything anyway."*
>
> *"I'm just going to have to think about letting you stay overnight at friends' houses in the future."*

There's really not much more that Lila's mother needs or wants to say. The next time her daughter wants to go on a sleepover, she will have to decide whether she will let her and, if so, what safeguards she can put in place. That is the issue. Notice that Lila's mother does not even bring up the lying issue. The unadorned fact is that she cannot rely on her daughter's truthfulness. But Lila's mother is not alone.

To be the parent of a teenager, you need a certain permanent degree of skepticism. Parents significantly underestimate the extent of their children's involvement in risky behavior: sex, drugs, and drinking.

It would be a whole lot easier to be able to trust one's teenage children. But the reality is that they lie. So parents of teenage children are stuck with having to make judgments about what they will or will not allow with incomplete information. It is part of the difficulty of being the parent of a teenager. If your aim is to have a teenager whom you can trust, that would be great, but you are not doing your job if you count on it too much.

So how do you teach children not to lie? More by example than anything else. Children don't learn honesty through enraged parents or big punishments. That only teaches them to try to be better liars.

Seven

CHARACTER DEVELOPMENT

The behavior of some teenagers really makes you wonder at times.

"Where the fuck is the remote? Who the fuck took the remote?"

Girard rose from the couch to look for someone to yell at about the missing remote, when he immediately stepped on it. It had been lying there all along on the floor right next to the couch, where he had left it.

"Who the fuck put it there?"

Now on his feet, however, Girard thought he might as well go into the kitchen and get something to drink. Reaching into the back of the refrigerator for a half-gallon container of apple cider, he knocked over an open jar of pickles. (A few days earlier, he had thrown out the top instead of screwing it back on because that had seemed like too much effort.) The contents of the pickle jar spilled onto the two lower shelves—a fact that Girard ignored—and he was heading out of the kitchen with the apple cider to return to the couch, where he could now watch his favorite show, *Real Police Beatings*, when he realized that his father had come into the kitchen.

"Girard, you just knocked over a pickle jar inside the refrigerator. Aren't you going to clean up the mess?"

"I didn't spill it," said Girard.

"Girard, I just saw you do it."

"I didn't spill it. I gotta watch my show."

And Girard barged past his father, hurrying back to the TV so he didn't miss any of his show.

TEMPORARY CHARACTER FLAWS

Teenagers, as you can see, display a lot of rather serious character flaws.

Maybe you're thinking: *I don't know what to do. I have so little time left. When he was eleven I thought maybe I was getting somewhere. But since he got to be a teenager it seems like everything has gone backward. He's fifteen now. I have three years—no, it's really more like two years and eight months—and then he's going to turn eighteen and be out of high school. What then? He's going to go out into the world like this? How can I change him? How can I straighten him out? I don't have nearly enough time. And besides, as things stand, I don't seem to have the ability to change him at all. What am I supposed to do? If he's my proudest creation, I feel like such a failure. I have to do something. Fast.*

Our job as parents is to try to shape our children into the best possible humans they can be. Make them into children that we are proud of. Children who reflect all of the best character traits we have worked so hard to instill in them. Children who will go out into the world and make that world a better place.

"Where the fuck is the jar of salsa? It was right here? Who the fuck took my salsa?"

Fortunately, it is not nearly as bad as it seems. In this chapter I will discuss the negative character traits that so often trouble parents when they look at their teenage children. I will also address where these traits come from, what they mean, and what their presence portends. And I will tell what you need, or do not need, to do about them when they appear daily in your home.

"WHO THE FUCK TOOK MY SALSA?"

Much of what follows is based on a developmental premise described earlier: with the great majority of teenagers, what you see is not what you get. For the most part, parents are privy to their child's baby self, which is an immature, at times very bratty, side of their teenager. But there is a very different, mature self that exists out in the world and most often *that* is who they become as an adult.

The following is a fictitious but definitely-could-be-true story:

Starting when Amber was eight years old, it was her job to clear the dirty dishes from the dinner table, rinse them, and put them in the dishwasher. And every evening, when dinner was over, it was always the same thing.

> *"Amber, where do you think you're going?"* asked her father.
> *"To my room."*
> *"Isn't there something you're supposed to do?"*
> *"Do I have to? I'm really tired. Why can't it be somebody else's job for a change?"*

Finally, one of her parents would get her to clear the dishes, but only after protracted fussing.

Years went by. The autumn leaves fell from the trees. The snows came and went. And then the first blush of spring, inevitably followed by summer with its withering heat. And then it was autumn again. But still, every evening, after every family meal—without fail—Amber left the dinner table without clearing the dishes.

> *"Amber, where do you think you're going?"*
> *"I don't know. I'm finished."*
> *"No, you're not finished. You have to clear the table."*
> *"Do I have to?"*

And then one day Amber was sixteen. It was a Tuesday night, to be exact.

> *"That was very tasty,"* said her father, wiping his mouth with his napkin as he rose to leave the dinner table. And, as he started away from the table, Amber also got up from her seat and picked up a couple of the dirty dinner plates.
> *"What are you doing?"* asked Amber's father.

"What do you mean?"

"Just what I said. What are you doing?"

"What does it look like? I'm clearing the table."

"You're clearing the table? Is this some kind of joke or something?"

"No. Why? What are you talking about?"

"But, Amber, you're clearing the table. You've never cleared the table without first putting up a fuss. Never. Ever. I don't get it."

"I don't get what you don't get. I'm clearing the table. It's my job. Is that okay?"

"This isn't a trick?"

"Why do you keep saying that?"

And from that day forward, Amber cleared the dishes immediately upon the meal's completion.

This is the way that it works. Not always. Not with all kids. But with most. All of those good character traits that you work to instill in them, they're in there. It's just that you don't get to see them. But, eventually, with most teenagers, most of the time, the tree bears fruit.

If only there was some way to speed up the process!

ENTITLED TEENS

Fifteen-year-old James was sitting in the kitchen eating a cheese and pickle sandwich when who strode into the room but His Majesty, King Thomas the Fourth. The king went directly over to James.

"I, King Thomas the Fourth, do hereby decree that you, James, because of your exalted birthright, are entitled to everything. Because of who you are, anything that you want, you deserve, and by your rights you shall get. Above all, James, let none declare that you must do anything in order to earn what you want. All things should come to you. Nothing by your effort, but only by who you are, James.

That's right, thought James. *It's in the Bill of Rights. They taught us about it in school. Everybody knows it: "We the People of the United States hold these truths to be self-evident blah blah blah something something something." Which means that everybody has a right to get good stuff. It's only fair. It also means that if there's stuff I don't want to do, I don't have to. It's called freedom. Everybody knows that too. Nobody can tell me what to do. Well, duh, this is a free country, I can choose to do something if I want to, but if I don't want to, nobody can make me. That's the law.*

Actually, feeling entitled is not bad. But there is good entitlement and there is bad entitlement. Good entitlement is when you feel that just because you are a human born into the world, you deserve an equal shot at everything and are equal to everybody else. It is when you believe that you should be treated well. That you should be respected. That you should have the same chance of getting good stuff as everybody else. Furthermore, it is feeling that you automatically have an unalienable right to be cared for, loved, protected, and to get your fair share of good stuff just because you are a kid.

That is good entitlement. People should feel that, as humans, they deserve to be treated well. It's their birthright—just because they are human.

But there is bad entitlement too.

I am special. And the nature of my specialness is that, just because of who I am, I deserve more. Special treatment. Just because of who I am: more deserving than others.

William and his mother were in the supermarket. They were in front of a dairy case that held hummus. William's mother reached down and picked out a plastic container of Waving Palms Sweet Red Pepper Hummus. Waving Palms was the least expensive of the three brands in the supermarket case.

"No, Mom," said William, *"we have to get Star of the East. It's the only kind I eat."* And William picked out a container of Star of the East Red Pepper Hummus. It just so happened that Star of the East was the most expensive of the three brands, literally almost twice the price of the same-size container of the Waving Palms.

"No, I'm sorry, William. *I'm not going to pay extra money for Star of the East."*

"But, Mom, you have to. *I hate Waving Palms and I hate Satifa* [the middle-priced brand]. *Star of the East is the only brand that I eat. I hate the other two. I won't eat them. They make me want to throw up. You have to get me Star of the East."*

"No. I'm sorry, William. If you want it so much, you can use your own money to pay the difference in price."

At which point William got very mad and started shouting at his mother.

"No, Mom! I'm not going to use my money! That's not the deal! That's not fair! You have to get me Star of the East! It's the only one I eat! You have to! YOU HAVE TO! You can't not get me Star of the East!"

"No, William. I don't have to get you Star of the East. "

"You don't understand! You have to!"

The good news about entitled kids is that it really is not so bad to want what you want. And if you really feel you're entitled to everything, that's your business. It only becomes a problem if others—e.g., your parents—go along. But if not, there is no problem.

Hence, all William's mother has to do to draw the entitlement line where it needs to be drawn, is not to buy the more expensive hummus. What she does not need to do is deliver Lecture 16A:

"William, you don't get it. How many times do I have to tell you in order to get it through your head? You are not entitled to everything just because you want it. You are no more special, no more deserving, just because you are you. That's not the way it works. There are seven billion other people in the world."

This is unnecessary and not very useful information, as all it will get in return is:

"But it's not fair! I hate the other kinds of hummus! It's not fair!"

That is: Willliam doesn't get it. Continuing the lecture will only make him argue more and feel that his parent is being a bitch.

Well, she is! She can afford the extra money! What am I supposed to do? Go without hummus? Or maybe she thinks I should eat the other hummus, which will probably make me throw up!

If William's mother sticks to her guns and doesn't get him the hummus, he will learn the only lesson that is necessary.

I am special. But nobody else seems to recognize it. What is their problem? I am entitled to special treatment. It's just that nobody seems to know it. And I explain it to them, but they're not even interested. So what I'm going to have to do, because I certainly don't want to have to go without stuff, is that I'm going to have to do stupid work—which I hate and which I already explained is completely unfair. But it looks like I don't have a choice. That's the way it is. It's the only way that I'll ever get anything. So I'll have to play along. Until they understand who I am.

Bad entitlement—feeling that they should get what they want just because they want it and everybody else be damned—basically comes from three sources. The first is when they too regularly are able to get their way by intimidating, cajoling, and arguing with you.

> "I think I'm allergic to the two cheaper kinds. That's why they make me nauseated. I have a delicate digestive system."
> "William, you are not allergic to the other brands of hummus."
> "I am too! You don't know anything! How do you know I'm not?"
> "Oh, all right, William. But this is the first I've heard about your problem digestive system."

Another way that they learn bad entitlement is from you. Do they see you act as if all people do not deserve equal respect?

Do they see you being intolerant with a salesperson, for instance?

"Oh, for Chrissake, don't you know anything about the products that you're selling? Don't they train you?"

Do they see you making fun of others?

"If there's a bigger idiot than your uncle Arthur, I'd like to meet him."

Or being impatient with people who can't help it?

Honk! Honk! "Come on! Come on! Look at that guy in the car in front of us: he must be over ninety! They shouldn't allow old people on the road! Come on! Come on!" Honk! Honk!

And last, they learn bad entitlement if normal demands are not made or insisted upon over the course of their childhood:

> "Tie your shoelaces, Cindy."
> "No, you do it."
> "Oh, all right, Cindy. But don't you want to be a big girl?"
> "No."

"I need you to bring in the blankets from outside before they get rained on."

"I can't. I'm busy."

"You never seem to help around here."

"That's because you always ask me at bad times."

"You have to do your homework for tomorrow."

"I can't. I'm too tired and I have a headache."

"I'm sorry you have a headache. Do you want me to write you a note?"

"Yeah. No. You do my homework for me."

"Again?"

"Yeah."

Entitlement is good if it means that you feel that, just by being born into the human race, you are special and deserve to be treated well and that you should get your fair share of everything in life. Feeling entitled is not so good if you feel that your version of "special" means that you should get a better deal than others just because of who you are.

SPOILED TEENS

Another common complaint about today's kids is that they are spoiled. Being spoiled is obviously a close cousin of feeling entitled, but here I am specifically referring to getting stuff. The classic image of the spoiled teen is one who too easily gets too much, such that their world revolves around getting and owning cool stuff.

"What? I get a lot of stuff. But what's wrong with that? My parents can afford it. Why shouldn't I get nice stuff? Do you want to see my sweaters? So what, I spend a lot of time going to expensive brand clothing and accessory websites? It doesn't make me a bad person. Do you want to see my charm bracelet?

"I know that this is going to sound greedy. And I understand how lucky I am that my parents can afford to get me really nice, expensive things. And I do care about poor people. But I really need to have a pair of Kismet jeans. I know they're very expensive. But my parents don't understand what will happen if I show up at school with a pair of different jeans. My friends

will immediately notice, and they will either feel sorry for me—you cannot know how mortifying it would be, their feeling sorry for me—or they may actually feel they need to distance themselves from me. You don't know my friends. 'Tina, it's not that we don't like you and all. But if certain people saw us hanging out with you and you were wearing those jeans, I mean, I know it's not right, but that's the way it is. It would reflect really badly on us. I'm sure you understand how it is. It's just that, what does it say about us hanging out with someone wearing those jeans?'

"I mean, I know it sounds overdramatic, but if my parents don't get me the Kismet jeans, it will ruin my social life. Actually, it will ruin my entire life. Trust me.

"Okay, I'm going to put on each pair of jeans. And I'm going to look at myself in this mirror and I want you to tell me that you can't see the difference. First, me in the Kismet jeans. Okay? I look good. I am now looking at myself in the mirror and I look good. Now me in the crappy jeans. Do not try to tell me that you don't see the difference! I don't look good. I couldn't go to school wearing these jeans. I could not go!"

Or Myron's plight:

It is not a good day in school. I have become a lesser person. I didn't used to be a lesser person. I used to be fine. In fact, as recently as this morning, I was not a lesser person. I was not a lesser person right up until precisely 10:13. It was at 10:13 between classes when Jamie Aldowitz showed me his new Delta Whisper [the very latest do-everything communication device]. Unfortunately, since that moment I have been a lesser person. It is not fun. And I will continue to be a lesser person right up until the time that I get a Delta Whisper.

Just then a small package was delivered to Myron right in class by a messenger from the principal's office. The package had just been dropped off at school for an emergency delivery to Myron from his mother. Eagerly Myron opened the package.

Omigod, it's a Delta Whisper. I can hold my head up. I am once again a person of value.

The way the world works is that there are large numbers of very smart and very creative people who get paid very large amounts of money to think up and produce products that are very desirable. These products either look very good or are just different enough to possess the perfect panache at the moment. The other kinds of extremely desirable products are those that can do stuff that takes "cool" to the next level—stuff that you didn't even know existed or that you wouldn't so desperately want until these very smart and creative people thought them up.

People should not be defined by what they look like, and especially not by what they have. It's not good if you need to have lots of cool stuff in order to feel good about yourself. But, at the same time, cool stuff—so long as it's out there—does exert a strong pull. Wanting stuff does not make you a bad person. If most of your friends have a nice cell phone, it's normal to feel left out if you don't have one. And if you really want an expensive cell phone and you get it, that doesn't make you a bad person, either.

We don't want to raise kids who feel that their lives are defined by what they have. At the same time, living in the world that they live in does make it kind of hard for them not to, at least to some extent, feel exactly that way.

What can you do? Don't get them obscene amounts of stuff even if you can afford it. Don't let them too often pressure you into getting things that they really don't need. Don't let them pressure you into getting lots of stuff you can't afford.

Probably above all, try to make sure that they interact with the world, that they strive to *accomplish* rather than just *have*. In effect, try to make sure that they are active in a way that they feel effective in their lives, separate from what they have. Which is what most parents try to do anyway.

Last, you want them to have at least some guilt. They get this to a large extent from you. Do you genuinely communicate that they live in a world where there are lots of people who do not have any stuff at all? And that the reason they *do* have stuff is that they are lucky to have been born where they were? No other reason. Nothing else separates them and the people without stuff other than their good luck. If they do have the good fortune to be able to own nice things, they should feel more than a little guilty that others do not have their good fortune.

INCONSIDERATE TEENS

"Mom, you have to drive me to the store right now. You know my project for history? It's due tomorrow and I need a packet of those

little stick-on tabs because Ms. Tremblay said we have to use them to separate the sections."

"Darryl, I am in the middle of finishing a report for work tomorrow. You knew about this all week, and now you're coming to me at the last minute. You cannot simply expect me to drop everything and instantly be at your service."

"But, Mom, you have to! What am I supposed to do? I need them now!"

"Darryl, you knew all week. It's not fair to come to me at the last minute like this. Everything does not revolve around you."

"But, Mom, it's due tomorrow!"

An unattractive teenage trait is that they really don't seem to understand that the universe does not revolve around them and their needs. We ask Darryl:

"Don't you feel you're being a little inconsiderate?"

"Well, I know I shouldn't have left it to the last minute. But, I'm sorry, I need the stick-on tabs."

"But don't you think it's unfair to your mother?"

"I don't know. I mean, she'll just have to stay up a little later. It's not such a big deal."

"You don't feel at least a little bad for your mother? How you've left this to the last minute and you are not even thinking about the way interrupting her work on her report causes her significant inconvenience?"

"To be honest, actually, I don't feel that bad. After all, she's my mom. That's what you do if you're a mom and you have kids."

They take you for granted.

Teenagers often act as if their parents are slaves—that they must be ready to serve at a moment's notice and have no lives of their own. How can kids be so inconsiderate? How can you teach them not to be?

What you want, as they go about their day, is for them to have at least some little part in their head that thinks about you, about how you might feel, or about what your needs might be. A permanent little place in their heads that considers you—at least a little bit.

What effect will this have on Mom? How will this make Mom feel?

How can you get them to understand that they are not the center of the universe?

Hello. I'm here. I exist in the universe. Same universe as the one you're in. Hello. I'm here.

If you want to accomplish this goal, do *not* try to impress upon them how inconsiderate they are.

> *"Darryl, does it ever occur to you to think about somebody's needs other than your own? You cannot simply go through life only thinking of yourself. You know what? Stop sometimes and just say to yourself, 'What effect will this have on Mom?' Is that so difficult? It is not always about you."*

The above is actually fine to say, and the words probably do go into his head. The problem only occurs if you expect to get a positive response.

> *"Okay, I know I can be a little self-centered sometimes. I'll try to be a little more thoughtful. I know you have a life too. I forget that sometimes. I need to think about that in the future. Sorry."*

Doesn't happen. Instead, what usually happens is that they will respond, but not the way you want:

> *"That's not fair! I do think of other people! I do think of you! I got you flowers on Mother's Day. But I guess that wasn't good enough! What's the point of my doing anything nice if you don't even appreciate it?"*
>
> *"I can't believe you, Darryl! You just don't get it! You don't understand a word that I'm saying to you!"*

Unfortunately the net result of such interactions is usually,
My mom doesn't appreciate anything I do. What the fuck's the point?
Not the lesson you wanted. And for you:
He's impossible. He's totally impossible. It doesn't matter what I say. What's the point?
Not what you wanted either.

The main lesson—and the only one that counts—comes from what you do, not what you say. The real lesson comes from whether Darryl's mother takes him to the store or not. It's okay if she decides to take him. Perhaps she feels that, as inconsiderate as Darryl is being, his need for the stick-on tabs is real, and she does not want him to get a lower grade.

But if she does that, then the main lesson for Darryl will be:

If I can make it sound urgent enough, she'll give in. She'll be ticked off at me, but she'll give in.

Which is fine, as long as it is not always the case. For example, let's say his mother was feeling very pressured about the report she was writing and didn't want to take the time out, right in the middle of what she was doing, and the store was going to close soon.

> *"No, Darryl, I can't."*
> *"But, Mom!"*
> *"I can't, Darryl. I'm sorry."*

And he did end up handing in the history project without the stick-on tabs and did get ten points taken off his grade.

Or a completely different time, when Darryl's mother simply chose not to be inconvenienced:

> *"Mom, I invited T.J., Lanny, and Melanie over for supper."*
> *"I'm sorry, Darryl; I only bought enough for you, me, and Kimmy, and I don't feel like running out and getting more at this point."*
> *"But, Mom, I already invited them."*
> *"Well, you'll just have to disinvite them."*
> *"But, Mom! That is so unfair!"*
> *"Next time, ask me in advance."*

Teenagers need to learn that your servitude has its limits. You can give in to their demands sometimes, but that becomes a problem if their self-centered side starts to rule you too much. Sometimes they have to experience not being the center of the universe. It is not so much that they learn to be considerate of your feelings. What they learn is a different but necessary lesson.

If I ask her to do something for me, maybe she will and maybe she won't. And if, in the future, I am going to ask her, I will have to consider the possibility that she won't, and to think about how, if it's too inconvenient for her—if it's asking too much—it might not happen. That is, there is this other variable in the universe besides simply what I want. There's also what she wants. That sucks.

So how do they get to be considerate? How do they develop a part of them that actually thinks of the feelings of others and genuinely does not want to cause unnecessary suffering to them? It is the trait we call empathy—putting yourself in the place of the other person.

How would I feel if I was really busy and somebody asked me to do something right away that they could have asked for at another time when they knew I wasn't so busy? Oh, I probably wouldn't feel happy. I would feel very put-upon. Oh.

How do they learn that? From having been loved unconditionally and treated considerately and not cruelly. All of that is internalized and then creates the capacity to genuinely care about others.

A last powerful component of teaching consideration to your child is your being considerate of them—regardless of how they may or may not act toward you.

Lindsay's mother picking up Lindsay after school:

> *"Listen, do you want me to drop you off at home before I do my errands? It's a little out of my way to do that, but I know it's boring for you being dragged along for an hour and a half."*
> *"Yeah, thanks, Mom."*
> Lindsay thinks:
> *That was considerate of Mom.*

A little of that goes a long way.

It is important to teach teenagers that we are not their slaves. But we also need to show them that we are sensitive to their feelings.

And, of course, as repeatedly noted in this book, if you have already been a nice and considerate parent most of the time, you probably have already won the battle. Existing inside of your teen is a nice considerate part of them that has been showing itself out in the world all along.

Darryl is always so nice with that elderly Mrs. Tuttle down the street. I wish I got to see some of that.

You will. But you have to wait.

OBLIVIOUS TEENS

Not only can teens seem wholly unaware of your existence other than as an object to serve their needs, but they can also at times be oddly oblivious of themselves and of how the way they act can sometimes cast them in a distinctly unfavorable light. It can seem very much like a movie that had parts edited out, removed as if they never happened.

Kayla's mother would not let her have Steven, her boyfriend, over to do homework with her, as her mother was going out and was not comfortable leaving Kayla and Steven alone in the house.

> *"Omigod, we're not going to do anything! We're going to study! You're obsessed with the idea that I'm some kind of sex-crazed slut, which I'm not!"*
>
> *"No, I am just not comfortable with the two of you here alone."*

The discussion continued downhill from there, ending with Kayla having a full-fledged tantrum and screaming at her mother with much profanity, including,

> *"I hate you! I hate this fucking house! You treat me like a fucking two-year-old. I hate you!"* but at considerably greater length

and with considerably more profanity.

At which point Kayla stormed off to her room.

Later that evening, when her mother returned from her outing, she confronted her daughter.

> *"Kayla, you were way out of line earlier when I said you couldn't have Steven over. You can't behave that way."*
>
> *"What way?"*
>
> *"Kayla, you had a major tantrum this afternoon and were swearing at me when I said you couldn't have Steven over to the house."*
>
> *"No, I didn't. You always exaggerate stuff."*
>
> *"You had a major tantrum."*
>
> *"No, I didn't."*

It is as if it never happened. Not only that, but:

> *"Kayla, I want you to watch this."*
>
> *"What's that?"*

"It's a video of your tantrum earlier this evening."
And then her mom shows Kayla the video.
"That's not me. That's some kind of trick video, like it was computer generated."

Are they lying, or can they distort reality that easily? The answer probably lies somewhere in between. When dealing with their family, many teens (and many adults as well) can be surprisingly oblivious to their own behavior. It is as if at home they are in an altered state of consciousness whereby anything unpleasant somehow gets screened out. They just don't seem to get it. So what do you do?

What you should *not* do is expend a lot of energy trying to get your child to own up to what actually transpired. Attempts to get them to see the truth very rarely—and I mean *very* rarely—meet with any kind of success. But what invariably happens instead, which directly prevents any positive outcome at all, is that you and they end up in an increasingly angry argument about what actually happened.

> *"Kayla, you had a major tantrum and were swearing at me because you couldn't have Steven over."*
> *"I didn't have a major tantrum! You always totally exaggerate everything I do!"*
> *"No, you were way out of line."*
> *"You were out of line! You were yelling at me!"*
> *"No, Kayla, you were shouting and swearing. It was awful."*
> *"I was a little mad; who wouldn't be? That was all that happened! You just exaggerate!"*
> *"I don't exaggerate."*

Unfortunately the more that Kayla's mother focuses on getting Kayla to see or admit what actually happened, the more Kayla becomes combative, defending her position and getting increasingly mad at her mother. The more defensive Kayla gets, the more evil she considers her mother to be and the more she feels accused. She does not reflect on what may or may not have been her behavior.

We ask Kayla,

> *"What did you just learn about your behavior from your discus-*

sion with your mother?"
    "That my mother is a bitch."

This is how she will see it.

It is far better not to get caught up in trying to convince them of the real story. It is far better to simply state what happened as you saw it, and go on from there.

> *"Kayla, I did not like the way you acted earlier this evening."*
> *"What way?"*
> *"You had a major tantrum and swore at me when I said you couldn't have Steven over."*
> *"I did not! You're exaggerating!"*
> *"I don't want you acting that way in the future."*
> *"What way? I wasn't acting any way!"*
> And Kayla's mother ends her participation in the discussion.
> *"You're not listening to me! I didn't have a tantrum! You exaggerate! You think I'm yelling when I'm not! You're too sensitive!"*

That is, Kayla's mother, more or less oblivious to Kayla's denials, states her piece and moves on. She has made her point and needs to say no more.

Kayla does hear her mother. She may or may not change her view of her own behavior. But there is no argument over what happened, only a statement by her mother that Kayla hears and has to contend with in her own mind.

Will she change her behavior in the future? Maybe. Maybe not. But there is a far better chance of her reflecting on her own behavior, rather than seeing it as just another instance of her mother being a bitch.

I don't know; I have this dim, hazy memory of me just maybe kind of yelling and maybe saying "fuck" a lot. I don't know. The memory is very dim.

WHY IS IT NEVER THEIR FAULT?

Not only do teens seem to have selective memory issues, but when they do remember something, their account never positions them at fault.

"Where's Major? Oh no! He got out again!"

Half an hour later:

"Elena, I had to run all over the neighborhood to find him. One of these days, we won't be so lucky and something bad could happen. How many times do I have to tell you that the screen door has to be closed and you have to make sure it clicks?"

"It wasn't me!"

"Of course it was you. You were the only one in the house."

"It wasn't me!"

"Stop saying it wasn't you."

"It wasn't me, and besides, how am I supposed to be able to close the door right when I have so many books that I have to bring home from school? I didn't want the dumb dog anyway!"

When it comes to teens, it's never their fault.

"My D+ in history? I told you about Mr. Terwilliger. He hates me! I don't know what his problem is. From the first day, he's had it in for me!"

"Just because I had friends over when you weren't home, how is it my fault that Stevie Quinlan stole money out of the emergency drawer?"

"It's that dumb refrigerator. It's slanted or something. Every time I open the door, something falls out."

Why can't they ever just say, *"Yeah, it was my fault. I'm sorry. I'll really try to do better in the future."*

Well, it isn't *my* fault. My parents always blame me for stuff. They automatically think it's my fault. I mean, I do stuff wrong sometimes. Everybody makes mistakes. But—really—they blame me for everything.

The normal human response to blame is to try to deflect it. It makes sense: if you did something wrong and somebody finds out, usually there are unpleasant consequences. At the very least, they're mad at you. Or maybe you get punished or you have to make restitution.

"You broke the lamp. You're going to have to pay for it."

"I didn't!"

Not only do teens deny blame in order to ward off the wrath of others, but they also deny their blame even to themselves. Most people do feel remorse when they know they have done something wrong. It's an unpleasant feeling.

Yeah, I know I should have been more careful. It really would suck if something happened to Major and it was all my fault. I don't want to feel guilty. It sucks.

Not only is remorse an unpleasant feeling, but admitting guilt to yourself means you need to change your behavior in the future. You have to be more careful in closing the door each time you come into the house; you have to be more diligent about doing homework in order to get a better grade in history. You can't have friends—or at least not Stevie Quinlan—over after school. You have to be more careful about taking food out of the refrigerator. You would rather not have to do any of those things. It takes effort.

So most teens prefer to argue and deny any wrongdoing and, hopefully, in the process, take the focus away from what they may have done. In their minds it is much better to blame somebody else, or unfortunate circumstances will ensue.

"The wind did it."

So how can you teach your teen to take responsibility for their own bad actions? What can you do to get them to understand that what they did was a problem, and that they will need to change their behavior in the future?

What you do not want to do under these circumstances is anything that will let your child avoid facing the simple truth of what they did and its consequences.

Unfortunately, it is very easy to unwittingly head in the wrong direction. This occurs when parents spend too much time and effort trying to get their kid to admit their guilt. Parents put far too much stock into getting their kid to own up. And into saying that they're sorry too.

"I did it. It was my fault. I wasn't careful. I'm sorry."

Great. But what does getting them to say the above really accomplish? Does their saying *"I did it. I'm sorry"* mean that that's what they really think? Or does it mean that you have successfully broken them down so that they will say the words you want to hear just to get you off their back? Unfortunately, the process of trying to get them to own up actually works against that goal. In their own minds it enables them to shift the blame away from themselves.

> *"Elena, it is your responsibility to always make sure that the door closes firmly."*
> *"I do! It's not my fault if the stupid door doesn't close right! You should have it fixed!"*
> *"Elena, the door is fine; it's just that you don't take the time to make sure it clicks."*
> *"I do take the time! You don't know anything!"*
> *"Elena, when are you going to learn to be more careful? You just think of yourself all the time. Never about what might happen."*
> *"I do too think about what might happen! You don't want to spend money to fix the door! Everything is automatically my fault!"*
> *"Well, it was your fault, Elena."*
> *"No, it's your fault because you're too cheap to have it fixed."*

In her own mind, Elena effectively shifts the blame to her mother: *Mom is such a jerk. She never believes anything I say. They should get a new door. It's too hard having to make it click every time. They're just too cheap.*

And the more that Elena is blamed, the more defensive she becomes and the less she looks at her own behavior. The more she sees her accuser as the bad guy and counterattacks, the further away she moves from seeing and accepting responsibility for her own actions. She becomes convinced that the responsibility lies outside of herself.

So what should you do?

Say what you thought they did. Say why you thought it was a problem. And, if you want, say how you felt about it. But say all of this briefly. And then shut up.

> *"Elena, Major got out and I had to run all over the neighborhood to find him. You have to make sure the screen door shuts correctly. Every time. One of these days, we won't be so lucky and something bad could happen."*

She, of course, will continue.

> *"I didn't leave the door open! I didn't do anything wrong! I don't know how it happened! You don't believe anything I say! You*

should get a new door anyway!"

But Elena's mother has said all she needs to say. At this point she definitely wants to stop talking. Even when her daughter continues,

"You are such a control freak! Nobody can do anything right to please you!"

Elena would like to blame everything on her mother, but her mother, by not arguing, is giving Elena nothing to rail against. Elena is stuck with the cold facts: she did not close the door tightly; as a result, Major got out and something bad could have happened. Period.

"You never believe anything I say! You don't! Ever!"

But with no one arguing, Elena is just talking to herself. And so, in her head—because her mother does nothing to get in the way of this—she cannot help but think:

That stupid door, why can't it just shut itself better? It's such a pain having to be so careful all of the time. Nobody understands what a big effort it is. But I would have felt terrible if anything had happened to Major.

With no parent playing the role of the villain, Elena cannot deflect blame. She has to accept the fact that she was not careful and that she probably should try to be more careful in the future.

Children do not learn responsibility for their actions from their parents convincing them they were at fault. They learn by seeing the consequences of their own actions.

And, as so frequently is the case, it comes back once again to that all-important skill in parenting: knowing when to shut up.

WHY ARE THEY ALWAYS SO NEGATIVE?

Then there are the kids who always seem to be so negative. If they have anything to say, it's usually something unpleasant.

"Mom, this orange juice tastes sour. It's gross. It's disgusting."
Evan's mother takes a sip. *"It tastes fine to me."*
"Well, it's not. It's gross. You should throw it out."
His mother thinks, *He is always complaining. Mr. Negativity. Like, last night, I reminded him that we were going over to his aunt*

Reba's, and immediately it was, "Oh, that's so stupid and boring."
But then he always has a good time—which he never would admit
later. If there's anything that comes out of his mouth, it's always a
complaint or a put-down.
"This car smells weird."
Anything I say gets a negative response.
"Doesn't the yard look nice?"
"What do you want me to say? It's a yard."
What is his problem?

Evan's problem is adolescence. Until their teenage years, kids seem to be openly enthusiastic about everything.

"Mom. Mom, you gotta look at this!"
"Evan, it's a dead bug."
"No, no, Mom, you don't get it! It's so cool! Look at it! It's the
coolest bug ever!"

But now, to be enthusiastic—especially with you—is very uncool. Showing enthusiasm means opening themselves up to you, inviting a sharing of their inner experience. Not exactly what they wish to do. Being closed off, negative, pushes you away. And that is a much safer thing to do.

Yeah, like I really want to share my inner feelings with my parents.

Yet as strange as it may seem, a lot of these kinds of comments may not be as negative as they appear. Many of these statements are just their way of making contact—their version of *"Hello, good to see you,"* only they can't possibly say that, so it comes out as *"This orange juice is gross."*

Another source of the negativity is that teens—like us, but even more so—use home and family as a place where all the pent-up stresses of the day finally have a safe place to come out. Not that they tell you what's bothering them:

At lunch today, all that the guys did was rag on me about how big a loser I was with Christine. And they wouldn't stop. They thought they were being so funny. But I wanted to smack them.

You don't hear about that. You hear about nasty-tasting orange juice. So how should you respond?

As always, here's my suggestion for what *not* to do:

The most normal response to teenage negativity typically runs something like, *"If you have nothing positive to say then don't say anything at all."*

There's also: *"You know, there are lots of starving children in the world who would be thankful to drink that orange juice."*

Which are both fine, if that's what you want to say. But, as you may know from experience, you'll typically hear something like the following in response: *"I'd have something positive to say if everything around here didn't suck, which it does."*

Or: *"But those starving kids aren't here, so we should throw out the juice."*

All you will get is more of the same.

I'd also advise against saying: *"Here's a list of all the negative comments you've made over the last week. You can see the degree to which you are Mr. Unpleasant-to-Live-With."*

The most normal response to their negativity is to point it out and explain how unpleasant it is. But all you're really doing is piling crabbiness on top of crabbiness. As I described earlier, that strategy almost always makes it worse.

In my experience it is far better to play it straight. To be matter-of-fact. Not defensive. But also not critical.

> *"I'm sorry if you don't like the orange juice. You don't have to drink it if you don't want to."*
> *"I don't. It's sour. It's gross. You shouldn't have gross orange juice in the house."*

But as you really don't plan to pour out the orange juice, you have nothing more to say. And so you move on. Even if Evan continues, still wanting more loving contact.

"The orange juice is gross! There's something wrong with your taste buds! It's really gross!"

Of course, all of this negativity is usually just a stage. Hence, twenty-two-year-old Evan might say:

> *"Remember the orange juice we used to get when I was a teenager? It was really pretty good."*
> *"Then why did you always complain about it?"*
> *"I don't know. To be difficult?"*

Jordan, his father, and his sister had been seated in the restaurant for about fifteen minutes when the waiter brought out one of the meals.

> *"Who has the Chicken Parmesan?"* asked the waiter.
> *"Me,"* said Jordan. Then he eagerly dug into his food as soon as the plate was placed in front of him.
> *"Jordan, wait until our meals come before you start eating,"* said his dad. *"The polite thing to do is to wait until everyone is served before you start to eat."*
> *"Mmpf,"* said Jordan, his mouth full of Chicken Parmesan.
> Later, as they rode home in the car,
> *"Jordan, when are you going to learn manners? You can't go through life acting like some kind of uncivilized savage."*
> *"Manners are bull. I'm serious, Dad; manners are bull. It's what snobby rich people do to show how superior they are to everybody else. Manners are phony. Think about it, Dad. Manners are exactly the opposite of acting like how you feel. It's judging people based on phony stuff, not on who they are."*

We want to raise well-mannered children; but for many teens, manners are to be disdained. They believe that good manners are not genuine. Many of the same teenagers also feel that manners require a level of effort they simply would rather not expend.

I believe in teaching children good manners. Manners are beneficial. They are good for a child to have as part of their daily repertoire. I am talking here about common courtesies, such as saying "please," "thank you," and "you're welcome." Looking people in the eye when you talk to them and not mumbling. Eating with proper utensils. Chewing with your mouth closed. Waiting to eat until everybody is served. Saying, *"Would you please pass me the peas?"* rather than grabbing.

There are some very real, practical reasons why manners make sense: first of all, manners make things more pleasant for others, who will, in turn, be more pleasant to you. Manners help start off interactions on a positive note—especially with people you're meeting for the first time. Manners provide a set formula, a script of how to act. Manners help you know what to say and do in a new situation. People who do not have good manners are often intimidated in new situations or with new people. As a result, they do not do as well in unfamiliar territory.

Having good manners gives you a foot in the door of a club of sorts—one that's very useful to be a part of.

"I'm not going to do it. It's too lame."

So what's a parent to do?

Keep insisting on "please" and "thank you" and "hold your head up when you talk to people." If they object, respond in a level manner: *"You may not agree with me. You may think manners are stupid. But I want you to use good manners anyway. They make a difference in how the world sees you. They are useful to have."*

Don't argue. Don't chastise. Just persist.

It can be frustrating. The best you may get is begrudging compliance. But then, when they get to be adults, most do understand the point of politeness. They may even thank you for teaching them proper manners.

> *"I won't thank you. I want to be in the Bad Manners Club."*
> *"No, you only think you want to be in the Bad Manners Club."*
> As I said, persist.
> *"Jordan, remember, offer to carry in one of these packages."*
> *"Fine, whatever."*
> *"Thank you, Jordan."*
> *"This is so lame and pathetic."*
> *"No, remember, the correct response is, 'You're welcome.'"*

WILL THEY EVER LEARN?

How will they ever learn? They have so many shortcomings, and time rapidly seems to be running out. What's more, nothing that you do seems to be changing anything at all. How will they ever learn to act in a manner that will allow them to go through the rest of their lives getting along with others and having enough good habits and a sense of responsibility so that they can survive out in the world on their own?

How do they ever learn? From what you teach them. From how you model adult behavior for them. From how you act toward them. From how you act toward others. And, as I said before, if you have been a basically good and supportive parent, the package that you give to them does become a part of them. And, with the miracle of maturation, they become an adult. With the great majority of teenagers, you don't have to worry about jamming it all in at the last moment. It is already there.

There is one last major factor in this area to be addressed: How will teens actually act when they are on their own in the adult world? Whether they want it this way or not, they will now have to be truly responsible for the consequences of their own behavior. That is, they will get to see the results of what they do. They will learn because there is no other choice.

Consider the example of Celine and her mother:

> *"Celine, what's this?"*
>
> *"What do you think it is? It's a cantaloupe."*
>
> *"No, I mean why is there a cantaloupe rind sitting in the refrigerator?"*
>
> *"I don't know; there's still some cantaloupe left in it."*
>
> *"No, Celine, it's just the rind. You don't eat everything out of the middle of a cantaloupe and then put the rind back in the refrigerator."*
>
> *"Well, there's still some left. You always say not to waste food."*
>
> Celine's mother thinks, *I don't care so much about the already eaten cantaloupe; but pretty soon she's going to go out into the adult world and there's so much that she doesn't have a clue about. If she doesn't learn to change, how will she ever survive on her own?*
>
> We ask Celine,
>
> *"Celine, what's with the cantaloupe? Nobody's going to eat it, and it's just going to sit there until it rots."*
>
> *"I don't know. Maybe somebody will eat it. It could happen."*
>
> Celine's mother: *That's what I mean. She totally doesn't get it.*

It certainly seems that way. Yet maybe she is not the total lost cause that her mother thinks she is. Will she ever learn?

Let's peek into the future. Celine is twenty-five years old and lives on her own in a small apartment. She works as a sales representative and has just broken off a three-year relationship with a boyfriend. We look in her refrigerator. In it is a similar cantaloupe rind, completely uncovered, with mold starting to show at its edges.

See, she didn't learn. I knew this would happen! I knew it!

But let's wait a little longer. Maybe Celine is starting to change. Maybe she has started to notice that whenever she buys a cantaloupe, eats just the middle, and leaves the carcass in the refrigerator, she never goes back to eat what little is left. After a week or two, the cantaloupe starts to look gross, and she ends up throwing it away. Maybe, one day, after she eats the middle out of a cantaloupe, rather than putting the remains back into the refrigerator, she realizes that there's no point in doing so, and she throws it away. From then on, Celine throws out the cantaloupe rinds rather than letting them rot in the refrigerator.

I don't believe it! She learned? My Celine learned?

How does this happen? Why didn't it happen before? Celine learned because she was no longer a child. She was an adult. Now it was just she and the results of her actions. As a teenager, taking responsibility can be a bit like a magic trick. If you put a cantaloupe rind in the refrigerator and you don't do anything, within a week, maybe less, the cantaloupe rind will no longer be in the refrigerator. It will have completely disappeared. Some adult—probably a parent—got tired of seeing the cantaloupe rind in the refrigerator and threw it out.

See, I knew the cantaloupe would go away. It wouldn't be a problem,

But if you live by yourself and put cantaloupe rinds in the refrigerator, all the magic is gone. The cantaloupe just stays there and rots.

A teenager thinks: *I don't really have to do it now. I'm still a kid, with other people to look out for me. I'll be responsible later—when I'm an adult. I just don't feel like it now.*

Later does eventually come. And when it does, not all kids learn, but most do.

So what's a parent to do in the meantime? What should Celine's mom do? The answer is more or less anything she wants. She can nag. She can throw away the cantaloupe. She can take pictures of the cantaloupe day by day and post them on the refrigerator to document for her daughter the gradual, moldy decline of the cantaloupe. She can stop buying cantaloupes.

Problems only arise when Celine's mom tries too hard to get her daughter to learn. She tries too hard because she feels time is ticking away.

"Celine, how many times do I have to tell you? Don't put canta-loupe rinds back into the refrigerator!"

"Celine, how many times do I have to tell you?"

"Celine, how many times?"

"Celine!"

It is the final lesson, and it is not one that you can teach them. People change, mature, even into adult life. And this happens because, as adults, they get to see—every day—the unadorned consequences of their own behavior.

"Hmm. Did you know that rotting cantaloupes have a kind of sickish sweet smell?"

And this happens even for those who are adults still living at home. Children no longer, they now have adult status. The deal is different. Also, they actually have matured. And perhaps surprisingly, they start to take on adult responsibility where they would not have before.

I suppose I should throw out the cantaloupe. It is getting kind of gross, and I was the one who put it there.

This is the way it is with so much of parenting teenagers. For all those undesirable character traits, you don't need to try too hard to shape your kids up. Many of those battles may be battles that you have already won.

WHEN YOUR TEEN IS NOT TURNING OUT LIKE YOU WANTED

"Harrison never did great in school, but he was always good at figuring out how to do things, coming up with ideas that most kids wouldn't think of. I remember one time, when he was just a little kid, he made these stairs out of books and chairs in order to reach a cabinet. It was amazing.

"I always thought he was going to do well. Not be one of those kids who, when friends ask you how he's doing, you have to mumble and hope they drop the subject. But that's exactly who he is.

"He's in his junior year and he's getting Cs and Ds with an occasional F. And he doesn't do anything. He just hangs out with his loser friends. I know he smokes a lot of marijuana. At home, he mainly tries to keep out of my way so I won't ask him to do anything.

"I used to nag him, but it was less than useless. They say how some kids are late bloomers, that they turn it around later in their life. But I don't see it with Harrison.

And Harrison thinks: *I know my parents want me to do better in school and to have more interests. But that's not who I am. I know I'm a disappointment to them. But I'm happy with what I'm doing. Maybe it's not enough for them, but it's fine for me.*

I don't like being with them because it always makes me feel that I'm not good enough for them. But I'm me. I can't help that I'm me. I want to be with people who are happy that I'm me. Who aren't judging me all the time.

It is normal to have expectations for your children. It is normal to feel disappointment when your child does not achieve—especially when a friend or relative is talking about their high-achieving child.

"Dexter was so disappointed when he got a B+ in honors history."

"My Harrison was so disappointed when it turned out there were only reruns on last night."

Grieve over not getting what you wanted. But privately. In the car. In the middle of the night. But in the morning he's still your kid. He needs and deserves your love and support just as much as high achievers.

You can still nag. It says, I expect more of you. But make a rule:

I am only allowed to lecture him a certain number of times per month. The rest of the time I have to be his loving, supportive parent.

And, in the end, maybe he will surprise you, or maybe he won't. Yet there is an irony about grown children: it is not necessarily the more successful ones who bring the most pleasure into their parents' lives or who are the most thoughtful ones.

Your child will always be your child. And is your child any less deserving of your love and support than a child who is more successful on the world's terms?

THE PERFECT CHILD

It was a Tuesday morning. Jason's mother was standing in the kitchen when suddenly she noticed that she was not alone. A boy who looked to be about fifteen years old appeared out of nowhere.

"Who are you?" asked Jason's mother.

"I'm the child you've always wanted."

"I thought you looked familiar. Now that you mention it, you do look like my Jason. But your clothes are so neat and tasteful and you're so well groomed."

"Oh, look who's coming down the stairs," said the well-dressed Jason. "It's actual Jason."

And, indeed, schlunking down the stairs was the real Jason.

"He didn't even look at me," said Jason's mother.

"Watch this," said fantasy Jason, and he bounded to the top of the stairs, only to start walking down them.

"Hi, Mom. Love you. What's for breakfast? And, by the way, I do very well in school and I write poetry. Would you like to hear my latest?"

"Who's that creep? Where'd he come from?" said actual Jason, just noticing the visitor.

"It's the 'you' I always wanted," said Jason's mother.

"I thought he looked familiar, except dorky."

"Hi. I'm you, except perfect. No, actually I'm you the way your mother always wished you would be."

"Why do you dress funny?"

"It's the way Mom has always wished you would dress."

"But you look dorky."

"Not to Mom I don't. Right, Mom?"

"It's true; he is dressed just the way I always pictured he would be."

"Mom, can I help you with anything?" asked perfect Jason.

"Why, how sweet!"

"I think I'm going to be sick," said the real Jason.

Suddenly a distinguished, gray-haired gentleman appeared in the room.

"Who are you?" asked Jason's mother.

"I'm the writer of this story. I can make anything happen. From this moment forward you can have one or the other of the two Jasons. It is your choice. And if you decide to pick the perfect Jason, you won't remember that your real Jason ever existed, or that you made this choice. So you won't have to feel guilty about relegating your real Jason to eternal oblivion. The only catch is that you have *just twenty seconds to make your choice. And if you don't decide within the twenty seconds, I'll turn them both into giant bunnies."*

"This is so cruel!"

"Twenty . . . nineteen . . . eighteen . . ."

"Can I speak to Dr. Wolf?"

"I'm he."

"You don't look like him. Your picture looks much younger."

"Yes, well, it was taken a number of years ago."

"You should update it. That would be more honest."

"Whatever."

"Can you promise me that my real Jason is going to grow up to be okay? That he'll be nice to me?"

"No, I can't promise that. But it will probably happen. And, by the way, you're running out of time. Three . . . two . . . one . . ."

"I'll take my Jason."

"Oops, sorry, too late."

And, sure enough, quite suddenly the two boys disappeared, replaced by two giant bunnies standing in the kitchen.

"What am I going to do with two giant bunnies?"

"Gdoink. Gdoink," said the two giant bunnies.

"Only kidding. Here's your Jason," said Dr. Wolf.

And, with that, real Jason was back, and Dr. Wolf and the remaining giant bunny vanished.

"I just saved you from oblivion because I love you," said Jason's mother.

"What are you talking about?"

"Forget it."

Eight

TEENS AND THEIR DILEMMAS

Seven-year-old Matthew was playing in the park with a group of other kids. His father was sitting nearby on a bench. Suddenly Matthew broke from the group and came running over to his father.

"Daddy! Daddy! They're teasing me!" sobbed Matthew. *"Daddy, make them stop!"*

Seven-year-old Reyna's mother had come in to say good night and was sitting on her daughter's bed when her daughter began to cry.

"What is it, sweetheart? What's wrong?"
"I miss Grandma Lucy" (who had died a year ago).
"I know; we all do," said her mother.

Eight years later.

"Matthew, you look a little down. Is something wrong?" asked his father.
"No."

"Reyna, you've seemed a little edgy lately. Is there something bothering you?"

"Mother, please!"

PARENTS AS HELPERS

It was so much easier when they were younger. If they had a problem, you almost always got to hear about it. You were the one they turned to to make it all better. But with the adolescent mandate that they must be independent, they find that turning to you for help is a very last resort indeed. And then, if there *is* a problem, it happens in crisis mode, where it seems so hard to know how to help.

"My parents mean well, but hugs to make it all better just aren't going to cut it. It's a little hard to explain, but the more personal anything is, the less I want them to know about it, since it would be, like, super embarrassing if they did find out. And I don't really think that there's anything they can do or say that is actually going to be useful. I just don't think they understand the world that I live in or what it's like being me. They just don't understand any of it."

For parents it can be very perplexing.

"It's so different from when he was a little kid. Now that he's a teenager, problems seem more serious. There's so much out there: drugs, sex, drinking. He thinks I don't know anything about his world. But I know that he's really naive, that he thinks he knows more than he does. It all scares me in a way that it didn't when he was younger. It feels like what happens now affects the rest of his life. It counts. I'm not really sure what to do, but I also don't know how much I should get involved anyway. How much does he need to learn so he can deal with stuff on his own?"

They may not come to you as much as they did before. And when problems do arise, events have a way of rapidly unfolding that can often seem overwhelming to you. But you definitely still can and still do play a significant and helpful role in their lives.

REASSURING A TEEN WHO CAN'T BE REASSURED

One evening, Erin comes to her mother, obviously very upset.

"I can't believe it! I made a fool of myself today at lunch! I got in a fight with Adam [her sort-of boyfriend] and I totally lost it! I was screaming and swearing at him! I made a giant scene in the lunchroom! Everybody was looking! I don't see how I can go to school tomorrow! I feel so humiliated!"

"Of course you can go to school. I know it was embarrassing. But kids get past it. It's like yesterday's news."

"You don't understand! It's posted on Facebook! Thank God somebody didn't take a video of it, or we'd have to move out of state!"

"Erin, I do think you're overreacting. You'll see. In a day or two it will blow over and everybody will forget about it."

"No, they won't, Mom! I'm going to have a reputation as a lunatic and everybody is going to look at me funny! I know how it goes. Kids aren't going to want to hang out with me!"

"Yes, they will. They already know who you are, and one scene is not going to change that."

"You still don't get it. My friends are fickle! They can drop you just like that!"

"You don't give your friends enough credit for understanding that people sometimes blow up. They all have had tantrums themselves—maybe just not in the school cafeteria."

"I'm not going to school tomorrow!"

Nothing I say seems to help. The more I try to reassure her, the less reassured she gets.

It can be very frustrating. To them, everything seems like the end of the world. And when you try to be reasonable, to add some perspective, all your reassurances only seem to make it worse. You can often feel as though your teen is fighting you, not wanting to feel better.

"You don't understand, Mom! If anybody thinks you're even a little bit weird, they don't want to have anything to do with you!"

"That's not true, Erin."

"Yes, it is true!"

The trick is in understanding the nature of teenage worrying. So often it can take on a life of its own. For every reassurance, for every reason why it might not be the disaster that Erin fears it is, her brain generates a never-ending stream of counterarguments. This is what brains do, and smart brains do it even more readily. As each reassurance from you inspires a new worry from them, they actually get more upset.

So what do you do? Understand that teenagers *can* be reassured by you. But it is not so much by your reasoning. It is that you *do* hear their concern and that you *are* sympathetic to their genuine suffering. They feel that you hear them and want to support them. But a major part of your reassurance is the fact that, hearing them, you are not nearly as worried as they are. Successful reassurance comes not only from your sympathetic presence, but also from your own conviction that your teenager's deeper concerns are not reasonable. You have that one useful piece of adult knowledge, which can't be transferred to children: namely, that much of what seems troubling at the moment has a way of fading into irrelevance over time. Not resolved, but somehow no longer nearly so troubling. But this is learned not through reasoning but through life experience.

To reassure, you do not want to rely on logic. What would happen if their logic were able to confound your logic? If they can convince you that all of your reasons why they shouldn't panic are not valid, then what?

> "So you see, Mom, even that reassurance that you just gave me does not hold up."
>
> "You're right, Erin! You've convinced me! It is a disaster! Omigod, what should we do?"

In effect, you are saying: I can't give you answers for all of your concerns. But from my experience, listening to what you are telling me, I'm just not that worried.

The fact that you hear your child's concerns and are not worried yourself is what ultimately reassures them.

> "I don't know what more to say, Erin. I know it's upsetting, but I think you will be surprised at how it does blow over. I'm just not very worried about it."
>
> "But they are going to look at me funny! I know it! I know them! I won't be able to sit with any of those kids at lunch ever again!"

Remember, the key is your reassuring and sympathetic presence, not your words.

"Erin, I don't know what more to say. I know it really does worry you, and I understand how upsetting it is. But I'm just not as worried about it as you are."

"But you don't understand! You're not listening to what I'm saying!"

But you are. And she knows that you are. And the fact is that you are not worried in the way that she is. And that does help.

"I have listened, Erin. I know that it is upsetting. I just don't see it the way you do."

"All right, I'll go to school! But you'll see. It's going to be a disaster!"

"It may be uncomfortable for a while. It will be hard, but it will blow over."

"But I won't actually know what they're thinking, because they now think that anything they say might start me off again! So they'll just gradually back off from being friendly with me, and I won't even know that it's happening!"

"I don't think so. But I know you worry about it."

"You don't know!"

Erin does go to school. And it is uncomfortable. But thankfully—as usually happens—the event soon becomes yesterday's news.

WHAT IF YOUR TEEN IS DEPRESSED?

A parent fondly reflects on his adolescence:

I remember when I was a teenager. Boy oh boy, what times we had! Yessir! Sowed a few oats. Painted a few fences. Those were the days. My teenage years, what times we had!

A current teenager sees it rather differently:

"That is such bullshit! You want to know what it's like being a teenager? I'll tell you what it's like! Let me tell you about school. It's boring! I have to get good grades if I want to have a future. But I don't really have good grades. I don't even know if it's really true

that you have to get good grades to have a decent future. But I don't want to take the chance. So I always have this pressure on me. But I hate studying and I hate homework, and I worry that I need to get it done, which sucks, but I guess I don't worry enough because that doesn't motivate me to do it. All it does is make me feel like shit, since just about all the time I'm not doing nearly what I should.

"And, yeah, I have a social life. But, to tell the truth, lately I think what I like best is getting drunk. And I worry about that, but I wouldn't tell anybody that I worry about it. And I know I'm only kidding myself when I say that I can not drink if I want to. Because I know if I'm not kidding myself, I really look forward to getting drunk, and I wouldn't not do it for anything. That's kind of fucked-up, isn't it?

"Anyway the main thing with my social life is that—except when I'm drunk—sometimes I seem to say stupid shit to people or I do stuff and it doesn't come out like I thought it would. And then I'm in some kind of drama because somebody is pissed at me, which really was not my intention. And I don't really have a clue as to how to make things better. Some kids seem to be good at that but I'm not one of them.

"Do I think about killing myself? I have. I wouldn't ever do it. At least I don't think so. But sometimes my life seems like such shit. Everything is so hard, and nothing really good ever seems to happen. And sometimes I just don't see the point of it if this is what it's always going to be like, except that when you're older they say it's harder. That's a lot to look forward to!

"My parents are nice and all, and I know that they love me. But what possible use are they to me, since they so don't have a clue, don't understand what it's like to be in my life. All they ever talk about—really—is bugging me about shit like chores, as if that's somehow important. But it's like, is that our whole relationship?"

Most teenagers will at times get depressed, even very depressed. It is normal. It is a frequent occurrence in an adolescent's life.

They can get depressed because of bad things happening in their lives: A love relationship gone sour. Problems with friends. Problems with school.

They can get depressed because life is not always easy or fun and it can seem that the bad outweighs the good, that everything just seems too hard.

They can get depressed because of an innate psychological predisposition toward getting depressed.

How can you know if your teenager is depressed? There are standard signs of depression—grades slipping, loss of interest in friends and activities, becoming withdrawn, sleeping a lot. Noticeable sadness, irritability, overall joylessness.

The problem is that the above can often describe any given teenager at any given time. Being a teenager can be hard, stressful, disappointing. The question is not so much are they depressed as: Is there something going on with them that you should be concerned about? You can ask.

> *"Katrina, you've seemed like you've been depressed lately."*
> *"You think I'm depressed? Living in this house is depressing, but I'm not depressed!"*
> If they are depressed, they may not realize it or may not want to talk about it. But sometimes they will tell you.
> *"Yeah, I guess so. There's a lot of different stuff going on. I've been feeling down a lot. Sometimes I'm not even sure why."*

But how do you know whether or not you should be concerned? The answer applies not just to the question of whether your child is depressed, but also to any concerns you might have about them experiencing a significant emotional or psychological problem, whether it be depression, anxiety, substance abuse, impulsivity (acting thoughtlessly in a manner that regularly creates trouble), or ADHD.

The rule is: be attentive to significant problems in any major area of your child's life. Ask yourself if your child:

- Has consistent trouble in school—with grades, behavior, or frequent school absences;

- Seems not to have friends, or is losing the friends they had;

- Has significant problems with eating or sleeping (doing too much or too little of either);

- Seems very withdrawn, or consistently unhappy.

All of these would be cause for concern. And, especially if these problems continue over time, then it is a good idea to seek out a mental health professional. Your child's pediatrician is often the best resource for referrals in your geographic area.

If a child is having significant psychological problems, mental health professionals can be genuinely useful. They can help indicate whether or not there is reason for serious concern, and if so, they can help with trying to alleviate the problem.

There is one issue where you do not want to wait: if you are worried that your child may harm himself or another, you need to consult a professional as soon as you can. If you worry that the harm might be imminent, then you need to call emergency services or bring him or her to a hospital, or if the situation seems unsafe right at that moment, you should call the police. You do not want to take chances by waiting and hoping that nothing bad will happen. When there is serious concern about possible imminent harm, something bad *can* happen. It is always a mistake not to seek help if you have serious concerns about the safety of your child or anyone else.

The other situation where you always want to consult a professional is if your teen talks about wanting to die. All such talk should be taken seriously. Whether it is seemingly in jest, part of a temper tantrum, or an apparently offhand comment thrown in as part of a litany of complaints, you do not want to let it pass. In response you should always ask,

"Are you seriously thinking of killing yourself?"

And unless you are fully reassured by their response that they are not actually thinking about doing it, you need to get help. Again, if you feel that the possibility may be imminent, then as just described, you need to take emergency action.

If you have a child who may be unhappy, regardless of how severe their unhappiness is or is not, there are always two other things that you can do that can make a positive difference. One is—as I have advised earlier—to regularly talk to your child.

> *"How are you doing? How's school? Anything going on?"*
> This may or may not get much in the way of a positive response.
> *"Do we always have to do this?"*
> Or perhaps,
> *"I don't know. Everything is fine. Don't worry about it."*

But persist. Sometimes you may get answers, sometimes you won't. Either way, your child will always hear the message: *I'm concerned about you and I care about you and I'm not going away.* Which is a very good message to reinforce.

Last, regardless of what the problem with your child may be, you always want to do your best to make your home a nice place. While a teenager may be miserable, they know that home is always there as a safe, and hopefully nice, haven to fall back on. Though they may not be happy, the very existence of this warm, safe place in their lives can make a significant difference in getting them through the bad times.

My life is currently shit, and I don't know if it's going to stay that way or not. But at least I have my room and my stuff, and most of the time my parents don't hassle me. I know that they love me, although that is of no use at all. Actually my home isn't so bad. And it's depressing to admit that the best thing in my life is being in my room. But that's the way it is. And I hate to admit it, but I'm glad I have my room.

WHAT IF YOUR TEEN GETS INTO TROUBLE?

Alex's mother is at work when she gets a call from Alex's school.

> *"Mrs. Crestman?"*
> *"Yes?"*
> *"This is Charles Neely, assistant principal at the high school. You are going to have to come down to the school and pick Alex up. He has been suspended for the day for fighting with another student."*

When Alex's mother retrieves her son, she gets the school's version of the story: a teacher on hall duty saw Alex push another boy, causing the boy to lose his balance and fall. The other boy said it was unprovoked. Alex would also be suspended for the following day—the automatic penalty for any fighting in school.

As soon as they are in the car, Alex launches into his defense.

> *"Mom, that was totally not what happened! Travis Bennett does this kind of stuff all the time, not just with me! He pushed me*

against a locker for no reason, and I pushed him away just to get him off of me! I was just defending myself! But that was all that Mr. Olivetti saw. Besides, Mr. Olivetti doesn't like me because he thought I was a wiseguy when I had him for gym last year. Which maybe I was a little, but that's not a reason to accuse me of something when I didn't do anything wrong! I swear to God, Mom!"

Alex begins to get teary. *"You've got to do something, Mom! It's not fair!"*

Should Alex's mother let the penalty stand, or should she get actively involved with the school, defending her son from what may be an unjust accusation, or perhaps even aggressively challenge the school over the perceived unfairness?

Parents often tell their teenagers that, now that they are older, they are going to have to start facing real-world consequences for their behavior.

But when your teenage child actually gets into trouble, things tend to seem a little different than you had imagined. For one, they always seem to have a very different story from the official version—plausible and invariably delivered with what seems to be genuine veracity.

"You've got to believe me, Mom! I didn't do anything wrong! I just defended myself! I swear to God!"

And not only does his story seem convincing, but perhaps the number one factor that undermines parents' tougher resolves is the anxiety that invariably and immediately kicks in:

Now that he's in high school, all this can count against his record. Not just for when he may apply to college, but maybe it becomes a part of his permanent record. They say that stuff like this doesn't follow you, but do I want to take the chance? What if it affects his future?

So what do you do? Where is the line between being too protective and looking out for your own child's best interests?

Every situation is different, so I would not give parents a hard-and-fast rule. But there is an important message in not being too swiftly protective. The message is that they are now entering a stage in their lives in which you cannot completely protect them. They cannot act with impunity. They cannot assume that, no matter what they do, they will be shielded from any consequences of their behavior. After all, in a short time, they will be fully on their own.

"It's not a matter of whether we believe you or not. It's that we can't

always protect you, whether you were right or wrong. Right or wrong, you have to figure out what you have to do so that you don't get in trouble. If they single you out—even unfairly—what can you do so they won't single you out again?"

What if your child really is being dealt with unfairly? If that is clearly apparent, by all means act. But often you don't know for sure. Frequently, it is next to impossible to discern exactly what happened. Under those circumstances, remember that even if your child unfairly gets into trouble (provided that the consequences are not too severe), the message may not be so bad: the world out there is a somewhat random, chaotic place, and you do need to watch out for yourself.

> *"Alex, I've decided that I'm not going to call the school. You'll just have to deal with what the school has decided."*
>
> *"You're not going to call the school and fight for your own son? You're throwing me on the mercy of people who are completely unfair, including one who hates me?"*
>
> *"I'm sorry, Alex. I may be wrong, but you're going to have to deal with this on your own. You're going to have to figure out what you need to do so you don't get in this kind of trouble in the future."*
>
> *"But you're abandoning your own child! You're actually abandoning your own child?!"*

Sometimes it can be for the best. But a humbling reality is that it is awfully hard when it is your own child.

Nine

TEENS AND SCHOOL

L ogan and Vanessa's father worries for his two children:
 "It's a jungle out there. I wish it weren't that way, but it is. The way the world is now, nothing is automatic anymore. Once you get out of school, you're going to need every advantage you can get. I want my kids to have a good time when they are teenagers. But the truth is that what they do now in school does make a difference. A big difference. It's their future. But they just don't get it."

Maybe some don't get it. But some definitely do.

"Every Sunday during the school year, it's the same. Saturday I have a good time. I'm relaxed, I can have fun. And Sunday starts out okay. But then, in the late afternoon, as soon as the sun starts setting, I get this sinking feeling. It's like a dark cloud. I start getting anxious, and it stays like that all through the evening and Sunday night. And it's there when I get up Monday morning. It doesn't go away until I'm actually in school on Monday. It's like I dread the coming of school every week. And during the school year it happens every Sunday. Always."

EDUCATION AND THEIR FUTURE

It is the way of school in the lives of teenagers. They have this very real sense—they are told this all the time—that once they get to be teenagers, especially once they are in high school, it now counts. What they do in school now determines their future. They all get this message. They all are very aware of it. However, what they do with this message can be very different from teen to teen. Some use it as a prod to make themselves do as well as they can. But many fight against it. Push it away.

> "Don't you have homework that you need to do?"
> "I don't need to do homework because I'm going to work at McDonald's for the rest of my life."
> "That's ridiculous, Timothy. You're not going to work at McDonald's."
> "Yeah, I am. I'm serious! Then I won't have all this pressure. You don't know! It's way too hard getting a good job now! McDonald's will be fine. You'll see!"
> "Timothy, you need to get started on your homework."
> "I told you, I'm going to work at McDonald's."
> "But you worked at McDonald's just this last May and hated it and quit after a day."
> "Yes, but this would be as a career. No, actually, I'm going to have my own rock band."

They feel the pressure. They resort to anything they can come up with to negate its effect.

> "What's the point of school? I'm never going to use any of this in the future anyway."
> "That's not true, dear. You will be surprised at how much of what seems irrelevant now will come in handy later on."
> "No, it doesn't! That's nonsense! Tell me one thing in any of my classes that I will ever use!"
> "I can't right at the moment, dear. I mean, I don't know everything you've learned this year."
> "You can't because there isn't anything! So I'm right. There's no point to it. So there's no need for me to do my homework."

But they don't even believe their own words. All kids, deep down inside, do believe the bottom line about high school. They do believe the words that they hear so frequently from the adult world: *doing well in school gives you better options in the future. Doing well in school gives you a better chance at higher paying and more interesting jobs.*

Teenagers may say otherwise. but they believe every word.

There is a basic truth about high school: if you do most of your homework, your time in high school will be okay. Your grades will be okay. Your parents won't always be on your case. You will feel that you are basically doing what is required of you. Conversely, if you frequently do not complete assignments, then high school is always going to be a struggle. You will always have a nagging sense that you aren't doing what you are supposed to be doing.

MOTIVATING TEENAGERS

So how do you get them to do their work? How do you motivate them?

The Petherbridge family got in line and, led by Mr. Petherbridge, marched out of the TV room, through the dining room, and into the kitchen, where they turned around and marched back into the TV room, chanting as they went:

> *"If we work like the devil*
> *We'll stay on the level*
> *And we'll get ahead*
> *Where others won't!*
> *S-U-C-C-E-S-S*
> *It has seven letters*
> *And five of them are different*
> *But together, together*
> *They're how to win!*
> *S-U-C-C-E-S-S!*
> *S-U-C-C-E-S-S!*
> *S-U-C-C-E-S-S!"*

Actually, if it works, I'm for it. But when it comes to sitting down and doing the work, studying hard for tests, and really paying attention in school, even though they may buy into the motivational pep talks—*I do want to do well in school. I do. I really want to do well in school*— the inspiration doesn't last very long.

> "*What about your homework?*"
> "*I started it, but I need a little break. I'll get back to it.*"
> "*But what about that pledge to yourself to really try, and really do well? Didn't you mean it?*"
> "*I do mean it! It's just that right now I'm really tired. I'm just going to take a little break. Okay? Would you back off?*"

When all else fails, parents start thinking about rewards and punishments.

> "*Now, Enrique, I want you to look out the window.*"
> "*Omigod! It's a brand-new Lamborghini.*"
> "*Yes, and it will be yours,*" said Enrique's father, holding out a set of keys. "*If.*"
> "*If what?*"
> "*If we like your year-end report card. What do you think of that?*"
> "*Vroom! Vroom!*"

> "*Mom, why are you holding that calendar, and why are the months of February and March taken out?*"
> "*Because you can forget about having any fun in February and March if your first-half-of-the-year report card is like the last one.*"
> "*Why can't I get a Lamborghini like the kid in the first example?*"

Rewards and punishments work. Especially rewards such as financial incentives, an expensive electronic device, even a car. And punishments—usually some form of grounding, making them stay in on weekends, taking away a cell phone or use of the car—also work. In response, kids will increase their efforts. They'll do better. But then, after a while, sometimes a rather brief while, rewards and punishments stop working. For schoolwork, as with most activities that teens don't like to do, rewards and punishments tend to be effective only in the short term. Over time—for example, during one's high school career—they don't work so well at all.

> *"What about the Lamborghini? Your dad's going to take it away if you don't pick up your grades—fast!"*
>
> *"Lamborghinis are really overrated. Besides, you don't understand how unfair they are at my school with piling on homework! Nobody can do what they ask!"*

WHEN MOTIVATION ISN'T THE PROBLEM

Contrary to how it may appear, I think that the great majority of teenagers are motivated to do well in school. They want to do well. And not only that, I believe that most would like to do their homework.

> We ask: *"You rarely do your homework, is that right?"*
>
> *"Yeah."*
>
> *"Why not?"*
>
> *"I don't know. I guess the main reason is just that I never feel like doing it. It's really boring. The fact is that I hate doing homework."*
>
> *"Do you want to do well in school?"*
>
> *"Yeah."*
>
> *"You're not just saying that?"*
>
> *"No. It would be a lot easier if I did better in school. For one, people wouldn't be on my case all the time. I know that kids who do well in school get better jobs and shit. But most of the time I just really don't feel like doing schoolwork. I just don't."*

Kids vary in how motivated they are to do well. But most do genuinely want to succeed. The main problem, however, is not about motivation. The main problem lies elsewhere—on one of two different planets. Let me explain.

I went to the same high school as my older sister. Both of us were very motivated. *Very* motivated. I did well in high school. But my sister did extremely well. I think one reason that my older sister did better than I did was because she was better in anything that had to do with English.

But there was one other teeny tiny difference between me and my older sister. I always pictured that, when she had two hours of homework, she would think,

Damn, I have two hours of homework.

And then she would sit down and do it.

On the other hand, when faced with two hours of homework, I would think,

Oh, look, there's a Sports Illustrated *that I've only read twice.*

And I would start to look through the magazine. Then maybe I would get up and go into the kitchen to get something to eat.

I really should be doing my homework. I will. I'll start on it in a minute.

And then I might go off and watch some TV. Maybe get another snack. Maybe check out a different *Sports Illustrated.*

Hmmm. This is really interesting. I didn't get the nuances the first two times I read it.

And if, upon rare occasion, I actually did sit down and do a little homework, it was not like I would then get into a groove and work straight through for a while. My style was a little different. When I finally did get down to work, I would get a little done and then pop right up and head for the *Sports Illustrated* or the fridge again. I don't think I was alone in that pattern of study either; there were—and still are—many kids not so different from me for whom the idea of doing two straight hours of homework was unthinkable. My sister and I were both highly motivated, but looking back, I have always felt that it was as if we were from two different planets.

People from my sister's planet cannot understand. They find it totally incomprehensible to wait before doing something that needs to be done—especially something where the consequences of not doing it are so clearly disastrous. And not only that, but people from my sister's planet also believe that if they will just do the darn task and get it over with, they will then be free to do all the other fun stuff they've been wanting to do without anything major hanging over their head to ruin their enjoyment. Those aliens look at folks like me and wonder, why don't they just do it?

As I said, to those from the realm of doers, this behavior is beyond comprehension. But to us from that other planet, it is a way of life. As soon as those of my kind are faced with something that we do not feel like doing, instantaneously—and I mean *instantaneously*—there arises in our breasts a force of insurmountable power. *"Noooooo! I don't feel like doing it! I really don't feel like doing it! Noooooo!"* It is a problem.

My main point is that lack of motivation is not the most important factor when schoolwork does not regularly get done. There are many teenagers who have genuine learning difficulties that make schoolwork harder for them than for other students. For them, the actual process of doing homework attacks their self-confidence—doing schoolwork becomes a constant reminder of its difficulty for them compared to their peers. But I believe that, above all, the main problem for those who regularly fail to begin or complete necessary schoolwork is the degree to which they have difficulty in making themselves do what they do not feel like doing.

There does seem to be a very noticeable gender difference. That is, most of the people from my planet seem to be guys. Most of those from my sister's planet seem to be girls. And not only do guys seem to be different from girls in their lesser ability to make themselves do what they do not feel like doing, but there is yet another guy-versus-girl characteristic that interferes with guys getting themselves to do homework. And that characteristic has to do with how one handles anxiety.

SWEEPING ANXIETY UNDER THE RUG

There are two distinct approaches to handling anxiety that every parent should know about. Let's listen in on some typical parent-son interactions, and then on some typical parent-daughter interactions:

> *"Tyler, what are you doing?"*
> *"What does it look like? I'm watching TV."*
> *"What are you watching?"*
> *"It's a nature special on animals who eat other animals."*
> *"Do you have any homework due for tomorrow?"*
> *"How is that your business?"*
> *"Just asking."*
> *"Yeah, actually, I do."*
> *"When are you planning to do it?"*
> *"Later."*
> *"But it's already pretty late."*

"So?"

"Are you liking the show you're watching?"

"Yeah, it's pretty cool. Actually, I've seen it before, but it's still pretty cool."

"Deirdre, what are you doing?"

"What does it look like? I'm doing my stupid homework."

"I thought there was a TV special on right now about confessions of high school kids who had their hearts broken by boyfriends or girlfriends who cheated on them. Don't you want to watch it?"

"Yeah."

"Wouldn't you like to watch it now?"

"Yeah, except I can't."

"You can't?"

"Yeah. I can't. If I watched it now I wouldn't enjoy it because I'd have this stupid homework hanging over me. I wouldn't be able to get into watching the show because I'd be worrying about the homework that I was going to have to get done. Actually, I'm recording the show, so hopefully I can watch it at another time."

"Alonzo, do you know where you're going to apply to college?"

"No."

"Have you thought about it?"

"No."

"When are you planning to?"

"I don't know."

"Zena, what are those big piles on the floor in your room?"

"Oh, those are the one hundred and fifty-seven college catalogs I sent for. I have to figure out where I'm going to apply, and also see if they have the courses that I'm interested in."

Teenage guys, to a much greater extent than teenage girls, have the ability to sweep anxiety under the rug. Far more than girls, they—to their detriment—are able to rid their minds of the normal anxiety, the normal discomfort that comes from having something that you need to do hanging over you. It is an anxiety that is useful, because it makes us do what we need to do. Girls more than guys are motivated by this anxiety. It mobilizes them to do what they need to do, even to do it well. Guys seem far more able to totally suppress this useful anxiety.

"Wow, look at that cheetah kill and eat that gazelle!"

Why is there this guy/girl difference? Almost certainly it is part of the many fundamental guy/girl differences. Is there some relationship between this phenomenon and the fact that four or five times as many boys as girls are diagnosed as having ADHD (Attention-Deficit/ Hyperactivity Disorder)? Is there something elementally different about the way guy brains are constructed? Probably. But regardless, the difference is there.

Belinda says to her mother:

> *"Look at my folder, Mommy. See how I divided it into seven color-coded sections? See how I added a topic sentence for each new section even though it wasn't assigned?"*
>
> *"Where's your folder, Jimmy? Oh, my. That's a folder?"*

SHOULD YOU LET THEM FAIL?

Let me talk about one thing not to do. When I first started seeing teenagers and their parents, I believed that parents should back off teenagers who do not adequately do their schoolwork. I thought that they need to do this in order to allow their children to experience what happens if they do not put in the necessary time and effort. When they did not do well, when they maybe even failed, I reasoned that they would learn to change their habits. How else would they ever learn the consequences of not working hard enough? Except there was a little problem: they didn't seem to learn. They just failed. And they kept on failing.

Consequently, I now believe that when kids cannot get their act together in regard to school, parents do need to be involved. For such kids, parents' involvement does produce better results than when parents are not involved.

If they never take the responsibility, how will they ever learn in the long run? What will they do when they have to go out in the world and there are no parents to oversee their behavior? My answer: maybe they will learn and maybe they won't. But hopefully they will develop the habit of working. And by getting stuff done, they will have learned significantly better habits than if all that they ever learned to do was nothing.

It takes resolve to practice this parental advice, as kids will invariably say,

> *"If you just backed off you would see! I would do fine! I would do better than with you always getting on my case! That makes it worse! Because all I do then is get pissed off, and then I am so totally not in the mood to do any work!"*

To which I would recommend that a parent reply,

> *"Fine. If I back off and you do okay, I will continue to back off. But if your grades drop and your school reports that the reason is due to work not getting done, or work done inadequately, then I'm back on your case."*

GETTING YOUR TEEN TO DO HOMEWORK

Like it or not, children who regularly do their homework and study for tests do far better and have a much easier time with middle and high school than children who don't. They feel that they walk on the right side of school and do not feel a permanent cloud over them, unlike teenagers who regularly fall short of doing their daily required work.

So what can you do to help? As I have discussed, the value of parents trying to motivate their teenagers as a means of improving schoolwork is very limited. At best it is useful in the short term, but it is not so useful at all in the long term, over a child's entire career through middle and high school.

The bottom line is that you can't actually make someone do anything that they do not feel like doing.

I don't feel like doing it. I'm not going to do it. I'm really tired. And you can't make me do it.

But you can structure their environment to create the greatest likelihood that the work will get done. Although you can't make them actually do the work, you can make sure that, at least for certain periods of time, they will not be doing anything other than schoolwork.

How is this done?

What I am about to describe is more or less what many boarding prep schools do. They have a set study time in the evening when students are not allowed to do anything other than schoolwork. The students may be in their rooms, they may be in a study area, but the rules are that there is nothing else they are allowed to do during that study time that might be a distraction. And the schools have proctors—school personnel—who go around enforcing the rule that if students are not working, they are at least not doing anything else. Some parents pay a lot of money to have their children go to such schools. Perhaps applying their approach will work for you.

Remember that above all, you want to provide the kind of structure for your child that he or she may not be able to create on their own. Here are some suggested first steps you can take:

- Have a set time—Monday through Thursday, and Sunday—when homework is to be done. It does not always have to be the same time each day, as schedules may vary during the week; but, for the most part, the more it is the same, the better.

- The rule is that during this homework time your teen is not allowed to do anything else. No watching TV, no checking out his Facebook page, no talking to friends on his cell phone.

- A public place within the house is the best place for this homework time. Even though there may be people coming in and out, that is less likely to be a distraction than everything he may have in his room. His room is a second choice—with the door open, so that he can be easily checked on.

- They are allowed to listen to music. Many teens actually study better while listening to music. Also, teens multitask. Some teens can get homework done while weaving in bits of electronic distractions—but definitely not as well as where homework is the exclusive focus. If your teen is doing okay in school—if there are no reports of constantly missed homework or low test scores where it is apparent that he has not studied enough—then you needn't get involved. But if not, the no-other-activities rule should stand.

- The homework time needs to be set at a time when you or the other parent are there. You are the proctor who periodically checks to make sure that they are not doing something other than homework.

- The length of homework time should be limited: an hour and a half to two hours, no more. When the time is up, they are free to do what they want. If they have not completed the work, the mandatory homework time is over nonetheless. If the homework time goes on indefinitely, the whole plan will fail. If the work seems too endless, they will give up. They must always be able to see the light at the end of the tunnel.

Some schools demand what would require even more time. Here you are stuck using your best judgment as to whether you want to extend the mandatory—not allowed to do anything else—time or not. I would suggest a rule where you still expect the required homework to be done, but that maybe you stay with the two hours of homework-only time—which you will enforce. The rest is up to them. But it is a judgment call on your part.

What will this accomplish? Maybe, little by little, they will begin to use the time to complete at least some homework. And maybe, over time, the amount of work produced during this finite time period will increase. As time goes on, if you stick with the plan, they will get better at doing the work. But do not think that their efficiency will ever rival the efficiency of those from that other planet.

Last, if you choose to follow this plan, you need to stay with it. Initially they may fight it tooth and nail. But if you remain consistent, night after night, they will see that the rule is not going away, and then—but only then—they may start to use some of it productively rather than using it to complain,

"This is stupid! I'm not doing it! It is a waste of time! I'm not accomplishing anything except getting to hate you more! Did I mention that it's stupid?"

WHAT, NO HOMEWORK?

We've all heard it before—it's the line that begins one of the most common circular discussions of all time:

"I don't have any homework."

"How can that be? I thought you had two assignments due tomorrow and a test."

"Well, I don't."

As we all know, he's lying.

"I don't know what the assignment is in Spanish and algebra, and I don't know any of the kids in either of those classes to call them and find out."

She's lying too.

"I left all my books at school."

Which he did on purpose, hoping that would make it impossible for him to have to do his homework.

"I did all my homework in fourth-period study block."

Which she didn't.

One advantage of having a set study time is that it offers a solution to the problem of teens lying about homework. If they have not been handing in homework regularly, but also have been dishonest about what needs to be done, you can have an addendum to the homework rule: the homework period stands regardless of whether they have homework or not, and during that time they are not allowed to do anything else. And if they say that they have nothing that they can do, not even a textbook to study, you can invent some busywork—which they may or may not do—but, regardless, they are not allowed to do anything else.

If they strongly object to all of this, you can simply say that all they have to do to get the rules changed is to show over a sustained period that they are getting acceptable grades. That there are no reports from their school that indicate they are missing assignments. In that case, you will be happy to have them be fully in charge of their homework. You will be happy to be off the case. But also, you are prepared to revert back to the old deal if they slip into not-doing-homework habits.

The bottom line is not about lying. It is about the fact that if you have a kid who—for whatever reason—is not doing homework, you have a choice: you can get involved with their doing homework, or you cannot. And if you do, the chances are that your child will do more homework than if you completely stay out of it. But this will also involve more of your time and energy and cause you more headaches. It is a choice.

"How about not? That's a good choice! Pick that one! I'll work hard! I will! You'll see!"

But maybe he will and maybe he won't.

COPING WITH STRESS

Children get the message about the need to do well. And with many kids it can turn into a true obsession.

"Everything I do counts. It wasn't like this when I was in grade school, but now it is. It's so competitive. If I screw up even a little, there's always somebody out there who does just a little bit better, and I lose out. That's the way it is."

There are parents who put excessive pressure on their children. But often it's not the parents.

"I don't know where he gets it. We don't put pressure on him. We always say that we want him to do his best. But as long as we feel he is putting in a good effort, then we're satisfied."

"That's what they say, and I suppose they mean it. But they don't get it. Have they looked out the window lately? Nobody hands you anything. I know that. It's a tough world out there, and if you can't get a good job, you aren't going to be able to make even a halfway decent life for yourself."

Of course, they are not wrong to perceive that school performance matters. The pressure is real and it is constant. With school, at any given time there is always work to be done. And it never goes away. Once schoolwork is finished, then the next day there is always more to be done. They can get overwhelmed. They grow to feel as if it is all too much. Too hard.

There is a problem. The problem is that it is necessary for the child to feel stress. Schoolwork is not fun. Often it is *really* not fun. So how do students make themselves do something that they very much do not want to do? The answer is simple: they must feel as if they have to. The pressure, the resultant anxiety, is what makes people work. Pressure is necessary.

"I don't feel pressure. I don't dread Sunday nights. That's because I know that, when it's time for bed on Sunday, I will have done all my work and done all my necessary studying. Mr. Tremmelman says that the E in my name—Emily—must stand for Efficiency. I think it may be true. That Mr. Tremmelman is such a kidder."

But the Emilys of the world are rare.

So what should a parent do? Back off? Nag? It is not a completely resolvable dilemma. The answer is that, with most teens, you have to do both.

When they get too crazed:

"Omigod, I've totally blown my life. I got a seventy-four on my biology test."

"No, you're going to do fine. You're a good student; you will do fine."

"No, I won't! You don't know anything! I have no future!"

"No, you are going to do fine."

They may not always seem to respond to your words, but your voice of reason can be very calming.

Maybe you can take a break until perhaps the next day when you ask again,

"I thought your history project was due tomorrow. When are you planning to work on it?"

You hear in response:

"Get the hell off my back! Stop yelling at me! I'd do better if you didn't always yell at me, which only makes me mad and nervous and depressed! It's Sunday! Look, I'm getting the impending gloom symptom! I can't feel my left arm! I'm having trouble breathing! Oooh! I think I better lie down!"

THE ULTIMATE LEVERAGE

"My Clayton is a good boy. It's just that he never seemed to get his act together in high school. Now he's in his senior year, and he's probably going to just barely graduate. And it's not because he's not smart enough. He's a smart boy. But he just never put any effort into his schoolwork. He just didn't seem to care. I used to be at him all the time about doing

his homework and getting better grades, but all that ever produced was a lot of arguing and even less homework. To tell the truth, I kind of gave up before the end of his junior year. I could see I just wasn't getting anywhere—except maybe making progress toward having a nervous breakdown. He hasn't gotten into any really big trouble during high school. Mainly he's just hung around with his friends. But I don't see him going anywhere."

Yeah, Clayton thinks, *Yeah, I want to have a good time in high school. What's wrong with that?*

"I just don't know what to do. I've tried everything, but nothing seems to have worked."

If you're a parent, your first thought is, *What's going to happen to him? At the rate he's going, he's getting nowhere fast. He's led his life like there was no future, nothing that he had to plan for. I just worry about him so much. What can I do?*

There remains the ultimate leverage: with the end of high school, a whole new ball game begins. He no longer has to go to school. Maybe he has a job, but almost certainly it's not one through which he can build an independent life. Months may go by, and what is very likely to become gradually apparent to him is that he has somehow landed at the bottom. Making little or no money. Having no really meaningful prospects. He will soon discover that while that was fine when he was in school, now, as most of the kids he knew from school have moved on, he realizes that's not acceptable. He acknowledges that he is now out in the real world—the working world. And he doesn't like where he is. Others seem to be moving forward with their lives while he's standing still. His is passing him by. And it forces him to think what had been unthinkable thoughts.

I don't know. There doesn't seem to be as much going on as there used to be. I always felt I was a cool dude. But I don't know so much anymore. It's that other kids are in college, or some of them are even starting to make real money. I don't see how I'm going to get stuff like other people seem to be getting if I just keep going like I am. It sucks.

It is the ultimate leverage. The world starts to move on without him, and he feels it. He feels pressure to do something. And as time continues, the world moves further on. And he remains standing still.

I don't know. I really don't want to have to do it, but maybe I should check out courses at KCC (the local community college).

Not all do this. Some continue to drift. But it is a powerful piece of real-world motivation that kicks in once they are out of high school. And you don't have to do anything to bring this powerful force into play. You just have to wait. You have a very big ally in moving your child forward. It has been there all along, waiting for its turn—if needed.

Chapter Ten

TEENS AND FAMILY

So far, I have talked mainly about issues between parent and teenager. But the life of a teenager is not limited to that twosome or threesome. It gets more complicated. Your teenager is part of a family. And families have their own issues.

BETWEEN PARENTS

I know you'll recognize this exchange:

> "*Ricky, turn off the computer and come to supper,*" says his father.
> "*I will in a minute. Just let me finish something. I'm right in the middle. It will only be two minutes. I swear to God.*"
> "*No, Ricky, turn off the computer now.*"
> "*But, Dad, it will just be two minutes. Just let me finish.*"
> "*No, Ricky, now!*"
> "*Dad, I said two minutes. Jesus.*"
> "*You heard me, Ricky!*"
> "*Dad, you are such a dick!*"

"Don't talk to me that way!"

"But you're being a dick!"

"You know what? You're grounded for the weekend!"

"DAD!"

Reluctantly, Ricky comes in for supper.

"Mom, Dad said I was grounded for the weekend and that's so unfair! I was going to come! He didn't even give me a chance! Now I'm going to miss Evan's party! I didn't do anything wrong!"

Ricky's mother—who was in the next room—has heard the whole scene between father and son.

"Carl, don't you think that's a little strict? I know his language was disrespectful. I'm not condoning that. But you could have given him the two minutes. Do you really think grounding him for the whole weekend fits his crime?"

"Stay out of this, Elizabeth. He knows he can twist you around his little finger."

"No, that's not it, Carl. Sometimes you just get too mad. He's a teenager."

"Stay out of this, Elizabeth."

"I'm not going to stay out of it if you keep coming down on him so hard all the time."

"No wonder he's growing up like a spoiled brat," says Ricky's father. He jumps up from his seat at the table, grabs his car keys, and storms out. *"You got what you wanted, didn't you, Ricky?"* his father calls out just before he slams the front door.

The number one problem in parenting a teenager where there is more than one parent in the home is that parents often do not agree on parenting decisions. This is normal and inevitable. Any two parents are bound to disagree over specific day-to-day issues—whether it's okay for kids to put their feet up on the couch with their shoes on, or whether it's okay not to turn the lights off when they leave a room. And they will often disagree on bigger issues—with one or the other being more or less strict about limits, or differing on the degree of back talk that they will tolerate. These disagreements can be a source of occasional irritation between parents or, as definitely can happen, they can destroy a relationship between two adults.

I'll admit it. I'm more lenient than his dad. In fact, I think part of why I give in as much as I do is that I feel his dad is too strict about a lot of stuff, and I compensate—maybe not consciously—by being less strict. Maybe I can make Ricky feel a little less like he's living on a military base, which is the way I think he often feels when his father is in charge.

Fortunately, this does not have to be a big problem. There are certain simple rules that, if followed, can head off most of the serious clashes between two parents in the arena of child rearing.

If the parent who steps in first makes a decision, the other parent needs to back them up—even if the second parent strongly disagrees. To do otherwise, as was the case with Ricky's parents, undermines the first parent's authority and demonstrates that the two of them are not a unified team. Ricky sees that he can get around or weaken any parenting decision by his father. This can seriously hurt the relationship between the undermined parent and the child, because the parent will harbor considerable resentment toward his child for circumventing his authority. It makes him feel like less of a parent. This reaction is inevitable. The undermined parent will also harbor considerable bad feelings toward his partner. Serious bad feelings. This too is inevitable.

Elizabeth doesn't even realize how much Ricky manipulates her. It's not just that Ricky is being taught not to respect me. She's not respecting me. And that really bothers me.

Last, there is a very real benefit from one parent backing the other, even if they do disagree. It forces the child to learn to deal with the stricter parent. It allows for that relationship to evolve—perhaps to a better place. That cannot happen when the child knows that he does not have to work on dealing more effectively with his father because he can always get around him. Should Ricky's mother simply keep her mouth shut if she disagrees with what her husband did? At the time, yes. But if it is something that really concerns her, then she should talk about it with her son's father privately at a later time. And then, as couples do, they can discuss or argue about the punishment, not to change it but so that Ricky's mother can express how she would feel about similar parenting decisions in the future. Couples will never completely agree about parenting, and it is not necessary that they do. But what *is* necessary is that, when one or the other makes a decision, the other parent backs them up. The exception is where a parent feels that there is actual abuse; then you do have to intervene. But not liking a partner's parenting decision is not a reason to intervene.

The following would have been better:

> "Mom, Dad said I was grounded for the weekend and that's so unfair! I was going to come! He didn't even give me a chance! Now I'm going to miss Evan's party! I didn't do anything wrong!"
> "That's between you and your father."

That is, leave it where it belongs—between father and son. It is the only way.

Again, if Ricky's mother really does feel that her son's father is too harsh too often, she should discuss it with him at a later time, out of their son's hearing.

And one last point: if Ricky's mother feels that her son suffers from too often being on the wrong end of his father's ire, she can empathize. But this is tricky, because she does not want to be critical of his dad. That would only take her son completely off the hook from ever trying to change his own behavior in interactions with his dad.

See, Mom agrees with me. Dad's a jerk. It's all his fault. I don't have to look at my own behavior.

It might be best to say something like,

"I know you feel that your dad is too strict. And I know sometimes it's hard for you." (She is recognizing his feelings, and perhaps he knows that his mother feels that way too, but she isn't saying it. To say it breaks the unified stance. But he also gets to feel that he is not quite so alone with what might, at times, be truly difficult for him.) *"But you could make my life and yours a whole lot more pleasant if you would do what your dad asks without making a fuss every time."*

Ricky's mother makes her point, and her son hears it. Her statement recognizes his feelings but does not absolve him from all responsibility. Saying the above would be enough. She would not want to say anything further.

PLAYING ONE AGAINST THE OTHER

Momma Amy is outside working in the garden when she is approached by her daughter, Melanie.

"Momma Amy, is it okay if I charge fifty dollars at the mall to get this really amazing top I saw last week?"

"No."

Melanie then goes inside to where Momma Jean is doing a crossword puzzle in the library.

"Momma Jean, is it okay if I charge fifty dollars at the mall for this really nice top I saw last week? It's on sale, marked down from a hundred and twenty dollars."

"I don't know—fifty dollars sounds like a lot."

"But, Momma Jean, it's really nice, and like I said, it's an amazing bargain!"

"Okay."

Later:

"Melanie, is that a new top?" asks Momma Amy.

"Sort of."

"Did you just charge that when I explicitly said not to?"

"Momma Jean said it was okay."

"Jean, did you tell Melanie it was okay to get that top?"

"Yes."

"Well, I had told her she couldn't."

"How was I supposed to know?"

Many teenagers who grow up to be wonderful people can be rather slippery in dealings with their parents, playing one against the other. Looking for the best deal. Resorting to half truths and total untruths to get what they want, as long as they think they can get away with it.

And they think nothing of it.

Well, if Momma Amy says no, and I know that maybe Momma Jean will say it's okay, I'd be stupid not to ask Momma Jean.

Obviously the best policy is to check with your partner before making a decision. But checking with the other parent is not always possible. And sometimes it just feels like too much trouble. This means that sometimes, even when you are careful, they will get away with it.

So what should you do if you catch them in a dishonest attempt at manipulation? Mainly you want them to know that you found out about it and you don't like it. But you also want to tell them that you will now have to be more careful about decisions you make when your partner isn't around.

What this teaches them is that they are not quite as smart as they think they are, and they will lose a degree of freedom because of their dishonesty.

It's a partial deterrent. But when it comes to controlling manipulative teens, that's about the best you can get.

How bad is it that teens will play one parent against the other, looking for the best deal? How hard should you try to make sure they don't get away with it? I think this is one of those issues that falls into the bad-but-not-very-bad category. I'm willing to be diligent so that they can't manipulate their way to the best deal—but only to a point. If sometimes they flimflam their way to a better deal, I'm not going to lose a lot of sleep over it. It is what teenagers do.

WHAT'S FAIR AND WHAT'S NOT

Making rules can be pretty straightforward when you are talking about a lone teenager. But it immediately gets more complicated when there are multiple children in the family. As soon as there's more than one, any decision about one child now has to be viewed in the context of another child.

> *"No, I'm sorry, Garrett. I do not want you having Timmy over after school when it's just the two of you at the house."*
> *"But that's not fair! You've always let Miranda have her friends over when there's no adult!"*
> *"No, I'm sorry, Garrett."*
> *"You can't do this; it's not fair!"*

It's a problem. A rule exists for one of your children, but then along comes another now-teenage child in the same situation. Even if they are the same age—let's say for the sake of argument that Garrett and Miranda are fraternal twins—you are not comfortable applying the same rule.

"Yeah, my father set the rule with Miranda. She could have friends over with no adults. Federal Statute 6388 clearly states that if it's the rule with one child, it has to be the same rule with a different child in the same circumstance. I mean, everybody knows that. It's the law."

Actually, it isn't the law. But the majority of kids today probably believe deep in their hearts that there really is an unwritten law that allows the same privileges to each child of a comparable age within the same family.

And it's not only the kids who worry about a lack of fairness. Parents feel governed by fairness rules too.

Well, yes. I try to make sure that any decisions I make will be fair. I do think it's important.

When kids say, "It's not fair," and we agree with them that it isn't fair, that it isn't equal treatment, it's troubling. After all, isn't being fair the backbone of what we teach them? How we raise them to be considerate of others? Isn't it important that we—of all people—be fair too? How else will they learn, if not by example?

"Because my parents weren't fair when I was a kid, I now rob jewelery and liquor stores. They never taught me the right way."

Isn't that how it works?

Not really. Sometimes there are other considerations that supersede fairness. But do not expect them to see it that way.

> *"Garrett, I know we let Miranda have friends over. But they're not going to make trouble. I worry when it's you and, really, any of your friends. Somehow you'll get into mischief. Like that last time, when you stole liquor, made prank calls, and broke the lamp in the TV room because of your wrestling."*
>
> *"What does that have to do with anything? You let Miranda do it and you say I can't. It's not fair!"*

It is a common problem. It can be about big things, such as when you will allow them to get a driver's license or go out on dates. Or little things, such as watching an adult-content movie or whether you buy them a bag of chips on impulse in the supermarket.

While fairness is a high priority, it is not our highest priority. Parents are guided by principles that may transcend fairness: for example, safety, or what you believe is in each child's overall best interests. Or even your own needs, taking into account that on a given day you may just be too tired to take your child to the store, despite the fact that you did the same thing for that child's sibling the day before.

I'm just really too tired today. I just don't have the energy to go out. But try getting him to understand.

So what should you do? Try to explain, but also know that, if it is genuinely unequal, they're not going to buy it—no matter what you say.

"But it's not fair! You let Miranda have friends over and not me! You can't do that!"

As you well know by now, there comes a time to disengage, and this is very likely the place to do it. *You* will have to be the one to end the discussion. Garrett is not going to get it. The unfairness will rankle no matter what. And trying too hard to get him to understand will only lead to increasing frustration.

> *"But it's not fair!"*
> *"I just explained it, Garrett."*
> *"But it's not fair!"*

Which it isn't. But no point you make will convince him otherwise. Hence, at that point, it would be best to say:

"I am sorry, Garrett, I know you feel it is unfair, but I am just not comfortable with you and a friend alone in the house."

"But it's not fair!"

You have nothing more to say. Your message will be heard. Not all decisions are exclusively guided by fairness. Sometimes other issues take priority— for example, that your judgment of risk may vary from child to child.

Over time, Garrett may well comprehend. It is part of the development of a more mature and nuanced moral system. Fairness is important, but sometimes there are more significant aspects to take into consideration. Someday he may understand. But not now.

SIBLING BICKERING

Two piranhas were having a nasty fight in a river. Just then, a pleasant-looking woman standing on the riverbank called out to them, *"Tell me what the problem is and I'm sure that I can help you work out a solution."*

The piranhas immediately stopped their fighting, swam to the surface, and called out to her, *"Oh, yes. That is an excellent plan. Please come into the river and we will begin our discussion. We're sure that it will be very productive."*

So the woman dove in to aid the piranhas.

Her family was sad when she did not return that evening.

For those families with more than one child, let me offer some advice that can eliminate what may be the greatest single source of parental wear and tear:

When siblings bicker, intervene only when you absolutely have to—when it has become too physical or the noise is driving you crazy. At those times your aim is to have them stop. You want to separate. You do not want to mediate or come down on one side or the other; you just want them to end the fighting. The one exception is where there is a threat of physical harm. If so, and the fighting does not stop immediately, do not back off from calling the police. As teens, they are now big, and injuries do happen. You cannot risk real physical harm. You may shout,

"The two of you, stop it!"

But don't get involved in the dispute itself. That's the big mistake. For as soon as you intervene, no matter what you say, you will immediately find yourself in the middle.

"Mom, that little brat Carly got into my makeup and she ruined one of my lipsticks!"

"I did not! I didn't touch Anne Marie's lipstick! She always thinks it's me! But she ruined it herself! She never lets me use any-thing of hers anyway!"

"Mom, she uses my stuff all of the time!"

"I do not! I do not!"

Don't touch it. This is not the place to be the all-knowing, resolver-of-all-conflicts parent.

"Time-out. Okay, Carly, Anne Marie, I want each of you to tell me what happened. You'll both get your chance to tell me your side. Remember, no interrupting. Let's see if we can come to a solu-tion that will work for both of you. Carly, you can go first."

"Okay, Mom, it was like this . . ."

Once again, we are taught that "fair" reasoning is the method of the perfect parent. But everything is different in the real world. It never gets past the "no interrupting" part. It is the way that leads to madness.

"Mom! Mom! Don't listen to her! That's not the way it was at all!"

"Omigod. Mom, Carly is such a liar! I'm gonna smack you, Carly!"

"Mom, Anne Marie says she's going to smack me!"

This is because, once you enter a dispute between siblings, a strange thing happens: the children are no longer interested in the issue at hand. With you in the picture, they become interested in only one thing: getting you on their side. They will be satisfied only with the complete capture of you.

"Yes, I have decided. Anne Marie, you are completely in the wrong. You are grounded to your room for one month, no, make that two months. We will have everything removed from your room to make it as unpleasant for you as possible. And Carly, my gem above all gems, I am raising your allowance by ten dollars, though I know this cannot compensate for the pain and suffering that has been caused by your sister."

"Yes!" says Carly.

"I'm going to kill you, Carly!" says Anne Marie.

It's much better not to listen. Listening only fuels the fire. It's much better to throw the responsibility of working out a solution back on them.

Useful phrases include: *"I don't want to hear about it."*

Or, *"The two of you will just have to work it out."*

Or, perhaps, where one or the other comes running to you for aid in a dispute,

"Anne Marie says she's going to hit me with a hairbrush if I even go near any of her cosmetics!"

"Gosh, that sounds like a problem (for you but not for me)."

Or, *"Boy, I'll bet that makes you mad."*

All of the above responses take you out of the equation and place the burden on your teens to work out a solution. Maybe they can, and maybe they can't. But they certainly won't if all they ever do is come running to you.

If you follow this procedure firmly and consistently, they learn that when it comes to solving their disputes, you are useless.

"All Mom ever does is say, 'The two of you will have to work it out.'"

But how will they learn to resolve conflicts if they are not shown the path to fair resolutions by you, their parent? you wonder.

Precisely. How will they learn to work out solutions in the real world, how will they learn to negotiate, unless they get practice? If anything, your intervention gets in the way of their developing that skill.

But the main benefit of abstaining from their fights—and it's a big one—is that, though they will continue to bicker, you will not get caught up in that most horrible of parenting activities: trying to resolve an unwinnable argument.

The stress-reduction benefits can be remarkable.

HOW TO DEAL WITH DIVORCE

I have often been asked, *"At what age is it least difficult for a child to deal with their parents getting a divorce?"* The answer is: no age. Divorce is difficult for children even when they are grown adults. The issues differ for each age, but it is always hard.

With regard to teenagers, there are many various issues, depending on the circumstances and on the child. But what follows are three big concerns for teens.

What's Going to Happen to Me?

A divorce adds a degree of instability to a teen's life.

To combat this you must, over the course of a divorce, be as honest and specific as possible about what is going to happen. Be clear about where each parent will live—recognizing that this may change. For teens, knowing where their home—or homes—will be is extremely important to them. They will also want to know how often they will see each parent and what the arrangements will be. This usually is not set in stone, at least early in a divorce. They will want to know if they have to move or change schools. To teenagers, the latter is a very big deal, and you will want to be as up front with them as you can.

"What's going to happen? Where am I going to live? What's going to be

the deal with visits and all? Am I going to have to change schools? Are there going to be new problems about money?"

Teens are very definitely going to worry about all of this. For their peace of mind, the best strategy is to be communicative, and whenever you are unsure of the answers to their questions, let them know that too—as truthfully as you can.

"For now, you're going to live here with me. You will see your dad regularly—we don't know how much. He has to get settled. I don't know about moving; I have no plans to move. Certainly, for now, there aren't going to be any big changes. If there are going to be, I will always let you know, and you can always ask me. We may not have as much money as we did before, so there may be some things we won't be able to afford that we could afford before."

Keep them informed, because the more they know about what's going to happen, the more they are able to manage the considerable anxiety they naturally feel about this new shift in their life.

Taking Sides

Virtually all parents will say—and genuinely mean—that they do not want their children to feel that they have to take sides. They say that they want their children to be free to have a good and close relationship with both parents. Although they may harbor ill will—even considerable ill will—toward their ex-partner, they really do not want that to factor into their child's interactions with the other parent.

The problem is that such sentiments and statements turn out to be tougher to maintain than most realize. Divorcing parents often start off well. But then the divorce settlement arrives, putting in writing the actual arrangements with regard to the kids and especially with regard to money, and now there is less to help them make good on those promises. There are almost always unwelcome surprises as to how much tighter money is than anticipated. Despite everyone's good intentions, disputes frequently arise. And, somehow, the kids end up in the middle.

Even though the parents are now divorced, it is precisely because of their children that they have to deal with each other over an extended period of time. Arrangements regarding visits—and the even more contentious subject of money—ensure their ongoing interactions. One parent may have to continually shell out money, while the other parent may continually feel that he or she is not getting enough of it. And with these disputes—no matter how good the intentions of all the parties involved—it is the kids who get sucked into the turmoil.

"Dad said that I can't play on the travel soccer team because you won't put up the money for it, which Dad says you do have. He says he already pays child support, so you get plenty of money. And he has no extra money because he's just getting by as it is, which includes the child support, which he says is more than what most fathers have to pay. He also says, 'Your mother had a very good lawyer.'"

It soon becomes about setting the record straight. The issue is pretty straightforward: your child will tell you the other parent's version of the facts, a version that casts you in a negative light and is patently untrue. The absolutely normal reaction—at least with regard to the untruths—is to want to tell your side of the story as well, to make your version known.

"Well, yes, all I'm saying is that it's not fair to me to have Jamie go around with this complete misconception, thinking all these negative thoughts about me because of lies that his father is telling him without at least telling him my side of the story—the true side."

The problem with this is simple. Let's say that Jamie's mother does tell her son her side of the story:

"No, it is your father's obligation to pay for extracurricular activities within reason, beyond the child support payments. The fact is that your father is not strapped financially, and even with my salary and the child support it is very tight to cover even basic expenses. Look at the car that I drive and the car that your father drives. And all that stuff about my having a good lawyer and how he got screwed is nonsense. He pays less than most fathers who have the yearly income that he does—which he never has been fully honest about."

And let's say that everything Jamie's mother is saying is true. What's wrong with Jamie's mother letting him know the facts as she sees them, so he at least can get both sides of the story and then decide for himself which parent is causing problems with his plan to be on the travel soccer team?

The problem is that when Jamie's mother responds to his dad's accusations, Jamie is now officially pulled into the debate. Both parents have essentially cast Jamie in the role of judge and jury reviewing the case as presented by the two opposing lawyers. They are putting him in the center of a court case—where his parents are the combatants.

But maybe that's not actually what Jamie wants. The net and inevitable result of Jamie's father's accusations and his mother's counterarguments is that, to the extent that the debate continues, Jamie is left with the ongoing question: *"Who is at fault, Mom or Dad?"* It stays in his head and is an upsetting ordeal for him. Who wants to be in the role of deciding which of their parents is a jerk? Or discovering that maybe they both are? What Jamie would prefer thinking is:

They hate each other. They don't agree about anything. That's why they got a divorce. Duh. But they both like me—at least I think they do. That's all I care about. I just want to have a nice life and not spend any time worrying about which of them is right and which of them is wrong and having to be careful what I say so that they don't get pissed off. I just want to have a nice time when I'm with each of them, and totally not have to worry about any of that shit. All thinking about it does is make me feel bad. Why can't they just—for my sake—work out this shit and not drag me into it? They're grown-ups and all, but they're not acting very grown up when it's about each other. That's for sure.

In the case of Mom versus Dad in the court of Jamie's mind, no matter what the final decision, Jamie is the loser.

I, Jamie Ramsbottom, have decided, and my decision is that my mother is a jerk. (No, that's not so great. How about this?) I have decided that my father is a jerk. (No, I don't like that either.) I have decided that they're both jerks. (I certainly don't like that, but it does seem a little closer to the truth.)

Regardless of the outcome, Jamie loses—he is the one having to participate in his parents' court case. It certainly isn't fun.

Why would parents want to do this? How does their child possibly benefit from being drawn into their fight? The obvious answer: he doesn't.

The way I think these conversations should have gone down is as follows:

> *"I will do all I can to work out travel soccer for you. But it's between me and your father."*
>
> The mother does not defend herself by presenting alternate facts to her son. Instead she tells him that she is not going to discuss his father's accusations any further.
>
> Even if the travel soccer does not work out because neither parent ended up paying for it, and the father maintained his stance, saying,

"Just like I told you. It's all your mother's fault because she wouldn't budge an inch when it comes to sticking it to me."

Jamie's mother should still not defend herself, saying instead,

"I'm sorry it didn't work out for you about the travel soccer."

Even if Jamie retorts with,

"Dad said it was your all your fault because you just want to stick it to him."

His mother should still say,

"I'm sorry it didn't work out."

What, then, is Jamie left with?

I don't know what to believe. Dad says it was all Mom's fault, and Mom says it was between her and Dad, and obviously they couldn't work it out. But I'm the one who's screwed. I don't know whose fault it is, but I do know that it sucks having divorced parents who can't agree on anything.

When I'm with Mom she won't get into it, which I like better than with Dad, who brings it up a lot. At least when I'm with her, I don't have to get into any of that shit. Not like with Dad.

Over time, when in comparable situations where Jamie's father bad-mouths his mother and his mother does not get into it, Jamie will almost certainly come away with:

I like Mom's way better. I don't know what the truth is in all the stuff that went on, but at least Mom didn't pull me into it the way Dad did.

In the long run, the parent who does not pull Jamie into the court case comes out looking better.

The End of Our Happy Family

"I know it's better this way. Neither Mom or Dad was happy with the other. And toward the end it was awful. There was this constant tension, if there wasn't an actual blowup going on. But I can't help it: I still miss that we were a family, and that it's never going to be that way again."

"You miss the good family times, huh?"

"Not really. Actually, there weren't any that I can remember."

"I don't get it."

"I don't either, but sometimes I get real sad about it anyway."

It may not always be apparent, but the majority of teens do grieve over the way it was. Even if the way it was wasn't so great, there is a sadness. These kids don't just grieve over the lost family times (happy or not). Many surprisingly harbor the secret wish that their parents would get back together again.

"But, Ricky, they hate each other now. It's been eight years. You say you really like Wayne (his stepfather of four years). *You're happy he's in your family. And you say it would never work if your parents did get back together. And that there's no way it's ever going to happen anyway."*
"Yeah, I know."
"But you still want them back together?"
"Yeah. I know it's stupid. But, yeah."
For all of the above reasons it is always a good idea for divorced parents of teens to periodically go to their child at a quiet time and ask,
"Do you sometimes feel sad about the divorce?"
And maybe you don't get anything back.
"No, I don't really think about it much."
Which is fine. But maybe sometimes, the child will say,
"I don't know. I guess. I mean, we were a family. And that's all gone. I know it wasn't great but I still miss it."

And they may even get sad. Which is not a bad thing. It is important to just recognize for them that the sadness is there and that it is okay.

Different Households, Different Rules

It's great when divorced parents work together for what they believe is in their kids' best interests, striving always to be on the same page.

"Hi, Diane, it's me. Did you say that it was okay for James to rent Bimbo Horror Night?*"*
"Why, that little devil! No, of course not! Thanks for checking with me, Brad."
But, often, that's not the way it happens.
"Mom, why do I have to go to bed at ten-thirty on school nights?

Dad lets me stay up as long as I want, just so I'm up on time in the morning. He says I'm responsible enough that I don't need a set bedtime."

"Mom, why do I have to clean the bathroom? I don't have to at Dad's."

"Mom, Dad lets me have Sherri Ann in my room. He says you're too uptight."

Of course, Mom is thinking:

His father doesn't just have different rules; he actually says anything he can to undermine my rules. He won't discuss anything. If I call him, he just hangs up or says, "You know the great thing about you and me being divorced, Eleanor? I don't have to listen to you. What about them *apples?" I genuinely think he does a lot of it just to spite me.*

And her ex is thinking:

No, I do it differently with Marcus because I think my way is right. His mother is way off. She smothers him. But I'll admit, if she gets really pissed, it does give me some pleasure.

It is always best when parents work together. At the same time, it is not necessary or realistic to believe that divorced parents are going to have the same rules. They do see things differently, which is partly why they split. That said, it can be very frustrating for parents to hear what goes on in the other home. And it's not just rules that cause concern. Various other behaviors your child is exposed to can cause worries too.

Marianne drinks a lot, which the kids get to see. I worry about the effect on them.

Many divorced parents have a lot of trouble dealing with the fact that, other than where there is real abuse or neglect, you can only control what goes on in your child's life when you are with your child. I have heard the concerns repeatedly from the many parents I counsel:

"But that's not right. Their dad does so much that qualifies as bad parenting, it has to have a negative effect on both of the kids. The stuff he says to them sometimes is so outrageous. And I don't trust some of his friends who are over at the house."

But you must remember: You can only control what goes on when you are with your child.

It is one of the hardest parts of parenting and divorce, if not *the* most difficult part. You have great influence on your teen, but there is also this other person in your child's life, who at least to some extent—and maybe even to a large extent—may not be such a good influence at all, but that person has continuing contact with your child and influence on your child's life as well.

You can always go to court. But that costs money every time, and courts generally do not like to make rulings about day-to-day parenting issues.

It's extremely frustrating when you genuinely believe that you are right. You may believe that what your ex is doing is definitely not in your child's best interests and is sabotaging what you are doing—yet because your ex's rules are more attractive, your ex seems to have all the leverage.

"Yeah, Dad's way more cool about stuff than Mom."

Parents often feel strong pressure to amend their own rules just so they're not too much of the bad guy. They find themselves defending their every action, even if just in their mind.

"He's, like, everything's fun. And I'm stuck in the role of the parent who's always making rules and handling the daily grind of parenting, like, 'Put away your laundry.' It's so totally unfair. But I can't win."

Despite the pressures that come to bear, however, I think it works best if you stick with the rules that you believe in: *"This is the deal when you are here with me. What goes on at your dad's is up to him."*

Teens will usually accept that the rules differ between the two parents. But that doesn't mean that they will like your rules any better, or that you won't regularly hear,

"But at Dad's . . ."

Switching Homes

Under such circumstances it is normal for a parent to worry.

But what if they dislike my rules so much that they decide to go live with their dad?

It is not uncommon for teenagers in divorced families to switch homes at some point. And sometimes they even switch back again. This can happen because they prefer the deal at the other parent's household.

"Yeah, like I said, it's way cooler at Dad's."

It can happen because battles at one home escalated to the point where it was just too much.

It's 2:30 A.M. on a school night and you find yourself making the call you least want to make: *"Robert, come get your daughter before I kill her."*

This is not necessarily a bad thing. Parents worry that if a teenager can switch homes, they are running away from responsibility.

Aren't they eliminating the possibility of ever learning how to work through conflicts? Maybe. But often it turns out that the other home is not quite the bed of roses they expected—that the greener pasture may be the one they left!

I didn't understand what a jerk Dad can be sometimes. And I way underestimated how bossy Lisa (the stepmother) *can be when you live there.*

These switches can be for the best when the situation at one home has gotten to be too problematic and for whatever reason things do go more smoothly at the other home. But even so, it can feel like a defeat:

Well, she got what she wanted, and so did he. Now I look like the impossible mother bitch who couldn't deal with her own daughter.

Just know that it really isn't. Often the contentious relationship between parent and teen actually improves because the child is no longer living there most of the time. Even if they don't say it, both sides are thinking,

Yeah, me and Mom are actually getting along a lot better now that I'm at Dad's.

Yeah, Isabel and I are getting along much better now that she's living mainly at her dad's. I hate to say it, but I actually like it this way.

Dealing with New Family Members

If you are no longer with your child's other parent, there's always the possibility of having new people in yours and their lives. New family members. New "sort-of" family members. Boyfriends, girlfriends, new partners, new stepparents, new half-siblings or stepsiblings. New people all around. This, of course, can elicit real resistance.

I don't like it. I wasn't the one who asked my parents to get a divorce. That wasn't my choice, and now they expect me to live with Sondra (his father's live-in girlfriend), *who actually isn't that bad, but also Louis, the asshole. I do not understand what Mom sees in him, and also the thought that they might actually have sex makes me want to throw up and they're all, like, hands all over each other—which certainly didn't happen with Dad. I mean, it's really disgusting. None of this was my choice.*

And, oh, did I mention Craig, the hyperactivity disorder poster-boy (Sondra's eight-year-old son)? *I don't know if he's officially hyperactive, but he*

really is a little wild man, which I know bothers Dad, and Sondra can't really control him. And can I tell you something else? Louis. He comes in and sits in the recliner in the TV room, which has always been where I sit. And he thinks he's so cool—you should see the jewelry he wears. He should be on the cover of Asshole Weekly. *Seriously. I mean the whole thing is completely unfair. And do you know what I can do about it? Jack shit. That's what.*

The addition of new partners or new siblings can actually be less of a problem with younger children than with adolescents. Teens are typically not going to see new people as true family members. They are more set in their ways and are not interested in changes that were not of their making. They must now share space. They get less of you—which they may not mind, except that they like to know that you would be available if they wanted you to be. And they are now expected to act cordially—on their home turf—toward people they could care less about or maybe even actively dislike.

I can tell you a lot more about Louis.

One important rule to keep in mind is as follows: always make sure that there is a regular time when it is just you and your kid or kids, alone together. They care a lot that the old family is not totally destroyed, and that they still can have full and regular access to you.

Of course, some problems arising from the presence of new family members are not always resolvable. This is especially true when the issue is one of dislike . . . and when teenagers are involved. Fortunately it is not necessary that everyone within a new family likes one another. You are not requiring that your child like their new family members. It often turns out that they do, but you cannot expect or demand it. You can, on the other hand, expect and demand civil behavior. But as with everything, here is where it can get very tricky.

Witness this exchange between Sybil and the fifteen-year-old who recently became her stepdaughter.

> *"Carlin, is this your popcorn mess?"*
> *"Yeah."*
> *"Would you please clean it up?"*
> *"I will, later."*
> *"No, I need you to clean it up now."*
> *"Who the hell do you think you're bossing around? You're not my mother."*

"What?"

"You're not my mother! You can't boss me around!"

"What did you just say to me?"

"You heard me!"

Later that evening, Sybil said to Carlin's father:

"You would not believe what your daughter said to me this afternoon." She then told him. "I do not deserve that kind of disrespect."

A little while later. Carlin's father spoke to his daughter.

"Carlin, Sybil said that you were rude to her today when she asked you to clean up some popcorn."

"Dad, you believe everything she says! She was the one who was rude to me! She can't just boss me around! You always side with her! I hate Sybil! Why did you and her have to get married?" And Carlin burst into tears.

A little while after that, Sybil asked Carlin's father:

"Did you speak to Carlin?"

"Yes."

"What did you say?"

"You have to understand, she was only four when her mother and I separated. It's hard for her having another parent in the house besides me."

"I can't believe you! You don't have a clue what a total little brat you're raising! You let Carlin wrap you around her little finger! I knew this would happen!"

"Shit," said Carlin's father under his breath.

"What did you just say?" asked Sybil.

You cannot necessarily change how family members feel about one another, but there definitely are certain rules for everyday situations that can make a big difference in avoiding conflict and unnecessary ill will. First, there are definite considerations to bear in mind:

A new partner living in the home is not the same as a parent. They do not have the same lifetime connection, the same history with your child as does a parent who has been there from the beginning. Nor do they have the same love or the same commitment to a child as does a biological parent—at least in most cases. What this means is that there is much that a teenager will accept—though not necessarily like—from a biological parent that they simply will not accept from a stepparent. Deep in their heart they feel that there is much in the way of discipline that a stepparent does not have a right to impose on them. When they say, *"You're not my parent,"* they are saying something that is very real to them. And that must be taken into account.

Another important principle: even though your teen may resent the fact that you brought a new person into her home and that she had no choice in the matter, she does need to treat your partner with the full respect that should be shown to any adult. Also, since your new partner now lives in the same home, your teenager must recognize that your new partner now has full rights in the household as well. Your new partner is not a guest. It is now their home too.

"No! No! It's not her home! It's mine! It's not hers! It's not! It's not!"

But it is, and that can be a tough reality for teens to swallow.

Taking the above into account, here are a few pointers that can ease some of the more common tensions between your teenager and a new stepparent.

Rule 1: Even if you don't agree, always back your partner in daily interactions with your child, just as you would with your child's original parent. To do otherwise will invariably cause your partner to harbor huge resentment toward you and your child. If you really don't like what your partner did, talk about it later.

Rule 2: Though your partner does have the right to give your children orders, you and only you are the boss when it comes to general parenting rules such as punishments, curfews, and bedtime, who they may hang around with, and who they may not. This is very important to a teenager. They may not always like your rules, but they have a very strong sense of who they believe has a right to make such rules and who does not. They feel strongly that it is only their "true" parent who has the right to make the rules that shape their lives.

Your partner may strongly disagree with your decisions, and may express that forcefully, and you may come to agree. But the ultimate right to set what are—in effect—policy decisions has to rest with you.

Rule 3: When your child is rude to your partner, always bring it up with your child. The rule has to be made very clear that being disrespectful to their stepparent is never okay. The rule has to require that—regardless of what they think of them—your child must always treat their stepparent with respect.

Rule 4: Regularly acknowledge to your child that you do understand that they may not be happy with the new family member.

> *"I know that sometimes it can be hard for you living with Sybil in the house."*
> *"No. Not sometimes, all of the time."*
> *"I know it can be hard. But I still love you, and I will do all I can to make your life as pleasant as it can be."*
> *"Good. Then get rid of Sybil."*

Recognizing that they may be unhappy with their new deal, and that they have a right to feel this way—even though nothing may change—means a lot to a teenager.

Here's a way that the previous sequence might have gone better:

The key lies in maintaining a standing rule that every time Carlin is disrespectful to her stepmother, Carlin's father must be told about it. And every time that he hears about it, Carlin's father must go to his daughter and say words to this effect:

> *"Sybil told me what you said to her this afternoon. I expect you to obey Sybil if she asks you to do something. And you may not talk to her the way you did—ever."*
> *"But, Dad, Sybil was being such a bitch! You don't know what she's like! She—"*
> *"I want you to listen to her and to talk to her in a respectful manner."*
> *"But, Dad—"*
> *"You heard what I said."*

This is not necessarily going to stop the disrespect, but it will lessen it. It says to Carlin that, although her father may be sympathetic to her feelings about his new partner, he is not supportive of her being disrespectful. If Carlin wants her father to be on her side—and make no mistake, despite all that they may say, kids very much do want their parent to be on their side—she will have to accept the deal as it is offered. The deal is that her father will understand her having negative feelings toward Sybil, but he will not accept the negative words. This is a deal that most teens will grudgingly go along with, once it is stated and reinforced. Their rationale is simple.

I hate Sybil. I'm always going to hate Sybil. But I want to be on good terms with Dad—unless of course he's acting like a jerk. So maybe—I'm not promising anything—I'll go along with Sybil some of the time, and I won't say really mean stuff to her, because she doesn't really matter anyway. She's not worth it.

And then later, you can answer your new partner with words that reassure them of your respect for them too.

> *"What did you say to Carlin?"*
> *"I told her that she needs to obey you and that she cannot talk to you in a disrespectful manner."*

And though Carlin's father might not punish his daughter—which may very well annoy Sybil—she is more likely to be appeased than not, because Carlin's father has made it clear that he is on Sybil's side with regard to Carlin's back talk. Again, it may not sound like that much, but it does make a big difference in the quality of day-to-day interactions.

A Note for Stepparents

You don't have to like your new stepteen, but you do have to treat them with respect. And vice versa—while they don't have to like you, you have a right to be treated respectfully by them.

You have the right to demand that your partner make it clear to their child that disrespect toward you is not okay.

But realize that a child's behavior is the product of an already established parent-child relationship, and for the most part, this isn't going to change. You can express your disapproval, but don't try too hard to alter your partner's parenting behavior. That only leads to frustration and bad feelings—and usually does nothing to change your stepchild's behavior either.

Chapter Eleven

TEENS AND SEX

There is an undeniable problem with teenagers that all parents must face. Teens want to have fun. And they are fierce protectors of their right to do so.

"Yeah, I want to have fun. What's wrong with that?"

Most of us can relate to their desire, as we like to have fun too. *I guess, nothing. I guess it's normal to want to have fun. I mean, fun isn't bad, is it?*

But not only do kids want to have fun, they want to have a considerable amount of fun. *"Yeah, I want to have a lotta fun. It's a lot more fun than a little fun."*

And that's when parents start to worry. *I don't know. I'm starting to get kind of nervous. Maybe we should limit them to a little fun.*

Have Scrabble tournaments.

Listen to Beatles music. (They're okay, right? I mean, kids like the Beatles—even today.)

Watch movies, but just the ones with not too much blood or sex or swearing. I mean, it's okay if there's a little blood, a little sex, some swearing, right? They're not nine-year-olds, for goodness' sake.

And dancing. Maybe dancing's good. Except I don't know if they dance much these days.

If you were to talk openly with teens about fun, you just might discover that they are having lots of fun, and in ways you may not think are "age-appropriate."

> *"Mom, I'm going out tonight and I'm going to have a lotta fun."*
> *"Oh, dear. Must you?"*
> *"Yeah."*
> *"What are you going to do?"*
> *"I'm going to get high—shit-faced—and I'll have sex with somebody. I don't know who. It will just depend on what happens. Yeah, it's going to be a great night!"*
> *"Oh dear! I'm just going to worry the whole night!"*

RISKY BEHAVIOR

It's not just a problem with teenagers. It's a problem with the whole concept of fun. Sex, drugs, and drinking are major ways that a lot of teenagers—and obviously adults as well—have fun.

So here's a question for you: Is fun that includes sex, drugs, and/or drinking more fun than fun that includes none of the above? A lot of people, teens included, seem to think so. What the adult world says to teens is that these ways of having fun *are* cool, but you can't enjoy them until you're an adult. Which, of course, only emphasizes to kids that these things must be significantly fun.

What teenagers like to do for fun—what is probably their number one preferred activity—is to hang out with good friends, friends with whom they are very comfortable. (In that way, they are no different than we adults.) But often in such circumstances, they want to augment their fun with substances, and if they do anything sexual at all, they usually want it to be heavy sexual activity.

Unfortunately, many of the activities that yield a high degree of enjoyment are risky. And the risks are very real, including serious harm, trouble with the law, humiliation. And, with many of the substances—to varying degrees—there is also the risk of addiction, whereby the substances can take over, and even ruin, a life.

It has to leave a parent wondering, *For goodness' sake, can't they just have a really good time, hang out, and kid around with good friends without using substances? And if they're going to engage in sexual activity, can't they just limit it to less advanced sexual activity?*

Apparently not. Teenagers engage in these obviously risky behaviors, in part, because they don't have as much fear as adults. They believe that the really bad stuff won't happen to them.

"Yeah, the truth is that I don't really worry about any of that bad stuff. I just don't."

For many teens, there is an added attractiveness to engaging in risky behavior.

"Yeah, if you want to know, the fact that some of the shit I do is dangerous makes it more fun. Risk is cool. Oh, and I forgot to mention, I especially like that adults think it's bad. That makes it even more fun."

But there remains one overwhelming reason why teenagers engage in, and continue to engage in, genuinely risky behaviors. And, contrary to popular opinion, it's not peer pressure. The single most compelling reason is that these behaviors *are* fun. Often they're *a lotta* fun.

If you are the parent of a teenager, you should know that sex, drugs, and drinking are problems that are not going to go away. There is no cure as long as teenagers seek fun in their lives, various substances are still available to them, or they have sexual feelings. These problems will persist forever unless some other activities more pleasurable than sex, drugs, and drinking surface. Trust me, there is no way that these risky forms of fun are going to fade into obscurity anytime in the foreseeable future.

So what do you do? Do you try to stop them from engaging in the riskier forms of fun? Do you do all that is humanly possible to make it *impossible* for them to engage in these risky activities? Or do you try to educate them as best you can, so that they truly understand the risks of what is out there? Obviously, the answer—in varying degrees—is all of the above. But if you are the parent of a teenager, you need to know that, despite your very best efforts to steer your child away from the kinds of activities that expose them to potential harm—even serious harm—there is the very real chance that they will do these things anyway.

WHAT PARENTS SHOULD KNOW

This reality leads us to ask the very natural question: What is a parent's appropriate role in their teenage child's sex life? And of course, that question leads to another: How much, if anything, do teenage children *want* their parents to know about their sex life?

"How do I feel about talking about my sex life to my parents? How do I feel about talking about my sexual feelings, what I actually do, what I maybe—I'm embarrassed to admit—don't do? How do I feel about sharing that part of my life with them? How much involvement do I want them to have in all of that? Let me think. How about none? I think that's about right."

You will recall that earlier I talked about the adolescent mandate whereby the vast majority of teens, as part of normal psychological development, become allergic to their parents. A big part of that allergy has to do with their sexuality. Sex and parents do not mix. Teens do not want to share anything about their sexuality with their parents. And they *really* don't want their parents to share anything about their sexuality with *them*. Every teenager "knows" that their parents had sex the exact number of times that there are children in the family. They also "know" that when their parents had sex they did not enjoy it, and that they were probably drunk at the time. All teenagers "know" that. To them, the thought of parents having sex is downright creepy.

Parents, on the other hand, are not "repelled" in the same way by the thought of their children having sex. But they find it disquieting on a number of levels. Sure, they get that there are very real problems that can come from teenage sexual activity, but the greater challenge for them is just wrapping their heads around the idea of their child's sexuality. They flat out find the concept of their child being sexually active too difficult to think about. Their son or daughter is no longer their cute little sweetie pie. They are now full-fledged sexual beings. But whether parents are comfortable with this notion or not, the fact is that sex is now a part of their teenager's life. And parents have to deal with that reality.

HOW ACTIVE IS YOUR TEEN?

Today's adolescents are exposed to a great quantity of sexual material. Much of it comes from the mainstream media: movies and TV. But another significant contributor to the explosive amount of information available to kids is the Internet, which provides easy access to videos and pictures with often quite graphic sexual content. Also, there is more back-and-forth dialogue about sex among teenagers over the Internet these days—including gossip as well as an exchange of real and valid information. Because they're not actually communicating face-to-face and have the added distance or anonymity of the written rather than the spoken word, kids will generally talk about sex more freely online than they would if the dialogue was happening in person. For these reasons, kids today are more sophisticated about sex—or at least they talk more about it—than in the past.

So what do they actually do? That's the question on most parents' minds.

The Kaiser Family Foundation, which regularly logs adolescent sexual activity, noted in their September 2008 report that 48 percent of all high school students acknowledged having had sexual intercourse. The Kaiser report further stated that this represented a decline from 54 percent in 1991. Could it be that kids are actually doing it less? It's difficult to say. We know that kids are certainly exposed to sexual material at younger ages via electronic media, as noted above. But it is far less clear that there has been a dramatic shift toward earlier sexual activity as a result of the availability of graphic and educational content online, or if this access to visual material has curbed actual experimentation.

Further complicating our ability to assess the situation is the fact that the data could be skewed by the semantics associated with the subject. There has certainly been much discussion in parenting and educator circles about how many teens today would respond "no" when asked about having sex, if the sexual activities they engaged in were anything other than sexual intercourse. And the media and entertainment worlds have certainly picked up on the whole "friends with benefits" trend. That is the trend where friends can be "couples" without being considered boyfriend and girlfriend. Teens also talk of "hooking up," a term meaning that they will engage in sexual activity with another teen—not necessarily sexual intercourse—for an evening, with the mutual understanding that this hookup includes no commitment beyond that evening.

One definite piece of good news is that kids are more aware of the risks of unprotected sex these days and they make use of contraception. Of course, many teens still do have unprotected sex, get pregnant, and have significant rates of sexually transmitted diseases (STDs).

My main point is that teens have sex. How much, at what age, and with what attitude varies somewhat from year to year. But the bottom line is that they do it. And, as they get older, more of them do it. (Not all of them, though.) And the risks of sexual activity remain. The younger they are when they do it, the more naive they are. However, the key thing for parents to remember is that the more knowledgeable teens are about the risks, the less likely they are to engage in risky sexual behavior.

How can you know if your particular teenager is going to engage in sex? The answer is simple: you can't. This means that if you have a teenage child, you need to assume that they may engage in some form of sexual activity, which carries inevitable risks. Does this mean that it is a good idea to be at least somewhat involved with the sexual side of your teenager's life? Yes.

How do most parents of teens feel about this? What do they want for their teen with regard to sex? I hear their thoughts on the subject frequently, and those thoughts are as complex as the situation.

"What do I want my kid to do about sex? That one's pretty easy. I want my kid to do whatever is normal—whatever that is—but I would just as soon not know about it.

"Actually, what I just said is not exactly true. What I want is that whatever they do—or don't do—doesn't create problems for them. No pregnancies. No STDs. I don't want them to be victimized. I don't want them to get hurt. I don't want them to end up in some big emotional mess. I don't want them to get into trouble."

I should say right here that, with regard to all aspects of sex covered in the previous paragraphs, parents—and really the rest of the world too—have very different standards for guys and girls. Over the years there may have been changes, with women increasingly claiming the right to their own sexuality. But certainly the deal regarding teens is still more or less the same as it always was: we consider interest in sex by a teenage boy to be healthy. We want him to be careful, but we're not particularly troubled by the idea that he may be sexually active. The sexual activity of teenage girls, on the other hand, makes us nervous. There is no question that most parents worry significantly more about their daughters' sexuality than about their sons'.

People justify the difference by saying such things as:

"Well, I wouldn't want her to get a bad reputation. You can say what you like, but once a girl is sexually active she can get a reputation, and it's going to stay with her all through high school. And don't tell me that kids don't look down on a girl who has had sex with a number of guys."

It's true. A girl who has sex a lot is considered a "ho" or a "slut" or a "nympho."

The female teen may argue against this stereotype with such statements as,

"No, I choose to be sexually active. I like sex. It is my choice."

While others think—or worse, say—such things as,

"Yeah, right. Which exactly proves my point that she's a slut."

On the other hand, a guy who has sex a lot is considered lucky, or a "stud." Maybe it shouldn't be this way. Maybe it's unfair. But this is the way it is. The questions and dichotomies, of course, don't stop there. Think about it: Do you purposefully teach your child ways or develop attitudes within them that allow them to enjoy a richer and fuller sex life? Isn't good sex one of the true joys of life? Don't we want to do all that we can for our teen so that they will experience that joy? Or are most parents ambivalent about that too?

"Do I want my kid to have a healthy, full, vibrant, enjoyable sex life as a teenager? Maybe mildly enjoyable is more like it. Just good enough so that their sex life will be okay in adulthood. No, actually, I just don't want them to do it. Maybe kissing would be all right."

THE CONSEQUENCES OF TEENAGE SEX

There are many potential problems that can come with teenagers engaging in sexual activity.

- They can get pregnant or cause a pregnancy.

- They can contract an STD.

- If they are girls, they can get a reputation as a "slut."

- If they are girls, they can be forced into sexual activity, or they can be subject to abuse in connection with the sex act.

- If they are guys, they may subject a girl to unwanted sex or abuse in connection with sex. (Guys can be subjected to unwanted sex and abuse too, but it is a significantly less frequent problem compared to what happens to girls.)

- Through having had sex, they can find themselves in a relationship that is more than they can handle emotionally. Either *they* are more emotionally involved, or their sex partner is more involved than they had expected.

- They can get confused by the sexual experience in such a way that it is disturbing to them; for example, they can feel ashamed or embarrassed by the event. Or because of their reaction during the experience, they can feel uncertain about their own sexuality.

Sexuality becomes a significant part of the adolescent's life. Ready or not, teens at this age become far more sexual beings—and hence are far more likely to engage in sexual activity. And with that sexual activity come far more potential problems. Sexuality is not bad. It is part of being a human. It can be one of the great pleasures of life. Besides, we cannot make sexuality go away. Though some parents might prefer it that way.

The number one reason why teenagers engage in sexual activity is because they are in a situation where it *can* happen. Where and when do they have sex? In their own home. At the house of a friend. At a party where a room is available. On study dates. In situations where there are no adults around, or at least no adults who are supervising what is going on. When do they do it? Anytime they can. After-school hours are just as likely times as late weekend evenings. The problem, of course, is that in today's world, most teenagers have a lot of unsupervised time and are often in situations where there are no adults around. Today many teens live in homes where both parents work. And parents of teenagers feel that it is finally possible to leave their kids alone in the house, that at last their children are at an age where it is safe to do so. Many parents have looked forward to this time.

"Yeah, finally Andrea is old enough that I don't have to adjust my work schedule so I'm home when she gets home from school."

Of course, it's good news for Andrea's boyfriend, Ricky, too.

My only point is that if your aim is to control your teen's sexual activity, the best weapon is to make it harder for sex to occur. Doing your best to supervise where they are and what they are doing will help. But recognize too that as kids get older, total supervision becomes more difficult and less appropriate. In the reality of today's world, if a given teen is hell-bent on having sex, it's probably going to happen. All of which means that if you have a teenager, you had better make some kind of peace with the idea that he or she may well have sex. If you don't, accept the fact that you may end up being bitterly disappointed when you discover that they have.

TALKING TO YOUR TEEN ABOUT SEX

The other way you can help control your teen's sexual activity is by talking to them. But talking is not really so much about stopping them from doing it. It's more about helping them to be able to make conscious decisions for themselves.

You can tell them how you feel:

"I will be really, really disappointed if I find out that you have had sex."

You can even lay down the law:

"You just better not have sex, mister, or you can forget about having your cell phone for the next three months."

You can try reasoning with them.

"Serena, can we talk?"

"Sure, Mom."

"I want to tell you why it is a good idea at this point in your life not to have sex."

"I'm all ears."

But whatever words you choose, just remember that as a preventive tool, words are limited. That said, talking to teens about sex—though no strong safeguard against their doing it—can make a big difference in the nature of their sexual activity. To the extent that they have your words in their heads when they are out there in the big world, those words increase the probability that their whole approach to sexual activity will be more thoughtful, and consequently less risky.

Ideally, you already have in place an established, easy, back-and-forth pattern of communication between yourself and your child. Yours is a relationship where they know you will listen, not just lecture. Where they know that, if they are genuinely honest, you will not go berserk.

It is *not* one where you will say,

"You did WHAT? Omigod, Lucinda—how could you be so stupid?"

It is instead a relationship where they know you will be open and not judgmental.

It is *not* one where you will resort to name-calling.

"Do you want a reputation as a slut? Is that what this is about?"

Ideally, you already have a pattern of good communication where what you have to say will be heard. But, if not, you should know that regardless of the prior nature of your communications with your teen, your talking to them about this important subject can still make a significant positive difference.

THE BASICS AND BEYOND

By the time your kids have reached their teen years, hopefully you will have made sure that they know about sex. You do not want to rely on whatever sex education their school may supply. School sex education programs vary greatly. You want to take the responsibility to make sure your child knows about sex before they turn thirteen. You can tell them. But you can also go online or to a bookstore to find material to help guide them. Don't be dissuaded by their claims.

"Oh, that is so embarrassing. I'm not going to look at any of it. Besides, I'm not two years old. Duh! I already know about that stuff."

Of course, they don't—at least not as much as they think they know. Also, their brains can often be excellent repositories of misinformation.

"If you've just had sex and you have sex again, you can't get pregnant because the guy can't make new sperm that fast."

Fortunately, there are many books and websites that provide frank and honest information about teens and sexuality. You may want to review these resources first to see if they are in keeping with your own beliefs about teens and sex, but they can be a good source of reliable information. Your teens may profess to have no interest. But if you make these resources easily available, they usually will look. Often.

Beyond basic sex information, there are certain things that may be very useful to share with your teen. As I said earlier, some of you ideally have had wonderful, open, and respectful communication with your child all along. But if the reality is that you are less communicative than that, I'm sure you are wondering what to do now. How do you start these talks? The answer is, you just do.

You don't have to do it exactly the right way. It may be awkward; it doesn't matter. The more they talk, the more it is a discussion, the better. But even if it is just you talking, that's fine. The point is that there are certain ideas that you want them to hear. And you are going to share those ideas. Maybe your kid will run and hide in a closet instead of listening. The trick is to persist. Try again on another day. And on a day after that. If you care enough, eventually you will get to deliver your message.

What follows is some specific advice that you may want to give your teenagers—for them to have in their heads as they go through the world of teen sex. There is advice for girls and different advice for guys.

These ideas can be presented in many different ways. Maybe you don't want to offer them all at once; maybe you want to dole them out a little at a time. Perhaps start by saying,

"Here's something to think about. . . . What do you think?"

Or maybe write a "teenage sex thought for the day" on a three-by-five card to be discussed with your child.

Or try the three-minute mobile phone call like Jason's dad did. Jason's cell phone rings. . . . His dad says,

"Hello, this is your father. Don't hang up. I'm going to talk to you for three minutes. Then you can hang up. But listen for three minutes, okay?"

Or text message. Anything. All methods are fine. Just so you do them.

ADVICE FOR GIRLS

As discussed, parents are of two minds when it comes to teens and sex. They are a lot more comfortable when their teenager is a guy. Traditionally, advice to guys regarding sex has been simple: *"Be careful."* Girls, on the other hand, have it very hard today—even in the most enlightened families. Wouldn't it be nice if the conversation went like so:

> *"Have a good time, Liana, and remember, if you and Elijah have sex tonight . . ."*
> *"I know, Mom, make sure he wears a condom."*
> *"That's my girl!"*

But it doesn't. Usually advice about sex given to teenage daughters, if delivered at all, is easily summarized in one word:

"Don't."

What follows is advice to teenage daughters that goes beyond the word "don't." It's about more than whether they should or should not have sex. It is about preparing them to enter, with their eyes wide open, that stage of life where sexual activity becomes a real possibility. It is about allowing teenage girls to be more thoughtful, hence more in control of their own sex life. It is advice intended to help them make better choices for themselves once they enter the world where sex is a reality. This advice enables them to have more control over their sex life and to avoid being victims. Hopefully, they can learn what to expect so that sexual activity is a choice rather than something that happens to them.

Warning: the advice below tends to portray guys in a somewhat cynical manner—as insensitive souls who are less interested in being considerate of a girl's feelings than in what they can get out of the relationship. This may not be completely fair—and, in fact, guys do mature and do become more considerate with time. But we are talking here about adolescent boys. They are good souls, but the world of sexuality is brand-new to them, and they are also very much creatures of their own culture—which many may learn to outgrow but have not done so quite yet. It is my hope that this advice to young girls is well taken.

- Sex does not seal a relationship. Don't assume that having sex with a boy makes a relationship any more than it was, other than that the guy now thinks he can have sex with you again.

• Guys often do mean what they say at the time, but don't assume they will feel that way later—even a little later. Sexuality, and the intimacy that comes with it, can powerfully influence how people feel. But once the physical intimacy ends, so can many of the feelings.

• Don't assume it will be private. In the age of Facebook, Twitter, and text messaging, what you did last night—or just this afternoon—can rapidly become public knowledge.

• Sexuality can create a flood of feelings that makes it harder for you to stay in control than you can in other situations.

• Drinking—by you, him, or both of you—makes the probability of sex considerably greater, and its meaning considerably less.

• If you are in a situation where sex *may* happen—alone with no adults around—it is more likely that it *will* happen.

• If he's always jealous and controlling, drop him like yesterday's news.

• If he in any way is physically hurtful—hits you, or grabs you hard—drop him instantly, then tell friends and adults. Do not keep that a secret.

• Prior to a situation where you think you might engage in some form of sexual activity, think about how far you want it to go.

Tell your teenage daughter to please ask questions, any questions. The more they know about the real world of sexual activity, the more their decisions are going to be based on prior knowledge rather than on reactions in the moment.

Also, make sure they know about contraception—if not from you, then from their pediatrician. A misconception that parents often have, to their later regret, is that teaching their kids about contraception condones sexual activity. It does not, but it does protect against unwanted pregnancy and sexually transmitted diseases.

I am frequently asked: *"Who should give the talk—moms or dads?"* I think it's probably more comfortable for both parents and the child if the talk about specifics is from the parent of the same gender. But the topic, in general, is not so sensitive that dads can't discuss it with daughters.

Last, use whatever words you want. I offer the above as a guideline, not necessarily as a script.

The point is for a girl's sexual life to be guided by active, thoughtful decisions, not by impulsive ones or by lack of awareness. But even then, it won't be 100 percent easy.

> *"Mom, Steven says he won't go out with me anymore because now I know too much. He says he prefers those dumb girls."*
> *"Excellent."*
> *"But I like Steven. Can't I go back to being dumb?"*

ADVICE FOR BOYS

It would be great if all dads could talk to their sons about sex.

> *"Son?"*
> *"Yeah, Dad?"*
> *"I think it's time that you and I had a little talk about responsible sexual behavior."*
> *"Cool."*

But even in today's world, despite the more widespread and open nature of sex, such conversations rarely happen. Parents think that a sex talk with sons means mainly telling their boys to wear condoms, but they often don't make the point that responsible sexual behavior also means being considerate and respectful toward others.

Parents typically avoid talking about sex with their sons for a number of reasons. They feel embarrassed. And political correctness notwithstanding, most parents still tacitly give their sons permission to do whatever they want with regard to sexual activity, as long as they don't make someone pregnant, pick up an STD, or do something with a girl that would get them into trouble.

But talking to teenage boys about sexual conduct is important. They are often unsure of what is good or even acceptable behavior. It's not the sort of scenario typically discussed among their peers or online. The messages that dominate these sources are as follows:

It's cool, admirable, a source of pride to rack up sexual conquests.

It's cool, admirable, a source of pride to do wild and irresponsible stuff.

Caring about girls as people is uncool, not something that you'd want to admit to.

Overall, the message they get from their culture is that sexual activity with girls is something that you do for what you can get out of it, and that the girls' feelings are not part of the equation.

Below are my suggestions as to what you might say to counter the above. Ideally, these suggestions would come up in the course of regular discussions that you have with your teenager. Even if you are confident that your kid knows all of these things and would not do otherwise, it does not hurt to bring these points up anyway.

When I'm asked, *"Should it be mother, father, or both who give the talk?"* my reply is that any way is fine. And when I'm asked, *"How old should my child be?"* I'd say, if he is already in high school, now is a good time. Otherwise, maybe have the conversation at age thirteen. But if he or his friends are into dating prior to thirteen, you would want to talk to him then. Last, use whatever words you want. Once more, I am offering the following as a guideline, not necessarily as something to be said verbatim.

- No means no. It's an iron-clad rule.

- Physical force is seriously never okay.

- It is not okay to have sex with someone who has a diminished capacity to say no—if they're drunk, drugged, or suffering any other impairment.

- If a girl puts herself in a situation where she is vulnerable—drinking alone with you, for example—it does not automatically mean yes.

- What you do sexually with a girl is a private matter between the two of you.

- It is never okay to have sex without a condom. It's dangerous to you and dangerous to your partner.

- It is never okay to make fun of a girl's body.

The fundamental theme is that no matter what the circumstance, no matter who the girl is, she is someone with valid feelings, and those feelings should always be considered. Sexual behavior should not produce harm.

What does this talk accomplish? If nothing else, it puts these ideas in their heads. They may or may not agree. But now—should they get into situations where these words do apply—there is a very real possibility that your words will enter their minds and quite possibly affect their choices.

"Hey, Jimmy," says Rhonda from the couch, acting like she's definitely had a lot to drink. Jimmy thinks—let's say correctly—that she's coming on to him. He is immediately excited by the possibility that he could end up having sex with her, especially since she seems pretty drunk.

But the following words pop into his head:

It is not okay to have sex with somebody who has a diminished capacity to say no—(like if they're drunk).

Shit, he thinks. She is pretty drunk. I don't know, maybe she would want to do it even if she weren't drunk. I think she's always liked me.

Maybe he will end up having sex with her anyway. Maybe he won't. But at least he had the moral debate. His parent's words entered into his decision-making process. His parent's words did exert real influence on him. Saying nothing exerts no influence on him whatsoever.

He may not agree. He may say to himself, Yeah. Yeah. Yeah. Like I'm going to seriously consider anything he's saying.

But you are taking a stand. You are saying that certain behaviors are not right—that they are bad. You are presenting yourself as a moral authority. You are leaning on whatever moral standing you have built up with your son over the years as his parent. In a clear message, you have described behaviors that you think are bad.

Will your talk have any effect on a teenage boy in the face of such strong countermessages from his culture? Perhaps it will. Perhaps not. But what the above can do is expose him to another view. Just by having the conversation.

"Thanks, Dad. Now I know the right thing to do, and I realize my friends are idiots and the stuff I see online is messed up."

Maybe not. But he hears every word you say.

MORE ADVICE FOR BOYS

I just described a prospective talk with teenage sons that addresses responsible sexual behavior. What follows is another talk. The first talk was about being considerate—always—of the wants and feelings of a potential sex partner. This next talk is different and should be presented separately, at another time from the above, so that it stands apart. It is specifically about abuse.

Many teenage boys are abusive to their girlfriends. Most boys are not, but many are. And most who are abusive do not even recognize that they are.

How can you know whether your teenage son is potentially or actively abusive with women? You can't. Hence, it is a good idea for parents to talk outright with their teenage boys about what constitutes abuse: which behaviors are abusive, and how these behaviors, if engaged in, are all seriously harmful. Many are against the law and many can get them into dire trouble.

"Abuse" is a word that has taken on a very specific and very strongly negative meaning. In today's parlance there are bad behaviors, and then there is abuse. It is a category—a very bad category—unto itself. The point of the talk is to spell out what abusive behaviors are. Many of the behaviors that I will list seem obviously to be abuse, but many boys still think they are okay. Most boys who abuse their girlfriends either do not think that what they are doing is abuse, or they think that it is somehow okay, even deserved.

Again, I present my proposed talk not necessarily as a script but as a guideline:

- Many boys abuse their girlfriends. I'm not saying that I think you will or that you do. But many boys abuse girls, and

I want you to know clearly what behaviors constitute abuse. Here are some rules. All the behaviors that I'm going to list are abuse, and you must never do them under any circumstances. It's a pretty big list, but they are all bad, and you must never do them.

- Never hit a girl—ever.

- You can't grab a girl hard—ever.

- If a girl gets physical with you—either hitting or kicking or threatening you with physical harm—leave. Leave right away. Hitting a girl in self-defense is not okay. Leave.

- If you are in an argument and are mad and you get very close to a girl, you must back away. An angry guy standing close is often genuinely scary to a girl, even though you may know that you will do nothing physical.

- If you find yourself getting very mad at a girl, leave.

- Do not get into an argument if you have been drinking. If you have been drinking and an argument starts, leave. These are potentially very dangerous circumstances, as they are often where the most serious abuse occurs.

The talk continues.

Some behaviors are controlling and abusive. Beyond physical harm, a way that guys abuse their girlfriends is that they can get very possessive and controlling. They do this because they want to be the boss. They do not know how to be in a relationship that allows the other person to be independent. These controlling behaviors are bad. They are never okay. The ways that guys do this are all bad and are listed as follows:

- They constantly want to know where their girlfriend is. Usually they do this by calling or texting many, many times during the day or night.

- They don't want their girlfriend to hang out with friends on her own.

- They especially do not want their girlfriend to talk to other guys, even if it is just friendly.

- They give them orders as to what they should wear.

- Never say verbal put-downs to a girl. For example, never call her "fat" or "stupid." Guys often think that the put-downs are a joke and that they don't mean anything by them. But all put-downs are abusive.

- If you think or know that she is cheating on you, your two choices include staying in the relationship and trying to get her to agree to stop cheating, or ending the relationship. You cannot retaliate or threaten her if she does not stop. This is also where people get hurt. This is never okay.

- If you are doing any of these behaviors because she is being aggravating and nasty (being a "bitch")—and she *is* being truly aggravating and nasty—that does not make these behaviors allowable. No matter what they do to you, women never deserve to be abused. What you can always do instead is leave, or end the relationship. These abusive behaviors are just as forbidden whether or not she is being abusive toward you. You still must not do them.

The above is a long talk, but what would you want to leave out? It may not be relevant for many teenagers. Many may never engage in any of the behaviors just described. Also, many teenage boys may hear the words but swiftly dismiss them. However, there are many teenage boys who really do not know which behaviors are acceptable and which ones are completely unacceptable. Nor do they connect these behaviors with the word "abuse," even though they should. It is good that they get to hear all of this.

TEENAGE LOVE

In adolescence, many kids don't just get sexual feelings; they feel love. There are two major developmental changes that, probably more than anything else, make up adolescence. One is the advent of strong and very present sexual feelings. The other is the turning away from the parent as the main source of deepest attachment, and directing of these strong feelings of attachment toward others in the world around them, separate from home and family. Put these two together and you get love. And these feelings are not to be trifled with. They can be very real and very intense. Never make the mistake of downplaying the objects of your child's affection.

Thirteen-year-old Jeannine couldn't wait to tell her friend Amy the big news.

> "Omigod, Cameron looked at me in science class. Should I put the mystery valentine on his desk like we talked about?"
>
> "I don't know, Jeannine. Are you sure he looked at you, and it wasn't Tessa he was looking at?"
>
> "I don't know! What should I do?"

Ryan's mom was talking to her friend about her seventeen-year-old son.

> "He showed me this necklace he bought to give to Elena for her birthday, and it was, like, four hundred dollars. I mean, that's a couple of months' worth of what he earns at his part-time job. I think he's way too serious about her."
>
> "Well, they have been going out for almost a year."
>
> "Thirteen months, seventeen days, actually. That's what he said this morning."

Teenage love is very real. It can range from the seemingly mindless crush of a thirteen-year-old girl on a boy in her science class to the far more mature love relationship of a high school senior with his longtime girlfriend.

Teen love is disconcerting to parents because it often appears to be so strong and all-consuming. Jeannine writes "Cameron" on her sneakers and all over her notebook. Ryan and Elena text each other nonstop throughout the day, and they're treated like a married couple by their friends. It's an outside force that seems to sweep away a lot of their rationality—and your influence on them.

As I have said before, their once-strong childhood attachment to you is now refocused on a new, sometimes intense, attachment to someone else, but with the power of sexual feelings added in. It's a good process—an important part of maturing. Your teen is learning to care deeply about someone other than themselves. It is the foundation of what, hopefully, will lead to mature love relationships in their adult life. Over the course of their adolescence you can actually see the maturing nature of the love relationships that they form. First, the early teenage crush that, with some, can shift in the course of a day. Later, the far more mature love relationships of late adolescence that not uncommonly end in marriage.

So what's your role in all of this?

Love, by its nature, is an obsession.

"I think about Cameron all the time."

"I think about Elena all the time."

The above is normal. But if you see the other parts of your child's life being adversely affected—their grades dropping, their contact with former friends dwindling, or their disposition changing to the point of being frequently unhappy or on edge—it may be time for you to intervene. A love relationship is supposed to be a mostly positive experience, not something that makes someone's life miserable. You may not necessarily be able to end your teen's relationship, but you can try to limit the amount of time during their waking day that they spend directly involved with their teen love.

Your best role is also as a supportive sounding board.

The big mistake I see many parents make is trying to downplay the seriousness of their child's relationship. When they do this they inadvertently demean their kid. And that will immediately turn their teen off.

Here are a few phrases that are simply *not* useful. You'd be wise to avoid them altogether:

> *"You'll get over it."*
> *"You'll see, honey, it's not such a big deal. It only feels like it."*
> *"This happens to everybody. It's just a stage."*

Such comments are invariably met with the cry: *"You don't understand."*

And maybe you don't, because to them their feelings are very real.

If you say, *"Ryan, four hundred dollars is a lot to spend on a present,"* I can assure you that he will be affronted.

"You don't understand. I want to get it for Elena. It makes me

happy giving it to her."

The problem is that you can't really influence the direction of your child's relationships. Mainly, you just need to validate their feelings and let them know that you are a sympathetic listener.

> *"You really like Cameron."*
> *"Yeah, I really do."*
>
> *"You're very serious about Elena."*
> *"I know you think I'm too young to be this serious. But I really love Elena."*

If there are breakups, you want to be there to commiserate, to give them support and comfort. But they will also have to ride it out, and for a high school senior in love, that can be a very painful and very slow process.

For infatuated thirteen-year-olds, recovery can be a little swifter.

> *"Mom, Mom, there's this really cute new kid in my English class. I think his name is Jerome."*
> *"What about all those 'Camerons' written on your sneakers?"*
> *"Oh, I can white them out."*

Sometimes teen loves can seem very childish. But they are a newly emergent, very adult, and important part of your teen's life. It is crucial to remember that.

IF YOU THINK YOUR CHILD IS GAY

Parents frequently ask, *"What if I think my son is gay? How can I know? How can I find out?"* My answer to all of these questions is, *"You can't."* Not all gay men fit into the stereotypes culture has of them. If you suspect that your son is gay, maybe he is, but maybe he isn't.

Under those circumstances, many of you will want to just ask your child. The challenge with inquiring, however, is that there is a potential downside to the question—no matter how you phrase it.

"I want you to know that I think you're great, and I'm happy with who you are. But there's something that I just want to ask. Remember, I'm going to love you and accept you no matter what. Are you gay?"

He may be gay, and he may be pleased for the chance to tell you. But you also might get:

"Omigod, you think I'm gay. Omigod."

The above response, by the way, is one he could say if he's not gay; *and* it is also one he could say if he *is* but is at a point in his life where he doesn't wish to disclose that to you. That is, your question might create more of a problem than it would generate goodwill. Many gay teens, for all kinds of reasons, choose not to disclose their sexual orientation. Perhaps he isn't ready to deal with your reaction. Perhaps—as a very normal adolescent boy—he'd rather keep all details about his sexuality private from you. I think the greater wisdom is to let your child be in charge of whether or not he chooses to come out to you, and when.

What do I suggest you do in the interim? First of all, if your child is gay, know that you can't change them. That is not the way it works. Nor is it a choice on his part, and thus something he could unmake. The world today for gay men is a more welcoming place than it was a couple of generations ago. Nevertheless, it is still a very difficult place for a gay teenage boy. Believe it or not, "gay" and "retard" are still the most used pejoratives in the world of kids. So what exactly can you do to help? Hopefully, what you have been doing all along—displaying an attitude of acceptance, demonstrating an understanding that being gay is a sexual orientation different from heterosexuality, but in no way shameful. If your child is gay, what makes the most difference to him, and ultimately to your future relationship with him, is what you have been doing and saying all of his life: your positive (or negative) thoughts and actions about being gay.

Have there been gay people in your life—friends or relatives—with whom you have seemed comfortable? Or have your past actions and words implied or outright stated that you think being gay is somehow bad? That being gay is distinctly less than not being gay? That it is something you frown upon or want to keep at a distance?

Bear in mind that the expression of such sentiments could have been subtle.

"Look at those guy cheerleaders. You know about them."

"Do you really want to buy the pink sweater?"

Or have you made clear that being gay is just another way that people are—not better or worse? This, more than anything, will send a message to your child that he will be loved no matter what his orientation.

"I think Mom would be okay with it. But Dad always puts down being gay. I'm pretty sure it would be a real problem for our relationship."

Of course, if you have not been so tolerant about being gay and now strongly suspect that your son is, you need to rethink your prior thoughts and feelings.

I have written here about gay boys, but most of what I have conveyed applies to girls as well. For whatever reason, however, parents of teenagers seem to worry less about their daughters' sexual orientation than they do about their sons'. Is this because there may be less of a stigma toward lesbians than there is toward gay men? Possibly. But it also indicates that parents tend to worry more about other aspects of their daughters' sexuality. Is their daughter actually having sex? Or worse, is she promiscuous? They even seem to worry more about the fact that she wears black, has odd-colored hair, and too many tattoos and piercings. The bottom line is: you need to be accepting of who your child is from the start, and just as accepting of others too—because you can't be completely certain who your child is until they more fully reveal themselves to you.

There is one last thing that you should do—whether you think that your child is gay or not—and that is to make sure that once he or she hits adolescence, they understand about the use of condoms. That is, if they have sexual relations, they know that using a condom is a powerful preventive, not just against pregnancy but also against STDs and specifically against becoming HIV positive—the precursor to AIDS—which is still very much of a problem with gay men, especially with younger gay men.

So the most direct answer to the question of what you should do if you think your child might be gay is: do not try to find out whether they are or they aren't; make sure that your attitude toward being gay is accepting and welcoming; and most of all, make it known to your teen through your actions with others as well as with them that if they were gay, they, their sexual orientation, and their lifestyle would be accepted by you.

Chapter Twelve

TEENS, DRUGS, AND ALCOHOL

What are teens who have made drugs or alcohol a significant part of their lives thinking? What are they actually doing? The following are fictitious interviews, but they could easily be real. They are, I think valid examples of how many of today's teens think.

An interview with Jesse begins,

"Tell me about your drinking. When do you drink? What usually happens?"

"Like a typical time when I drink?"

"Yes."

"How about last Friday?"

"Yes, that would be good."

"On Fridays I really like to drink. I don't usually drink during the school week. But I really look forward to getting wasted Friday nights. Or at least drinking a lot. Anyway, I called Anthony right after school—he's my best friend. We usually check in with each other at the beginning of the weekend. So I tell him that I'll come over to his house maybe around five-thirty—he has a part-time job right after school."

"You drive?"

"Yeah. Anyway I get over to his house a little before six o'clock and we start hanging out. And he has a couple six packs of beer and maybe half a pint of Jack Daniel's and we start drinking—not a lot. And we get something to eat at his house and we call around and see what people are doing. Anyway, we end up going over to this kid's house who Anthony knows better than me. And there are a bunch of kids there—"

"How many?"

"Maybe ten, including me and Anthony—guys and girls—and basically we hang out the whole time and everybody is drinking and we listen to music. And there's a girl there who I know a little, and we sort of hook up, but nothing too heavy. And basically it's cool. I have a good time. And I guess I drank the whole time I was there. I don't know how much, but I guess it was pretty much."

"How much do you think?"

"I don't know, really. I wasn't keeping track. But I could definitely feel it. I had a lot of beer and some of the Jack Daniel's, and one kid had tequila and I had some of that. There were two kids there, this kid Jason who's another friend of mine and some kid Clark, and they sort of got in a fight. It was stupid and no big deal. Just mainly pushing. But we were a little nervous that somebody might call the cops."

"When did it end?"

"You mean the party? Hanging out?"

"Yes."

"I don't know for sure, but I think we got back to Anthony's house maybe a little before three o'clock. He drove my car because I guess I was pretty out of it, but he had less to drink so it was no big deal, and the kid's house wasn't far from where Anthony lives. And I crashed at his place. But I had to get up at ten the next morning for my job at Rosario's Pizza. Jake wants me there so I can get the place ready when it opens at eleven."

"You weren't hungover?"

"Yeah, but I've done it before."

"Do you drink that heavily every weekend?"

"No. I usually drink every weekend. But I guess I drank more than I usually do because I was pretty out of it. But it's no big deal. Like I said, I'm not an alcoholic."

"Do you ever drink alone?"

"No, not really. Like I just said, I'm not an alcoholic or anything."

"Could you stop drinking if you wanted to?"

"I don't know. I suppose. But why would I want to?"

Now here's an interview with Emanuel.

"Tell me about you and marijuana. How old are you now? When did you start smoking?"

"I'm sixteen. I guess I started when I was thirteen. There was this group of kids I was friendly with, and we all started smoking around the same time. I guess I've been a smoker since then."

"Are you still friendly with those kids?"

"Some of them. There's this group of kids I smoke with pretty often. Some are from that original group."

"Any girls?"

"No. I know some girls who smoke weed, but not many."

"Do you ever smoke alone?"

"Yeah. Pretty much every day after school, if I don't go over to somebody's house and smoke with them."

"You smoke every day?"

"Yeah. Does that shock you?"

"No, I guess not. I know there are a lot of kids who get high every day."

"Yeah, well, I'm one of them."

"Why do you smoke every day?"

"I don't know. When I get home from school, if I don't smoke it kind of sucks."

"What do you mean?"

"I feel kind of depressed or anxious and shit. I didn't smoke for a while. I didn't like it. But smoking pot is cool. I like the way it makes me feel."

"How do you do in school?"

"Good. Bs and sometimes an A."

"Do you think your pot smoking interferes with your schoolwork?"

"Not really. Like I said, I smoke in the afternoon. But I don't

usually smoke at night, and if I have homework, I do it then."

"Are you addicted to marijuana?"

"No, marijuana's not addictive."

"Could you stop smoking if you wanted to?"

"Yeah, like I said, marijuana's not addictive. I've gone through periods where I wasn't smoking, or I smoked a lot less. But I don't want to stop. I like smoking and it doesn't screw up my life. They should legalize it. What do you think? Don't you think they should legalize it?"

An interview with Connell.

"You're a crystal meth [a highly addictive form of methamphetamine] *user, is that right?"*

"Yeah."

"How old are you? How long have you been using it?"

"I'm seventeen. I've been using it since I was fifteen."

"Is fifteen kind of young to start using crystal meth?"

"Yeah, I was young for getting into it. Though I know a lot of kids my age who are into it now."

"Do you think you're addicted to it?"

"Yeah, I guess. It's kind of the only thing my life is about. Getting high. Figuring where I'm going to get it, or how to get the money for it."

"Have you ever gotten into trouble with the law?"

"Yeah. A lot. I've been in juvie pretty often. And I thought I had kicked it. But I didn't."

"How did you ever get into something that got to be such a big problem in your life?"

"I don't know. I was already into a lot of stuff, and you could get it, and I didn't know a whole lot about it except that it was supposed to be this fantastic high. I knew maybe it was dangerous, but, what the fuck, I was already into some dangerous shit, like stealing. How bad could it be? Anyway, I tried it. It was a really good high. Way more than anything I'd had before. And that was kind of it. I could get it. But, like I said, money was a problem, which is why I got into trouble so much."

"Are you in school now?"

"No, I dropped out."

"How were you as a student? What kind of grades did you get?"

"Not real good. School was never exactly my thing."

"What do you do now?"

"I work part-time at this pizza place. It's actually not bad. And I do this other shit—basically anything I can do to get money. So I never know exactly what's going to happen."

"Do you like it when you use it?"

"Yeah. Of course."

"Would you like to stop using it?"

"Not really. Like I said, I like the effect. It's just that I don't like how my life is so totally just about getting high. I'd like to be able to use it but feel a little more in control of my life. I'd be lying if I said I really wanted to stop using it."

HOW PREVALENT IS SUBSTANCE USE?

The statistics on teenage drinking and drug use vary from year to year. Use of some drugs becomes more prevalent, while use of others seems to decline. But overall the patterns remain more the same than not. According to *Monitoring the Future*—an annual survey of drug and alcohol use by teenagers in the United States that is conducted by the University of Michigan Institute for Social Research and funded by the National Institute on Drug Abuse—over the last thirty years there has been a gradual decline in alcohol use by teenagers. (You may find this a little surprising, as it contradicts what is frequently reported in the media.) The use of alcohol by eighth graders has dropped over the last fifteen years from approximately 25 percent down to 15 percent. (They did not have statistics on alcohol use by eighth graders prior to 1995.) "Heavy" alcohol use, defined as "five or more drinks in a row at least once in the prior two-week period," has declined since 1995 by between 15 and 25 percent. But still, roughly 70 percent report having drunk alcohol during their teen years.

Marijuana use has remained roughly the same, with a little over 40 percent reporting usage of marijuana as of the 2008 survey. Between 5 percent and 10 percent of teens use hard (stronger, more addictive) drugs such as heroin, cocaine, crack cocaine, crystal meth, oxycontin—depending on the definition of hard drugs.

However, there has been one major change in illicit teen drug use: in recent years there has been a significant rise in the use of prescription drugs—pain relievers, tranquilizers, stimulants, sedatives—to get high. The Substance Abuse and Mental Health Services Administration, U.S. Department of Health and Human Services, reports that over 10 percent of teenagers, and possibly more, now abuse prescription drugs. Furthermore, there appears to be an increasing trend toward their use.

The bottom line is that if you have a teenager, there is a real possibility that he or she will drink or use illicit drugs. Drugs and alcohol are available to most teens. Most teens like the effects. And most teens have no strong objection to drinking or drug use—excluding the harder, more addictive drugs. They defend their choice with statements like the following:

"What's the big deal? I like how they make me feel. I know they can be a problem. But I'm careful. It's just not such a big deal."

Parents, for their part, are very clear about what they think regarding their teenage children and the prospect of hard drug use.

"Absolutely not! They ruin a life. A child who uses hard drugs is a parent's nightmare."

But most parents today are far more ambivalent with regard to their teenagers' drinking and using marijuana. Probably more than anything else, it is this ambivalence that characterizes parents' thinking about their teens and much of substance use. That is, they're against it, but they're not sure how against it they should be.

WHERE DO YOU STAND ON DRINKING?

Many parents of teens are totally against their teenagers drinking. But just as many others are less certain.

They're probably going to drink someday anyway. Besides, adolescence is supposed to be a time for fun. How bad is it if they drink? If I make a big deal out of how they shouldn't drink and drive, then at least I have put that idea in their heads as a protection. But as long as they're not drinking and driving, there's a lot worse stuff than drinking. And what control do I have? Besides, if they drink as teens and have had some experience with drinking, won't they become more in control, more responsible drinkers, once they become adults? I can't keep them locked up in their rooms all through high school. I mean, the big majority of kids who are in high school do drink. It's always been that way. And I know some become alcoholics, but most just go on to have normal adult lives.

It is not easy to know what to think. But let me present some of the real problems with teenage drinking. What follows may very well make you a little less ambivalent.

Regardless of what you may say to your kids about drinking and driving, teenagers who drink are significantly more at risk of becoming involved in a fatal car accident.

Alcohol consumed in large quantities can be toxic to the point of death.

Alcohol consumed in combination with other drugs can be more toxic than alcohol alone. (This is particularly troubling given that some teenagers experiment with prescription drugs to get high.)

Drinking significantly increases the chances that your teenager will do something that will cause a major problem in his or her life— something that he or she would not have done had they not been drinking. Examples of this include:

> 1. Getting pregnant or getting somebody else pregnant. (Teens who drink are more likely to have sex. And they are much more likely, if they do have sex, not to use birth control or to misuse birth control.)

> 2. Getting an STD (for the same reasons as above).

> 3. Getting into trouble with the law.

> 4. Forcing someone into nonconsensual sex, including the possibility of getting into serious trouble for it.

> 5. Doing something—usually of a sexual nature—that ends up being significantly humiliating. This is especially true for girls.

> 6. Getting into a fight where someone is badly hurt. This is especially true for boys.

> 7. Being more likely to die by suicide. When depressed, potentially suicidal teens drink, which causes them to feel more depressed. This, of course, puts them at a higher risk of killing themselves.

Kids who drink also encounter these other problems:

- When fun becomes defined as drinking, kids are less likely to have nondrinking fun, or even know that there is such a thing. Hence, they become dependent on drinking to have a good time.

- Teens say one big reason that they drink is to relieve stress, and this is not a good pattern to set early in one's life, as it gets in the way of developing other more reliable stress-coping skills. What kids are learning in this process is to drink rather than to cope.

- Last, alcohol has a power of its own. Teenagers, like adults, vastly underestimate that power. They almost all think that they can handle it.

In a later segment I will cover what you can and cannot do if you are concerned about your teenager and drinking. But first let me talk about that other ambivalence-inspiring substance, the one that parents are perhaps most on the fence about, maybe even more so than alcohol: marijuana.

WHERE DO YOU STAND ON MARIJUANA?

The following is a fictitious—but not very—interview with a parent:

"You used to be a heavy marijuana smoker and you still smoke sometimes? Is that right?"

"Yeah. I smoked pretty much every day for a number of years. I smoke occasionally now. Not often."

"Do you feel that it created a problem for you?"

"To be honest, I don't really think so. I have a good job and I make good money. I have done well in my working career, and I have a nice family, so I guess I can't really say that it was a problem."

"Do you feel that it was in any way harmful for you at the time?"

"It's hard for me to say. There was a time when marijuana was so much a part of my life that I really can't separate my marijuana smoking from everything else that was going on with me at the time. I think of those times and all that I thought and felt, and marijuana was a really big part of it."

"Do you think of it as bad?"

"No. I'd be lying if I said I did. For the most part, all of my thoughts about marijuana are good. But there definitely were people I knew, people I still know, who pretty clearly wasted a lot of years of their lives. They were cool, but they weren't really doing anything except hanging out and smoking. They were kind of just drifting. And I think that some of them—even today—don't really have such great lives. You can't help thinking that maybe they missed out on a different life that they might have had but for the marijuana. Maybe they would have turned out like this anyway, but I'm not so sure.

"The problem is that I really have no regrets about the role of marijuana in my life. I have good feelings about it. I would do it all over again. But I have no way of knowing how it will affect Derek. I just don't know. I was lucky. But I know what it can do to some people. Still, what can I say? I liked that part of my life."

Even though parents might be quite comfortable with the role of marijuana in their own lives, they also know that not everyone escapes without problems. Most parents today—whether they were marijuana users or not—remember people they knew as teenagers whose marijuana use did, in fact, cause problems and may have even changed the direction of their lives.

"Like I said, it was okay for me, but maybe it wasn't for everybody. There was this guy, Tim, at my school, who was always a straight-arrow kind of guy. But then he got heavily into pot in the middle of high school, and he just kind of drifted. And he's still drifting. He's always had kind of dead-end jobs. Maybe he would have ended up that way anyway. I don't know. I know it's a little hypocritical, but I'm just not comfortable with it for my son, Derek."

The problem, of course, is that there is a double standard. We were willing to take *some* risks when we were teenagers, whereas we're not nearly as comfortable with our kids taking many of those same risks. In fact, we much prefer if they took none.

The great majority of marijuana users do seem to be able to lead normal lives. Their marijuana use does not appear to have hurt them. Especially maddening and confusing are those cases whereby a teenager who is a regular, even heavy, marijuana user seems to be able to function at a high level and go on to live a successful life nevertheless.

So is marijuana a problem, or not? Let us dig a little deeper.

IS IT A PROBLEM OR NOT?

The following are what I believe to be the three greatest potential problems with marijuana use for teenagers:

Addiction

Marijuana *can* be addictive. This is a very contentious issue. Marijuana is not considered *physically* addictive. My understanding is that it does not produce a physiological craving per se, which makes it different from many other substances, ranging from cigarettes to heroin. But it is addictive, if indeed addiction means that the drug, by its power over a given individual, can make that individual crave the drug. In other words, if marijuana can make someone want it badly enough on a regular basis, if it can entice someone into planning their lives around making sure that they get it, if it entices the brain to crave it the way the body often craves other drugs, then marijuana can be considered addictive after all. It becomes not a choice, but rather a need—not a conscious decision over which they have control, but an urging that regularly exerts a powerful pull on them and controls their behavior. Your child will deny its addictive qualities with claims like the following, but just because kids don't recognize its addictive qualities doesn't mean that you shouldn't.

"You are so full of shit! You so don't know what the hell you're talking about! Yes, I smoke marijuana. I smoke every day. But you're not me. How can you know whether I can control it or not? How can you know what's in my head? What no one seems to understand is that I choose to smoke dope. I could stop smoking if I wanted to. Marijuana is not addictive. I choose not to stop. I smoke because I like it. I can stop it if I want to, but I don't want to."

And they will usually have an example of a brief period of time when, for one reason or another, they did not smoke for a while.

"And you know what? I didn't crave it. But I like smoking weed, so I went back to doing it."

Marijuana's Effect on Ambition

My main concern is that marijuana can absolutely decrease ambition in some kids. Many say that marijuana makes you "lazy." But it is more than that. What marijuana can do—at least with some kids—is cancel out the future. Marijuana has the power to take the clock off the wall, so that some (not all) kids who are regular users can drift and not worry about it. Most feel no pressure to do anything in particular. They do not have the sense that their lives are supposed to be moving along. They seem to think that what they are doing now will have no effect on what will happen to them in the future. Their lives often become all about now. They don't seem to have purpose or any sense that they are supposed to be doing something. And they drift.

Nor do they see that marijuana is influencing their thoughts and shaping—rather than just being a part of—their lives. This in-the-moment philosophy is very much the marijuana talking, even though the kids seem to think it's their own philosophy.

> *"At my high school, I see a lot of kids—including some I grew up with—who are incredibly stressed. All they're doing is worrying about grades and trying to plan for their future and they're not actually living their lives. What kind of life is that? They're going to look back on high school and they're going to wonder, what did I do? Their lives are not about now but about later. They're just totally uptight about everything. I'm not saying you're not supposed to do schoolwork, but you're also supposed to enjoy life. They'll end up with some boring job and feel that they missed out, but it will be too late. I don't want to be like that. What's the point if everything is about the future? Life is about now."*
>
> *"Do you think that marijuana is making you think that way?"*
>
> *"No, this is me. Maybe the marijuana has helped me see it. But this is what I think."*

Wasted Time

The last big issue with marijuana is that—again, for some but not all users—it can become an alternative to simply passing time. An alternative to experiencing the periods of boredom, low-level depression, and anxiety that are an inevitable part of a normal day. If marijuana becomes such an alternative in your child's life, it can interfere with developing a tolerance for the normal stresses of daily life. Marijuana users have to be high just to get through an ordinary day. They lose the coping skills necessary to deal with their everyday lives.

You may or may not agree, but I do think that teenage drinking and teenage marijuana use can present real problems. If teens can get through their adolescence without alcohol and marijuana, they are almost certainly better off.

WHAT PARENTS CAN DO

There are basically two things that you can do if you don't want your teenager to drink or use drugs. The first thing is to keep track of your teenagers. Know where they are. Know what they are doing. Know who they are with. Check up on them. Are there really parents home at the party they are going to? As they transition from being young teenagers to older teenagers, it can become increasingly more difficult to monitor them. But it is also a personal parenting choice: How much do you want to be involved in the supervision, or surveillance, of your teenager's daily life? On this question, parents differ considerably, not only in terms of personal preference, but also with regard to each specific child.

> "I always felt I could trust Phillip. He had his small transgressions, but I never really worried about him. I always gave him a lot of space. But Jerome is a whole other story. I trust him as far as I can throw a piano. With him, I always trust that he's up to something that he shouldn't be doing."
>
> To which Jerome responds,
>
> "Mom always thinks I'm doing something that I shouldn't be doing, which is totally unfair, because even though she's right—I actually do a lot of drugs, but she can't possibly know about all the

drugs I do—she never checked up on Phillip the way she does with me. It's just not fair."

The reality, of course, is that the degree of supervision you want to have over your teenager during their waking, nonschool hours is just not possible in today's world. You simply cannot be on top of their every move. Further, kids who are hell-bent on drinking or doing drugs usually end up finding a way to do just that. Supervision has its limits.

The other way that parents can make their children's substance use more difficult is by keeping track of the substances. Searching for marijuana or locking away alcohol in your house are examples of the kind of tracking I'm talking about. And perhaps the most significant thing you can do is to keep close track of prescription medications. It is especially important always to carefully dispose of medications that are no longer being used. This is particularly significant with prescription drugs, because home has proven to be a major source of these drugs for kids. Inadvertently, many parents are their kids' own drug suppliers.

Despite my recommended vigilance, though, you should bear in mind that the great majority of teens who refrain from drinking, smoking marijuana, or using other illicit drugs during their adolescence do so not because of firm parental supervision, but rather because *they* choose not to. It is the same as with those who do drink or use drugs. They choose that path. So if for the most part you can't control them, do you really have any role in teen substance use? Yes, you *can* have a meaningful influence on your children's choices about drugs and drinking. And that goal is accomplished by talking to them.

TALKING TO TEENS ABOUT DRINKING AND DRUGS

The standard parent-teenager substance-use talk basically consists of the parent stating their reasons as to why they just shouldn't do it. They can almost hear parts of the lecture now. . . .

"And reason number sixteen: teenage alcohol consumption sets a pattern that increases your chances of being overweight as you get older."

The problem is that these messages—especially when they come from an adult who also is their parent—often have very little, if any, positive effect. Teenagers tune them out. Parents' words tend to go in one ear and out the other. The kids just do not buy it.

"Of course that's what my parents would say! What else would you expect them to say? They're going to give the scariest possible warnings that they can come up with. They're hardly going to say things like, 'I mention this, but actually the chances of this happening with you are very slim.' Or how about, 'Actually, son, when you weigh the pleasures you get from smoking pot, they tend to outweigh the risks.' No, they're not going to say that. So why should I trust anything they say, when it is so predictable?"

Earlier I provided a list of reasons why alcohol and drug use by teenagers can cause significant problems. But I presented that list to illustrate why parents shouldn't be so ambivalent on the subject. I did not present it in a way that would necessarily speak to teens. However, if you want to use these as discussion points with your teenager, that's great. Despite knowing that teenagers tend to ignore antidrinking or antidrug talks, particularly when they come in the form of warnings, or when the source is an adult, or worse, when the source is their parent, I'm still a huge advocate of talking anyway.

Even if they only process a fraction of what you say, it can have a genuine impact on their drug and drinking behavior. The key is how you do the talking. It is the difference between having a conversation and giving a lecture. To the extent that it is a lecture, they won't hear a word. I will talk about how to have a conversation shortly.

And remember too that the end result, while positive, may not always be abstinence—though it can be. The great majority of kids who abstain from drinking do so because of factors separate from what their parents may or may not say. The main impact of talking is that their approach to drinking and drug use will be more thoughtful than if there were no such talks. They may still engage in these activities, but they are likely to do so with more consideration of the risks. Because you talked to them about it, your child may have a more reasonable, more realistic, and definitely safer approach to drugs and drinking. And their behavior might be safer too.

FOSTERING HONESTY

So what is this better way of talking? It's nothing so revolutionary in theory, but it can be in practice. It is open, honest, and adult communication. Basically this means talking to your teenager as if he or she were another adult in the room with whom you have decided to be completely forthcoming.

It is not easy. It takes practice. The gist of it is that when you are talking with your teen about drugs and drinking, you want to try to be as open and honest and adult as you can be. As I said, what you do not want to do is give lectures.

This type of conversation has certain basic rules, which you can tell to your kid.

The rules are:

"I can ask you questions, but you don't have to answer. Also, you can lie. But it is better if you try to be honest. You can ask me questions, but I don't have to answer. However, I will always try to answer as much as I possibly can, unless it is something that I am just too uncomfortable with. I will try to be as open and honest as I can. There is nothing that you are not allowed to say or ask. You will not get into trouble for anything that you say. You are allowed to get mad at me, but it would be nicer if you didn't. I will try very hard not to get mad or defensive. You can criticize me if you want. We can stop anytime you want. Also, I can end the conversation at any time—but hopefully that will not have to happen."

The idea is that if you are going to talk with your teen about a very serious, adult topic, you want to be as mature about it as you can. Let me give an example: what follows is a conversation between mother and daughter where the mother is trying very hard to be open and honest. The mother begins the conversation.

"Lisa, you can start if you want. But if you don't want to, I'll start."

"You can start."

"Okay, what do you think about drinking. Do you drink much?"

"I think maybe I don't want to talk to you about me and drinking. And I'm not saying that I do drink. But there's a lot of stuff that I think I want to keep private. No offense."

"That's fine. Those are the rules. Do you have any friends—you

don't have to tell me who—that you think might drink too much?"

"I don't even feel like telling you about my friends. Maybe I will some other time. I don't know."

"That's fine. Do you want me to talk? You can ask me anything you want to."

"When you were my age, did you ever get really, really drunk, like you threw up or did really stupid stuff?"

"That's a little embarrassing for me to talk about."

"I know. You said you didn't have to talk about it if you didn't want to. But did you?"

"Okay, I'll tell you one story."

"There were more than one?"

"I'm not answering that."

"Jeez, my mom was a teenage alkie."

"You want to hear about the one time?"

"Yeah."

"Junior year, three other girls and I decided that we were going to have a sleepover getting-drunk party. One of the girls had a way of getting alcohol, and there was one weekend that her parents were away. I remember she even asked permission to have the sleepover. Of course, she didn't mention the plan to get drunk."

"Do you remember what you had to drink?"

"Actually, I do. It was a bottle of vodka that we mixed with some kind of cola. I think maybe that was what made me throw up."

"You really threw up?"

"Yeah. But that was later. Mainly we sang songs, except for this one girl, Jenna, who kind of passed out and slept nearly the whole time. And at one point we went outside and sang, and I'm surprised we didn't get in trouble because it was maybe two in the morning."

"Were there times where you drank and you did stuff that was more than just going outside and singing?"

"Yes."

"Omigod! Did you ever get drunk at a party and end up having sex with a guy who you had no intention of ever having sex with and the next day could not believe that you actually did have sex with?"

"That's not even close to something I would talk about, whether it happened or not."

"Come on, tell me! You said you wanted to be open."
"No, that's not something I will talk about."
"Did you like getting drunk?"
"Yes, except I didn't like the throwing-up part."

In this example, the mother succeeds in being open, honest, and adult. Though at one point she does not give her daughter information about herself, she in no way attacks her daughter for asking the questions. Openness does not necessarily mean telling everything. But it does mean not getting defensive or evasive—and trying to say as much as you are comfortable saying. You leave yourself open, vulnerable. Which I think comes across in the dialogue. And I think comes across to Lisa. It is actually a very powerful talking technique, if you can tolerate it.

I am being open and honest. I am leaving myself vulnerable because I think what we are talking about is that important.

If you can actually have dialogues like this, there is no way that Lisa would not be encouraged to talk and think about whatever it is that she and her mother are discussing. The impact is that the conversation is now put into a completely different, gigantically more memorable form.

WHAT NOT TO DO

What you do not want to do is be critical or judgmental, or to teach. Doing those things will instantly kill the open back-and-forth dialogue you are aiming for.

Here's an example of what not to do:

Lisa asks her mother,

> *"Do you remember what you had to drink?"*
> *"That's not important."*

Lisa's mother felt uncomfortable answering, and her discomfort made her respond to her daughter in an off-putting manner.

A simple "no" or "yes" would have been better. If you are not comfortable with a given question, you can always say, *"I'm sorry, I'm not comfortable talking about that."* Which answer they will not like, but which is honest and will not impede further conversation.

Or, for example, Lisa asks,

"There was more than one time you got very drunk?"
"Don't push it, Lisa."

As I just said, if Lisa's mother is not comfortable answering, she should say that, rather than being critical of Lisa for asking.

Or let's say Lisa does end up talking about one of her friends.

"Okay, there is somebody, but I'm not going to tell you who it is because then you will kind of look at her differently. Anyway, she definitely does drink too much, and I know for a fact that one time she had sex with two different guys the same night."
"That's terrible. That's exactly what I worry about drinking making somebody do."

That last line, of course, is a big mistake. It's a lecture and will turn Lisa off right away.

It would be better to offer no comment or to say something innocuous like,

"Wow, she must have been pretty drunk."

Both of which will encourage Lisa to keep talking.

"Yeah, I can't believe she did that," says Lisa, and the conversation continues.

SHARING YOUR OWN EXPERIENCES

The talking that I am describing here definitely gets into the tricky issue of how much about your own life, and your own drinking and drug habits (past or present), you want to share. My thinking about this subject has changed over the years. I used to be less comfortable with the idea of parents talking candidly about their own personal history regarding drugs and drinking. I now think that if there are things that you are not comfortable talking about—for whatever reason (usually because it's too embarrassing)—then don't talk about them. Otherwise, it's okay to share them with your kids.

I believe that the value of talking openly is not so much in what lessons your child may or may not learn from knowing about your life or your experiences. Rather, the value lies in the nature of the conversations—open, frank, and adult—that you have with your teenager. It would be counterproductive if too often you feel that you have to be the adult authority, always in control and careful of what you might say, or if too often you feel that there always has to be distance between you and them. Because, if that is what it feels like to them, then such conversations simply are not going to have the same impact that a discussion on a more person-to-person level would have.

You might wonder: *But won't it undermine my authority if they feel that we are talking more or less as equals?* Don't worry. I think being a friend works in this instance. When you are parenting, you often play different roles. One of those roles is parent-as-authority—saying "no," making demands, etc.—and in that role you are definitely not your child's buddy. That does not work.

But being on the same level really does work when you are talking about the very adult topics of drinking and drugs. If you talk about your own experience—using substances or not—they know that you understand to some degree the complex issues and feelings they are encountering. If you talk in the most adult, mature manner that you can, they have to feel the respect that comes with that. What does all of this accomplish? It gives credence to any concerns that you do have—and perhaps it also conveys lessons you learned from what may have been your own negative experiences. But above all, it forces them to look at their own life experience in a more mature manner—because that is how you are interacting with them. Which is precisely what you are after.

THE SINGLE GREATEST RISK DETERRENT

There is a saying in the real estate business that the three most important factors in the value of a house are location, location, and location. I believe that to seriously curtail risky teenage substance use, the three most important prevention factors are: how much they think they have a future, how much they think they have a future, and how much they think they have a future. This consideration dwarfs all other deterrents to serious drug and alcohol abuse. Many teens who see themselves as having futures do not become substance abusers. But there are, in my mind, stark differences between these teens and those who believe that the future holds very little promise for them.

Either because of real socioeconomic barriers (being poor, living in the inner city, being part of a minority population), or having real difficulties with school, or just experiencing plain old depression, not believing that your future holds much promise makes some kids so much more vulnerable to serious drug abuse than others. They can't help but think,

"My life sucks and my future sucks. Why not take risks? What have I got to lose?"

Teens who feel that they have a reasonable chance of enjoying a good future also take risks, but most of them only do so to a point. There is always the thought in the back of their minds:

I don't want to do anything too risky. I mean, I don't want to do anything that's going to screw up my future.

What does this mean if you are a parent of a teen? It means that you want to do everything you can to steer your child away from potential problem substance use, including helping them to see and realize their future prospects. If they are headed for potentially serious trouble, you do not want them to lose sight of the fact that their life has great potential down the road and that they need to make sure they remain on the path to secure that future. Monitoring and informing their substance use is extremely important. And the way to preserve that future is to take action in the present by encouraging them such that they can continue to meet with reasonable success in their teenage lives. They must know that if they flounder too much now, they are putting themselves at a much greater risk for alcohol and drug abuse.

UNDERSTANDING THE POWER OF SUBSTANCES

There is a basic problem with drugs and drinking. Unfortunately, every time you take alcohol or drugs into your body, they can change how you feel and think. They can even make you perceive these changes as positive. You feel good. You feel relaxed or, in some cases, enjoyably energized. You may even feel strange, or think strangely, but in a way that you like. Otherwise no one would use drugs or alcohol. The bottom line is that drugs and alcohol can induce pleasure. And this pleasing effect can be made to occur at any point in the middle of a normal life. All you have to do is ingest the substance.

"Yeah, if I'm not high on anything, I'm just my normal self doing whatever it is I'm doing at the time. And if I'm doing something that sucks—like sitting in a boring class in school, or sitting at home with nothing to do that isn't boring or stupid, or even going out with buddies but what we're doing is boring and stupid and the same thing we always do—I don't like how I feel. But I know a way that I can change that."

More likely than not, if you try one of these substances for the first time you will like the effect. And if you try the same substance on another occasion you will like it then too, maybe even more.

"The first time I smoked pot, it was a little weird but it was okay. But the second time was better. I definitely liked how it made me feel. It was cool."

"The first time I did cocaine it was amazing. I'd never felt like that before. I felt great. Afterward, it was actually a little scary to think about—because of how great it made me feel."

"Yeah, I started drinking when I started hanging out with this bunch of kids. And I was way more relaxed and funny. And it was kind of a warm feeling. It was nice. I had a good time. The alcohol made it more fun. If I'm honest, it was definitely a better time than I would have had if I hadn't been drinking. That's just the way it was."

That is, all of these substances have a certain power. They can cause you to like what happens to you when you take them. In and of themselves, chemicals can produce an effect that makes you feel good in a way you'd love to feel again. These substances have no mind, no will; they are just chemicals. But in varying degrees, with varying drugs, and varying users, they can control you. They can blur the line between what seems like your choice, and what the substance and its effect are actually choosing for you.

And because drugs and alcohol are so accessible, and because they can have this enticing effect on you that you really like, they also soon have a real power and influence in your life. They just do. You want to encourage your child not to turn that power over to anyone or any thing, most of all not to a chemical substance.

Chapter Thirteen

TEENS AND ELECTRONICS

The most obvious change in the lives of today's teenagers is the degree to which the electronic world has become the very fabric of their day-to-day lives.

A MINUTE IN THE LIFE

Nanette is sitting in her room at home an hour after school has ended. She is listening to music through a headset.

> *I can see you*
> *You little fool*
> *Just walk away.*

As she listens to her music, the above lyrics echoing in her head, she also reads a text message that she just got from her friend Eden.

> *"U want 2 come over tomorrow afternoon?"*
> *"No, i have practice right after school,"* Nanette texts back.

Nanette then calls her friend Danielle on her cell phone.

> *"Hey,"* answers Danielle.
> *"What did you think of Valerie today?"* asks Nanette. *"Do you think she knows about Chuck and Marissa?"*
> *"I don't know. I think maybe Karyn might have said something to her. She looked kind of strange third period."*
> *"Do you think we should say something to her?"* asks Nanette.
> *"I don't know,"* responds Danielle.

At that point, while still in the middle of her conversation with Danielle, Nanette sends a message via her Facebook page to her friend Gavin.

"That is so cute, you and Knight," she writes to Gavin, regarding a picture of him and his dog she has just seen while going through a group of pictures Gavin posted on his Facebook page that afternoon.

> *It's only lightning*
> *I tried too hard*
> *Just walk away,*

continues the song.

> A new text from Eden comes in. *"How about thursday?"*

> *"I guess,"* Nanette texts back.

> *"I think maybe we should say something. I hate for Valerie not to know when everybody else does,"* says Nanette, continuing her conversation with Danielle.
> *"Shit!"* says Nanette.
> *"What?"* asks Danielle.
> *"Nothing, sorry. I just lost my fucking page in my fucking biology book that I have to study for a test tomorrow."*
> *"Maybe it's better that she doesn't know,"* says Danielle.

Eden texts again. *"You guess? what's that supposed to mean?"*

> *"Yes. thursday is fine. Okay. Yes,"* Nanette texts back.

Right at that moment, a different text message comes in.

"I love you," texts Nanette's ex-boyfriend Chas, who randomly sends similar messages to her as a sort of ongoing joke between the two of them regarding their current still-close-but-somewhat-ambiguous relationship.

"Fuck you," texts back Nanette affectionately, like she usually does.

"Maybe you're right. I guess we shouldn't say anything," continues Nanette with Danielle.

"I think it's better if she finds out on her own—or not," responds Danielle.

"Thursday. but thursday's definite. right?" texts Eden.

"Yes," Nanette texts back.

You're not my boss
Just don't keep looking
Just walk away

The song plays on.

"Shit," says Nanette. *"I lost my fucking place again."*

"You're an idiot," says her friend Danielle.

The above represents what might be a typical moment in the electronic life of a teenager. One difference, however, is that in real life there might well have been even more simultaneous entries: pictures, online comments, unfolding dramas, all within a single moment. Our kids are living in a vast network of flying images, words, and sounds. A universe hooked up to their brain. And they are in the middle of it—seeing, hearing, and reacting to it every moment. It is what they do. When teenagers are not in school, the great majority of their waking hours are spent in some manner connected to the electronic universe. At any given moment, they have multiple connections. This is their reality.

The burgeoning electronic world, specifically with the rise of cell phones, the growth of the Internet, and the prevalence of video games and other such sophisticated computer technologies, has caused a dramatic shift in the way teens exist, function, and thrive today compared to previous generations.

They stay connected, talk to, or send messages to friends 24/7. They can immediately access a vast range of information and entertainment sources. Their world is simply not the same as the world of prior generations of teens. Some of this is good, some of it not so good, and the rest—who knows? Regardless, it is what it is, and it's not going away.

So what does it all mean? What should and can you do about it? It is a major concern for many of today's parents.

> *"Yes, I worry about it. Really, other than when she is in school or asleep, it's her life. I can't possibly follow everything that is going on, everything that she does. I worry. You hear about these sexual predators. Kids just don't understand how exposed they are. They are way too trusting. They're far too vulnerable, it's easy to see how they might be taken advantage of. And God knows what she's up to. Sex, drugs, drinking. That's all they talk about. You don't know what kind of trouble they could be into. And that's not the half of it. Try to get her to come to dinner. To participate in any family activity. To help with anything around the house. Just to get her to talk to us. It's a major battle."*

The kids have their views too.

> *"Excuse me. What my mom doesn't understand is that I really am in the middle of something important. Nina—who is my best friend in the world—was really upset about what Denise said about her today. I mean really upset. And I can't just leave Nina hanging—she's my best friend. My mom just wants to talk to me about something that is almost certainly some chore that does not absolutely need to be done right then. I mean, really!"*

To which parents naturally would respond,

> *"That's what I mean. I just don't know what to do. How much should I be concerned? What can I do, anyway?"*

As always, I think taking the mystery out of things can help parents deal more effectively. So let's look together at what your kids are actually doing when they are digitally connected.

WHAT *DO* KIDS DO ONLINE?

I've taken the liberty of actually asking teens what they do in this electronic world they are immersed in. What follows are fictitious but very representative samples.

"Sara, what do you do?"
"I don't do anything really wrong. It's no big deal. I talk to friends. Yeah, we swear a lot, talk about sex, drugs and drinking—and gossip. But that's what teenagers do. I've never done anything really bad.

"Most of the time I talk about what's going on. And who I talk to is people I know. I don't talk to strangers. Why would I want to?

"What's the worst thing I've ever done? Probably a couple times when I did say real mean things to this girl, but she deserved it. And maybe some sexual stuff that I'm embarrassed to talk about. I mean it was just sex stuff—if that's bad. It was with people my own age. Maybe the worst thing that I do is that I probably waste a lot of time, when maybe I should be doing homework or getting exercise or something productive. What I do, it's just not really that bad."

"Sam, what do you do?"
"It's not a big deal. I go to different websites. Sometimes there will be like really funny videos. There's this kind of car, a DeLorean, that they used to make and I'm really into it, and I go to websites about that. And this rock band that I like. I go to porno sites. I'd be lying if I said I didn't. But what's so bad about that? That's normal for guys my age, right? I use my cell phone a lot to stay in touch with kids about what's going on. And before me and Maya broke up, we used to text each other about a billion times a day. Usually stupid shit."

"What's the worst thing you've done?"
"I guess maybe drug deals. I arranged to buy some marijuana. It was just marijuana. But I don't do that anymore. I got nervous when this kid who I was friends with got into trouble."

"What about cybersex?"
"I'm not sure what that really is. But when me and Maya were still together, we used to send pictures back and forth. You know

what I mean. But she was my girlfriend. Was that even wrong? What I do, it's just not really that bad."

Repeatedly, kids say that what they do online is not that bad. Which would be great if that were totally true. But, certainly, many teenagers do cross over lines into areas that are not so good. And their judgment about what is safe or acceptable is not always the best. As I have said before, what teens will tolerate as risk in their lives is certainly more than the degree of risk that their parents will tolerate. This fact causes lots of parents to worry. Let me list the main worries before we tackle them one by one.

WHAT PARENTS WORRY ABOUT MOST

Cutting right to the chase, there are a few things that parents of teens unanimously worry about. They include:

- Sexual predators.

- Cyberbullying.

- Engaging in or planning to engage in problem behaviors—anything to do with sex, drugs, drinking, and illegal activity.

- Getting so caught up in the electronic world that it interferes with necessary life activities such as schoolwork and sleep.

- Being so connected with others via the electronic world that it interferes with family activities such as joining family meals, doing chores, spending quality time with family, getting ready to go places, and just talking to loved ones.

There are other problems too, of course, some of which I will talk about later. But I think the above list summarizes the biggest worries. These concerns fall into two general categories. One speaks to what kids actually do on the Internet and on their cell phones—meaning the content of their interactions. The other category speaks to how much time kids spend connected to the electronic world, and the powerful pull this world exerts on them. I will discuss these two categories separately.

Let me begin first by addressing the generally troubling things—the overall dangers and bad behavior that occurs while kids are using electronic media, and what you can do—not just to alleviate your anxiety but to minimize your child's risk too.

PARENTAL CONTROLS

One source of protection from the things you worry about most are the parent controls designed and provided by the makers of the very technological devices that concern us. The best way to learn about these is to check them out on the Internet under "parent controls." You can discover what is available, what they guard against, and how to best set them up in your home.

One common control is the website blocker. These are programs that you can install to prevent access to websites that are undesirable, such as sites that are too sexually explicit or violent in content. Computer-savvy kids may learn how to circumvent these blockers, but for the most part they are really very effective. Remember, however, that they do not always work *perfectly*. The adult world tries to keep their children away from potentially harmful websites, yet kids keep doing their best to outfox us. Nevertheless, the website-blocking programs on the market today tend to serve their function well with most teenagers. The Internet companies are smart too—they pay people good money to keep the website-blocking programs up-to-date. Of course, there will always be the kid who says,

"Not for me. I can get past anything. It's a challenge. But I'm good. Really good."

Fortunately, most teens are not expert hackers.

Another major way to control electronic use is surveillance. It is actually quite easy for you to view what your child has sent or received through their cell phones, via e-mail, or through their social media accounts. It's all there. Texts. Internet messages. Pictures. Videos. You can learn which websites your teen has visited, and even how long they stayed on that site. You can get information about who they have had contact with—though sometimes you can only access screen names, not real names. Again, you can find out how to do all of this by Googling "parent controls." You can also contact your child's cell phone maker or service and ask how you can review your teen's phone activity. Understand, however, that there is no way that you can completely keep track of everything that your teenager does over the phone or online—it is too big a job. Also, some information is protected. For example, in order to guarantee privacy, some phone companies will allow you to see times and sources of sent and received messages but will withhold all other information, disallowing the viewing of actual sent or received material.

Another obvious surveillance technique employed by many families requires that all Internet use take place in a public area of the house. Teens hate this, but they hate it for precisely the reason that many parents value it: kids want the freedom to do what they know their parents would not approve of, and to do it unobserved. You've heard the argument, I'm sure.

> *"No, that's not it. I just don't like people looking over my shoulder. It's called privacy, if you didn't know. Which, actually, I, as a teenager, deserve."*
> *"But you do naughty things."*
> *"Yes, but shouldn't I have the privacy to do them with no one knowing about them? That would certainly save my parents a lot of worry."*

So what will this surveillance accomplish? Assuming that your child knows about it—I will talk about secret surveillance (aka snooping) shortly—they will probably try to limit, censor, disguise, or get around sending or receiving anything that you would not approve of. The net result is that fewer troubling communications will actually be sent and received. But will surveillance eliminate these troubling correspondences entirely? Probably not. When a teen knows or suspects that what they communicate online or by phone will come under your purview, they will almost certainly tone down their problematic communications—at least to some extent. There is no assurance that this will lead to less unacceptable behavior, but at least less of it will be transacted over the Internet.

"Yeah, I'll do lots of bad stuff, but I won't be stupid enough to talk about it over the Internet."

Now that we've introduced the notion of increased surveillance, what do you do if you discover that your teen is engaged in unacceptable behavior? If the behavior is directly connected to their Internet or cell phone use—if the unacceptable activity is actually taking place via their electronic communication, for example, sending sexual pictures of themselves, making arrangements to get marijuana from a friend, spreading nasty rumors about another child over the Internet—then you would want to temporarily suspend their means of engaging in these activities by taking away cell phone and/or Internet use. And if their problem behavior is very serious and continues—if they persist in regularly harassing other teens, or connecting with inappropriate partners, or regularly engaging in illegal activities—you would need to take away their access altogether.

Assessing the value and dangers of your child's electronic media use is not an easy thing to do, since it is such a new reality, but let me try to field some of the many questions that may have been cropping up for you lately.

Many parents ask: *"What if the problem behavior is not directly taking place over a cell phone or the Internet? What if it is just something you happen to learn about because your child is discussing it with a friend online? What if you learn that your daughter is having sex with her boyfriend after school at your house? What if you learn that your son has regularly been harassing another child in his class at school? What if you learn that your son and a friend have been regularly stealing energy drinks from a convenience store? What if you learn that your daughter got very drunk at a recent weekend party? Is suspending Internet use going to be a meaningful response to your teen's bad behavior elsewhere? If not, what do you do?"*

You would probably do the same things you would do if you learned about the problem behaviors by means other than surveillance of their electronic records. You would do what parents have always done when they learned of their children's unacceptable activities, even prior to the explosion in the digital realm. If they came home drunk, or you caught your son and his girlfriend unclothed in his room, or you heard from a parent of your son's friend that three boys—one of them being your son—were smoking marijuana in your son's friend's basement, you would deal with each situation based on your child and the specific transgression in question. You would consider the problems independently, recognizing that each requires its own parental intervention.

That is, conducting electronic surveillance is but one aspect of a parent's overall awareness of their child's behavior.

Other frequent questions I receive include the following: *"Is there more need for surveillance today? Do today's teenagers engage in more problem behaviors than in the past (that is, prior to the Internet and cell phones)?"* Granted, there does seem to be a greater variety of bad behavior—new and different behaviors that did not exist in the past. For instance, there was no cyberbullying before, no going to inappropriate websites, no sending embarrassing photographs of yourself or others over the Internet. But is there really more bad behavior occurring today than before? Or is it just different kinds of bad behavior kids are engaging in? Are we just living in a different world? Does the electronic explosion require more surveillance, or just a different kind of surveillance?

Of course, all of this naturally leads to the larger question: How much surveillance should parents be conducting anyway? This question remains one of the most discussed dilemmas in teenage parenting circles. To what extent do you need to know about everything your child is doing in order to steer them in the right direction or to best protect them from harm, versus how much do you need to know in order to allow them the freedom and concomitant risk that enables them to navigate future situations better on their own? How can they ever learn to live in the world if they do not make their own choices and experience the consequences of those choices? How can they learn to survive in the world when they are not in control of their own lives, mistakes and all? And then of course there is the slightly nasty question: When is a parent's need to know about all of their child's activities based on what is best for their child and when is it more about their own need to free themselves from worry? You've had this thought yourself, no doubt, many times:

If I know exactly where he is and what he is doing in every area of his life, then I don't have to worry.

Parents might prefer literally being there every moment of their kids' lives because then they wouldn't have to worry. But their teenager is not likely to be thrilled about that prospect.

"No, you're wrong. I actually like it that Mom comes to parties with me. And the guys are getting used to having her along when we drive around. They think she has a cool sense of humor. And you should see what she's like when she's really high on weed."

The answers to all of the above questions, of course, vary from child to child and parent to parent. Some parents are far more comfortable with keeping a tight rein on their teenage child. Others prefer to give their kids more independence and to react to problems as they arise. I would not recommend one way over another—you will have to choose what you are comfortable with. Kids that are hell-bent on bad behavior will usually find a way to engage in that behavior. The bottom line is this: surveillance almost certainly curtails unacceptable activity to some degree. But, depending on the extent of the surveillance, there can also be losses, namely in your teenagers' ability to take responsibility for his own life and to learn from his own experiences. For this reason you need to carefully weigh how and when it's used.

SECRET SURVEILLANCE

So far I have been discussing the surveillance of teens' electronic communications when teens *know* that the surveillance exists. But what about *secret* surveillance—aka snooping? Here's an example of what can happen when the child finds out:

> *"Tori,"* asks her mother, *"how does Jerilyn feel, now that her stepfather is no longer living at their house?"*
> *"What?"*
> *"Uh—"*
> *"Omigod, Mom, you've been reading my messages!"*
> *"No, I haven't."*
> *"Yes, you have! I never told you that her stepfather left! Omigod! How could you?"*

Clearly Tori feels as if her privacy has been violated, and it has.
So should you secretly snoop on your teenage child?
One frequent response from parents is:
"Yes, of course I should do it secretly. If they know I'm going to do it, won't they keep it all better hidden?"
The answer is: probably. The obvious argument for secret snooping is that you might discover something serious that you would not have known about otherwise. Maybe they are having sex with much older

partners. Maybe they are selling drugs. Maybe they are thinking about suicide.

Because these would be serious discoveries, many parents wonder if covert sneakiness actually provides benefits beyond other risk-prevention steps. They often ask: *"Do the benefits outweigh the negative aspects of going behind my child's back?"*

My answer to that is simple: secret snooping has a definite downside. It is dishonest. And if your child finds out—which they often do—they will very likely feel betrayed.

> *"I can't believe it! My mom lies to me! The one person I'm sup-posed to be able to trust! She can't do that!"*
> *"But you sneak around and lie to your mother all the time."*
> *"Yeah, but that's different! That's what kids do! When you're an adult, you're supposed to be honest. Especially to your kids. How will I ever learn to be honest if my mother lies to me?"*

The biggest challenge with secret snooping, as you can see, is this dishonesty factor. It says that, in the adult world, being dishonest is okay, provided you have a good enough reason to be. No question about it, parental snooping does send the message that dealing with others honestly and openly is not such a high priority. And that is not a good message to send to your child.

So where do I stand on the subject? I don't like secret snooping. Ultimately, snooping is one of those "do-the-ends-justify-the-means?" deals. If I could be convinced that sneaky snooping was a significantly useful instrument in a parent's arsenal for protecting children from significant harm, then I might go along, reluctantly. But I don't think it is.

GUIDELINES FOR TEENS

I have just been talking about parents trying to oversee their teens' interactions in the electronic world by keeping track of what their child is doing. But you can play another role regarding your teens' connection to the electronic world, which is to be proactive. You can give your teenage child a set of guidelines—safe and fair rules—that they will be expected to comply with. And you can also turn yourself into a resource for your teen when problems arise.

You can say these rules aloud or you can write them down. It doesn't matter. But either way, it's information that you will want to repeat, and that you should regularly repeat. Maybe your teen gets it, maybe he doesn't, but you will want your child to hear or see these rules continually. Here, also, the Internet is a good resource. You can start by looking up "Internet safety for teens." Let me suggest a possible set of rules for you to share with your teen:

Predators

This issue seems to crystallize parents' greatest fears about the dangers of the Internet. It is the most prominent concern in their minds—and certainly one that has gotten much publicity.

It is here that you want to give a simple, unequivocal warning:

"Under no circumstances should you meet in person with someone you met online. Under no circumstances should you give out—other than to people whom you already know—any information about yourself that would allow someone to identify who you are or where you live. Do not give them your phone number, your address, the school that you go to, or any other information they could use if they wanted to find you.

"There are people out there on the Internet who are not who they say they are, and who could harm you. Unless you know the person you are giving such information to, do not give out any personal information about yourself."

It is a warning that you want to reiterate again and again. Your teenager may never have any contact with a predator over the Internet. But those predators are out there. And trust is not something you want your teen to rely on when they are communicating with others on the Internet. As I said, the warning needs to be simple and unequivocal—and repeated often.

Privacy

The issue of Internet and cell phone privacy is a big and ongoing one. For starters, teens (especially younger teens) do not adequately understand how anything that they communicate can end up *not* being private. Even people whom they absolutely trust to keep information and images discreet cannot always be trusted. You've heard this lament all too often before:

"Ivan and I broke up on not very good terms and he sent around a very humiliating picture of me and him that I never dreamed anyone else would see."

Any entry—whether comprised of words or pictures—made or sent via electronic media can become part of a permanent record that can be used in ways that one would not want.

"I said I liked a whole bunch of movies, and it turned out my social network gave that information to different companies who started sending me all kinds of spam designed for people who supposedly, if they liked those movies, would like these products. Really, it's like people can get to know anything about me. Nothing's private."

The younger teens are, the less careful they tend to be about privacy and the less motivated they are to do anything about it, not that they know what to do about it anyway. As teens get older, and as they get increasingly Internet- and phone-savvy, the more aware of privacy issues they become. They are less trusting, far more skeptical, and better at (even more, interested in) employing privacy protections—not all of which are so easy to put in place retroactively. You simply cannot count on younger teens to adequately protect their own privacy.

Again, it is useful to go online and search "Internet safety for teens" to learn about specific steps that you or your teen can take to control online privacy.

Here are some basic rules and cautions to provide to your teen.

"Unless it is to someone you know, you shouldn't give out any identifying information about yourself or our family. (The same warning as offered above regarding predators.) You should use screen names that do not incorporate your own name or initials if you are in a chat room. And you shouldn't give out any passwords.

"Realize that whatever messages you write or pictures you post, they are not as private as you may think they are. You cannot count on the people receiving them to keep these things to themselves. Before you write anything or send any kind of picture, think about what it would be like if other people—people whom you wanted it to be kept private from—saw it."

You need to constantly remind your child that privacy cannot be counted on and that they must be careful to take whatever precautions they can. You do want privacy concerns to be a permanent part of their electronic media consciousness. A sad fact is that this new consciousness now needs to be part of *everyone's* awareness. A great deal of your online communications become permanent record. Any written words or images that you send over the phone or the Internet are now out there. And those communications do have the capacity to come back and haunt you. Teens need to know this.

Dangerous Secrets

It is not unusual for teenagers—through contact with friends—to become party to information that involves potential serious harm to another. More often than not such information comes with the expectation of complete secrecy. But for teens to feel bound by this secrecy is a mistake. Where there is the possibility of someone doing real harm to themselves or others, a teen's keeping it secret can end in tragedy. Teens often mistake an oath of silence as having moral precedence over revealing the possibility of serious danger. They are wrong.

For the above reasons, you need to instruct your teen to tell you about any of the following occurrences. Emphasize that not doing so potentially puts themselves or others at risk of getting hurt.

Tell them not to keep any of the following scenarios secret:

"If someone is threatening to harm or even kill themselves, tell me. You may have pledged secrecy, but kids do follow through on these threats, and many who harm or even kill themselves have told friends beforehand, but unfortunately their confidences were kept secret. If adults know about these plans and are able to intervene, it could prevent serious injury or even save a life.

"If you hear that some kid plans to seriously harm somebody else, the same thing applies. Keeping it a secret increases the chance that it will happen. Letting adults know about it makes a big difference in putting a stop to it.

"Tell me if you get any kind of message that worries you or scares you in any way.

"I can help with all of these things. You should not keep them secret from me. Telling me absolutely reduces the chance that something bad will happen."

Cyberbullying

Cyberbullying is the sending of messages or images that threaten or humiliate another child. Kids do it out of pure maliciousness, but they also do it thinking that it is funny and not understanding how it may affect the recipient. Either way, a lot of it goes on.

A problem with all of the nasty, embarrassing things that kids communicate to one another over the Internet is that there is nothing guaranteeing it will not continue to happen. If kids are going to communicate with one another over the Internet and through texting, the only foolproof way of eliminating nasty communications is by eliminating Internet and cell phone use. For the vast majority of today's teenagers this is not going to happen. Which is to say that if you have a teenage child, it is highly likely that your child will, at different times during his or her adolescence, be on the wrong end of such communications. Furthermore, there is much that may go on that your teenage child simply will not tell you about. Either they think they can handle it, or they fear that your involvement will only make it worse. But they are wrong.

If they are truly overwhelmed, if they cannot deal with what has been going on, telling you will help provide significant protection for them. Often you can help by removing the source of the nastiness. This may mean contacting your child's school, contacting the parents of the message sender, or even contacting the law. Also, you can make suggestions to your child about what they themselves can do about it—for example, you can suggest that they delete messages from possible bullies without reading them, or that they report problems to their Internet service provider. Perhaps you can suggest ways to look at what's been happening so it is less disturbing to them. Here is an example of one dad helping his daughter put the nastiness in perspective:

When Elena got a mean posting from her classmate Jeannine, Elena's father said to his daughter:

> "All of your friends know that it's not true. So what Jeannine posted doesn't really change anything with all the kids you hang out with. They're not going to look at you any differently. All that will happen is that they'll feel bad for you because Jeannine was so mean. Really, nothing changes. And then everybody forgets about it."
> "You think?"
> "Yes. You'll see, tomorrow nobody is actually going to say anything except in support of you."
> "You think? You're not just saying it?"
> "Yes."

But let's say that the nastiness already happened and it created a situation that is tougher to deal with: an embarrassing picture sent out over the Internet accompanied by details that were unfortunately true and now everybody knows. The meanness has already gone out and had its effect. We can feel Elena's pain:

"Too many kids know what happened. They know what I did Saturday night. And now they're saying all this mean stuff. Kids I thought were my good friends. They've been saying stuff and they do look at me differently. I can tell."

This is one of those situations where you can't make it "all better." Yet you can still have a very powerful role in helping your child get through it. You can make a big difference by simply getting them to share the event with you. Then you can help them know that they are not alone with it. That you are there for them. That you are unequivocally on their side. And that you genuinely understand how it makes them feel.

The secret to getting past the really bad things that can happen in your kids' lives often has less to do with figuring out good resolutions and more to do with the inevitable passage of time. You do not want to invest too much effort in trying to resolve the problem. You simply want to be there for them. And the situation—just with the progression of time—will get better. Although this is not something you can convince them of.

"You'll see. In a week it will feel different. People will start to move on to other stuff. Gradually, you will feel different. You really will, even though you can't see it now."

"No, you're wrong! You don't understand! Everything has changed! Nothing will ever be the same!"

Although you may feel as if there is nothing you can say to comfort them, you can still potentially be very useful in helping them get past the moment—just by being there and being sympathetic.

All of this, however, is predicated on your child telling you about it. You can't help if you don't know. So what should you say to ensure that your kid will talk to you? What should you do to maximize the possibility that they will come to you? Here's a suggestion: every so often, just remind them.

"Because you're a teenager and are often online, you may end up on the wrong end of cyberbullying. If people say things to you or about you, or people post things that are embarrassing or hurtful to you, and if it's really upsetting to you, I really want you to tell me about it. Let me know. I can't promise that I can make it all better. But I do know that, even though it might not seem like it, if you share it with me it can help make it easier. It will help make it not hurt as much. It really will. If it's really upsetting, don't try to deal with it all on your own. It's too hard. Please tell me about

it. I promise you that you will not get in trouble for what you tell me. If it's upsetting, please tell me about it."

I strongly recommend including the part about their not getting into trouble for what they tell you. You have to decide if you are comfortable with that. But bear in mind that if this is not part of the deal, they will be much less likely to confide in you. Again, you can be significantly helpful to them in the face of cyberbullying, but you cannot help if they don't tell you about it.

Bullycide

The great fear regarding bullying, of course, is that whether it is done in person, texted, or over the Internet, it will ultimately become so painful that your teen may think about killing himself. An overwhelming fact about adolescence is that the adolescent mandate tells kids it is no longer acceptable to experience yourself as a dependent little kid. Ready or not, they must cut themselves off from what has previously been their number one source of support—namely, you. Now, in dealing with all of the pain that the world dishes out, they often feel very much alone—too much alone.

What am I supposed to do? I just can't continue to go out in the world and face what I'm supposed to face. It's too hard. I'm sorry, but I just can't deal with it.

The tragedy is that some kids cannot imagine how they can go out into the world and continue to exist being on the wrong end of such hate and scorn. They feel they are alone and do not see how they can continue into the future feeling as they do, being in their world and experiencing it as they have. They feel that their future is impossible. Yet there is a hopeful piece in all of this. If they can just feel attached at this time to others who they know are on their side, who do not see them at all as defective, who like them and support them—this can make a big difference. These others can be friends, but they can also be parents. This connection can go a very long way toward their not killing themselves. The problem, of course, is that they have to be willing to share their thoughts—their intense pain and their humiliation. This is why, despite how hard they may try to push you away or keep you out of their lives, it is always good to be there anyway.

"Hello. Is there anything bothering you?"

"No, and I can handle it if there were, which there isn't. And even if there was something bothering me you would be useless because you wouldn't understand. And I'm not planning to kill myself, if that's what you're worrying about, so please get out of my room."

"No. I think I'll stay a little more, just in case you may feel like talking. I'll just wait around a little. You and me."

"You just don't get it. Of all your stupid things that you do, this is the stupidest."

But it's not.

Which is why if there is bullying going on, you definitely want to hear about it. Maybe you can be helpful, and maybe not. Maybe you can understand what it's like, or maybe you can't. But you are there working on it *with them*. They are not alone with it. Which is a very big deal.

It is hard to know whether more teenagers kill themselves these days due to being bullied than they did in the past—though it is true that you hear about these instances more often. Either way, the problem of teenagers killing themselves because they have been the victim of bullying, or because they fear the bullying, is very real. There will always be bullies and meanness. That is not going away anytime soon.

Teens as Perpetrators

It's difficult for many parents to acknowledge this, but the truth is that your kids are not always just the victims. Your teenage child may at times do the very things you absolutely do not want them to do. It's a good idea to tell your teen exactly what he may not do when using electronic media. It's possible that he'll do some of these things anyway, but telling him what the rules are does make a difference. I offer the following rules as a suggestion, but you should use your own discretion when deciding which rules you think are important for your teen to hear.

"You may absolutely not threaten any kind of harm to anyone else.

"You may not say anything that would be hurtful to, or about, someone else. You may not spread rumors about somebody. You may not talk about others in a way that would embarrass them. You may not show pictures or videos that would embarrass them either. It is wrong. It is cruel. It is as bad *as if the same thing happened to you. Also, you can get into serious trouble if you do any of these things.*

"You may not send or receive any messages that would involve your getting any kinds of drugs or alcohol for yourself or for someone else. Also, if you do, you could get into serious trouble.

"You may not send or receive any pictures of yourself or of anybody else that are of a sexual nature. This includes any pictures of naked body parts. You cannot assume that they will be kept private. Also, you can get into trouble for sending or receiving them. In many states it is a crime to send or receive underage sexual images, and since you and your friends are all underage, sexual pictures that you might send to each other are considered child pornography. In many states that is against the law.

"You may not send or receive messages that describe sexual behavior. The main reason here is the same as with pictures and videos: you cannot be sure that they will be private." (It is less clear whether sending these messages is against the law. However, since they and their friends are underage, sexual communications may be categorized as child pornography as well.)

Last, regarding an issue that applies more to teenage guys than girls, a guy should never send sexually tinged messages, even if he believes the message to be inoffensive, or even if the message is intended as friendly teasing or is extended in a way he perceives to be a nice way. For example:

"You've got nice tits."

Even though he may know other guys who sent similar messages and it seemed to be fine for them, there is always the possibility that the girl who receives this message may not find it the least bit friendly or amusing, and in fact may report it to an adult, which can lead to charges of sexual harassment against the guy who sent the message. You want to expressly warn boys:

"If you send what you think is a friendly message to a girl, but it includes what could be considered sexual content, there is a risk. You may think that it is harmless. That you are only joking. That you are being friendly. You may know other kids who have done the same thing and it wasn't a problem. But you cannot count on the girl's seeing it that way. She may not like it at all. And if she reports it to an adult, you could get into serious trouble for sexual harassment."

Sexting

A more specific problem that is not going to go away anytime soon also involves "sexting"—the back-and-forth sending of frankly sexual material among teenagers. One of the greatest challenges with current technology is that it allows for the very easy, instantaneous sending of any messages and images that one feels like sharing at that moment. These words and images can be sent to someone's cell phone—or over the Internet so that anybody can see them. The impulsive and immediate nature of the medium does not encourage kids to think first before acting.

To complicate matters even more, just about anyone can now take out an electronic device and snap pictures or capture brief videos of whatever they choose to point their lens at.

> *"Cool, I just took a picture of my school desk. Cool, I just took a picture of the ceiling."*
> You can take a picture or video of another person or persons.
> *"Cool, I just took a picture of Melissa."*
> You can take a picture of yourself.
> *"Cool, I just took a picture of me making a silly face."*
> *"Cool, I just took a picture of my stomach."*
> In an instant you can send the pictures to anyone you want.
> *"Cool, I just sent all these pictures to Sondra."*

Besides visual images, you can send word messages via your device. All you have to do is type in text, and then those words are sent or posted for others to see. These words can include any obscene expression or a description of any of a range of sexual acts that you can think of. And all you have to do to communicate these messages to another person is hit the send button.

"Cool, I just sent a private message to this girl I'm friends with where I used a lot of obscene words and described two cool sex acts. Really cool."

Whether we like it or not, teens are sexual beings. Teens have always been sexual beings. But now the technology makes it very easy, *extremely* easy, to communicate words and images of a frankly sexual nature to anyone, anywhere, anytime. It is a problem that is pervasive and persistent. The best that parents can do is to try to monitor what goes on and warn their teenage children about the inherent risks of sending such messages themselves. But advanced communications technology combined with inherent teenage sexuality makes for what is always going to be a certain amount of trouble. Here again, as elsewhere advised in this book, communicate your concern to your child so they hear the message. You never know if the echo of those words will keep them from making an impulsive mistake that can have long-term effects.

ACCESS TO THE WORLD

So far, in discussing teens and the world of electronics, I have mainly been talking about what they do—addressing whether it is a problem or not, and what you can do about it. But separate from the issue of content is the subject of just how much waking time our kids are spending connected to the electronic world. It is more than integral to their life—it has become part of the very fabric of their lives.

Teenagers today can gain access to a vast quantity of information in ways that did not exist even in the relatively recent past. Very quickly, they can learn about:

The prices of different headsets

Specific Civil War battles

A rock star's current activities

The newest look in fashionable jeans

Answers to very specific questions, for example:

Question: What are the names of the members of the 1970s rock band KISS?

Swift Answer: Paul Stanley, Ace Frehley, Gene Simmons, Peter Criss

Question: Who was the king of France in 1748?

Swift Answer: Louis XV

Kids today are a different kind of creature than they were in the past. It's as if their brains extend outside their bodies and are linked to a giant sea of information via millions of tiny invisible wires. Without going anywhere, just by giving instructions to a small machine, even a very small machine, they can call up this vast reservoir of information. It is what their brains do naturally now—giving themselves constant instructions to pull up specific information—but the data collection process goes on outside of their bodies rather than inside their heads. They can know a lot of stuff—quickly. The bottom line about easier access to all this information is that, if knowing more is good, then this is very good.

"Yeah, my dad thinks he knows everything. But, actually, everything that he knows I could know if I wanted to, but most of it is stupid shit, so why would I want to know it? But I could know it all if I wanted."

The interesting thing about kids gaining such easy access to all this information is that the world of their future requires that they be fluent in these skills. Their current extensive involvement in this electronic world means that they are acquiring this fluency almost by osmosis. Reading, writing, and arithmetic were once the three basics of learning. Now there is a fourth: technological fluency—knowing how to use these devices, and also knowing how to navigate and mine their content.

Also, in case you hadn't noticed, virtually all kids know how to type out messages, swiftly—with their thumbs and on teeny tiny keys no less!

MULTITASKING

Not only are teens better at getting information than the rest of us, they also seem able to receive and react to a great variety of information all at the same time. Their multitasking abilities are legendary!

"Yeah, it's cool. I can watch a video, text a friend, go over my football picks for this coming weekend, and yell at my mother to get off my back about taking out the trash—all at the same time."

Multitasking is not new, of course. People have always juggled busy lives. Preparing supper while talking on the phone to a friend and also watching one-year-old Herman crawl around the kitchen. It is just that now, however, with the expansion of the electronic world, today's teenagers have developed the capacity to multitask well beyond what we were able to do before. Very well beyond. Again, this is not a bad thing. It is good. Multitasking is definitely a useful skill.

But there is a criticism of today's multitaskers. Although they may be better able to deal with an increased amount, variety, and speed of incoming stimuli, they may now actually *require* that intense level of stimuli. They actually seem to need more and more diverse and fast-paced information and activity to keep themselves occupied and entertained. It's as if they have much less tolerance for a slower, one-track world.

This account of Dwayne trying to watch an ancient rerun of *The Jimmy Desmond Show* says it all.

> "*It's* The Jimmy Desmond Show *with your host, Jimmy Desmond*" (audience applause).
> "*Hey, everybody.*"
> "*Hey, Jimmy,*" responds the audience.
> "*Do we have a great show for you today, or what? The Curdie Brothers with their talking dog Frances and, straight from Mongolia, the Mongolian Fire Dancers—you're in for a treat with them! And, for you kids, Slappy Lappy and his clown cousins and, this is really going to be great—*"
> "*Jesus,*" says Dwayne as he switches to another program. "*Is he going to announce the whole show? I tried, but I just can't watch it.*"
> Dwayne had been fidgeting wildly almost as soon as the show began. "*Maybe the Mongolian Fire Dancers would have been cool, but I'm never going to find out. There's no way I can wait.*"

It is said that we have created a world of short-attention-spanned teenagers—an ADHD (Attention-Deficit/Hyperactivity Disorder) generation. That they have grown accustomed to a constant barrage of images, words, thoughts, and concepts, which has made them less tolerant of anything that is not as fast-moving. That they do not have the same degree of patience as those before them.

This may be true—at least to some extent. Teens today may have less patience for "nothing." For "dead time." Less patience for that which moves slowly. There's no question that they read less—that is to say they read fewer books and magazines. And maybe, just maybe, they have less patience for work—which would be a problem for a productive society. To see the impact of this trend better, let's look at some of the differences between boys and girls.

GUYS, GIRLS, AND VIDEO GAMES

A very noticeable trend in the United States during the last twenty years or so has been the shift in who is attending college. It used to be that significantly more guys went to college than girls. But now the trend has reversed. One possible reason for this shift may be that women increasingly see the need to be self-supporting and to get good jobs in order to have a fuller and more secure adult life. But there is another possible reason.

Guys—at least as kids—tend to be more hyper, antsy, and less patient than girls are. I have already mentioned the statistic, which has held up over the years, that four to five times as many guys as girls are diagnosed with ADHD, and before the existence of that diagnosis, as having hyperactivity disorder in childhood. If you're a guy, you somehow have to overcome being antsy and force yourself to patiently do schoolwork so you can excel enough to go on to college. But what if there were something that actually interfered with a guy's ability to exert that patience? Might that be a problem?

Let me talk about one specific electronic medium that has impacted the lives of boys in recent decades: video games.

It really is pretty obvious that when it comes to video games, guys as a group are profoundly different from girls. Video games are definitely a guy's medium. Teenage girls also play video games, but for whatever reason, this genre of game playing simply has not captivated girls to the extent that it has guys. Not only are video games extremely entertaining but their game design also naturally appeals to guys, so you can easily see why they are so compelling. Which they are.

The people who make video games do a very good job. The best video games can be years in the making. And they just seem to be getting better and better. The graphics are more realistic; the story lines more imaginative, complex, and sophisticated; and the game play—how you control the action—is ever more challenging, ever more clever. The video games marketed to guys are very good. Excellent, in fact. Very entertaining. Very absorbing. I'd even venture to say very, very absorbing.

Anyone with a teenage son knows how difficult it can be to get them to interrupt their video game playing even to come to supper.

> *"I will. I'm coming,"* they assure us over and over while we wait.

And how angry they can sometimes get.

"Listen, just leave me the fuck alone! I'll do my homework. Just get the fuck off my case! Get out of here. Leave me alone!"

I mean, they can get really mad.

So is playing video games addictive? If "addictive" means that this is something that has a powerful hold over them, leaving them with little control over it, then maybe the answer is yes.

"That is such bullshit! I'm not addicted to video games. I choose to play them because they are fun. If there was something else that was more fun, I would do that. I could stop playing if I wanted to, but I don't want to."

"But you do play a lot, don't you?"

"Yeah, so what? Your point is?"

"Do you think it affects your schoolwork?"

"No."

"But you have homework tonight that you need to be doing, don't you?"

"Yes, and I will."

"You don't sometimes fail to study when you should, or miss assignments, or more often than not rush through them?"

"You're getting really aggravating, you know."

"Just a couple more questions. What's the worst thing about school?"

"That's easy. The work."

"What's so bad about the work?"

"It's fucking boring."

"Last question."

"It better be."

"Do you think you'll want to go to college?"

"I don't know."

My only point is that something is causing the shift in the number of guys versus girls going to college. Could video games be a significant factor? It is certainly a thesis worth bearing in mind for the sake of the young guys in our lives.

PRODUCTIVE VS. NONPRODUCTIVE TIME

I would like for you to imagine something along with me for a moment. It is the year 2071. Fifteen-year-old Bradley is in his room. He is always in his room, as all that exists of him is his head. Like all of his friends, at age thirteen he has had cyber-head-transplant surgery, whereby his brain has been directly hooked up to the Internet without the need for intermediary devices.

They probably won't really have head transplants by 2071—but we sort of already have the equivalent. Kids' brains don't have to be wired up to a central computer—they can now carry the means to be connected at all times with them everywhere. And their little mobile devices even come in cool little cases, in personalized colors and designs.

"Do you want to hear my ring tones?"

So is all that time that they spend connected to the electronic world—just the time itself, the large proportion of their waking hours—bad for them? Are they somehow missing out on having a richer, fuller, more productive life? Let me pose a few other questions that might help answer this larger one: If they weren't linked into those devices, what would they be doing instead? What did teenagers used to do before the world of electronics was so accessible and pervasive? Was what they used to do really so much better?

When I was a teenager, we didn't have the Internet or video games. What did I do to pass the time? I'm not saying I was typical. But here's what I enjoyed.

I played outside, mainly by myself, at whichever sport was in season—baseball, basketball, football—even in bad weather. I watched TV; I went through periods of watching a lot, or watching very little. I didn't talk much on the phone with friends. But when I turned sixteen I got a driver's license, had access to a car, and spent a great deal of time over at different friends' houses, hanging out. I rarely read—occasionally I picked up science fiction stories. I often looked through the world almanac at sports statistics. I listened to music a lot—on the radio and on a 45 rpm record player. I had minimal contact with either of my two sisters (once we got to be teenagers, we seemed to have stopped our incessant fighting), or with my really quite nice parents—my choice.

Was what I did—what kids used to do in the days before the Internet or cell phones—any better than what they do now? I don't know.

Does being connected to the electronic world so much of the time take away from physical activity? Yes. Does it take away from family time? Yes—to some degree. But it's not as if teenagers were dying to hang out with their parents before the Internet entered the picture either. I certainly wasn't, and like I said, I had nice parents.

"This family time has already gone over three minutes. Can I leave now? Please."

Does their constant connection to the electronic world intrude, at least somewhat, on a teenager's willingness to participate in after-school activities or maybe to go over to friends' houses, because they can't wait to get home to resume their online or video game activity? Probably. But they still do like to go over to friends' houses.

One criticism is that so much time on the Internet eliminates the possibility of developing skills and interests that require a lot of consecutive time. Getting good at playing a musical instrument. Getting good at a sport. Learning how to fix a car. Developing skill at carpentry. Working on a creative science project—though any science project today would almost certainly utilize the Internet. Probably, at least to some extent, this is true.

Another criticism of being so constantly hooked up is that kids become less skilled at knowing how to entertain themselves, knowing how to fill their time without having to rely on outside resources. This, almost certainly, is true. Of course, kids would argue,

"Yeah, but why do I have to know how to find stuff to do that isn't on the Internet or playing a video game? The Internet has so much more stuff on it—and not all of it is stupid. You can really find out a lot of stuff about a lot of stuff if you know how to find it, which of course I—or any kid my age—can. They say I should read a book. Did they read a book? Besides, I read stuff on the Internet, like about how escaped Burmese pythons—that get close to twenty feet long—are now showing up in many parts of Florida, and are becoming a problem. How is that worse than reading Harry Potter books, which I actually did when I was a kid?"

The above, I think, is a valid counterargument. The bottom line is about the quality of time. Many kids challenge us to show examples of how being hooked up to the digital world so much of their waking time is any less productive, less fulfilling, less meaningful, or less contributing to a richer life than what teenagers did before the current electronic explosion. I think it is helpful for each of us to think back to the activities of our own childhoods and ask: Is whatever our own kids are doing instead, as they move back and forth within the electronic universe, somehow less good for them? If you really are concerned about it, maybe you can think of and direct them to Internet activities or websites that you believe would be of interest to them and that may contain a little more intellectually broadening substance. What do you find interesting? Yet the question remains: Are today's teens learning true skills—skills relevant to a richer and more productive life?

"I have a skill: I can do Dragon Buster III to the eleventh level. Trust me, you have to be really good. It is a real skill that takes lots of practice to get to the eleventh level of Dragon Buster III."

On another more serious level, today's teenagers are learning the skills necessary to succeed—and in some cases, just survive—in their universe. They're learning how to communicate with others in the language of the world they will inhabit. They're learning how to find information. Most kids are better at navigating this world and maximizing its resources than we are. Will what they do now, with whatever skills they acquire as they chart these new frontiers, be less productive, less enriching, less useful in the future world—the world where they are going to live *their* adult life? I honestly don't think that it is possible to answer that question yet.

STAYING CONNECTED

One profound way that teenagers' lives have been affected by their connection to the electronic world is through their connection with others.

Besides connecting teenagers to the universe of information, the world of electronics connects them to a universe of people. And not just any people: it connects them to the people who make up their daily world and network of friends—their peers. In addition to connecting them with other kids, the electronic world also connects them with events involving people they are close to or interested in. People they like. People they don't like. People they think are noteworthy— like the very popular junior basketball player whom they don't know personally but whom everyone knows about. Or the girl in the grade before them who they heard was a great singer and now has videos of her performance posted on her Facebook page. It's where kids find out what went on today. Especially, who said what to whom. Unfolding story lines with many, many interwoven plots and characters can be found. This universe is richly textured. And every day, every evening, the drama unfolds further—sometimes with visuals—on a screen right in their own room, or via a phone right in their hand. These are real-time plot twists they're engaged in.

"There's this kid Eddie, and he really liked this cousin of Kay's, but she broke up with him and he was really upset. And Eddie started talking to Kay about it. But then Eddie and Kay sort of started liking each other, except that he is apparently into serious drugs—at least cocaine—and is a pretty tough kid. But now maybe Kay's cousin is back to liking Eddie."

"Today in school there was this almost fight between Danny and Cameron because Cameron called Danny a punk bitch at some party Saturday night where he had been drinking, and Maria, who is Danny's younger sister, has this wicked crush on Cameron."

"Gaby and Greg are maybe breaking up again like they always do. But today at lunch Greg was talking to Karina, and was like being consoled and Gaby got really pissed at Karina because she thought she was coming on to Greg which she wasn't, because I [Amanda] was there and I saw that it wasn't that way. But now Karina is really upset because you know how she is if she thinks anybody is mad at her. And I just got a text from Karina saying that Gaby wants to talk to her—on the phone—like Gaby is going to call her in five minutes, and I don't know what that's about."

It is a world of continuously fascinating stories. You can't miss out. You can't *not* be part of it. It is always out there happening at every moment, and maybe you are even directly connected to it, a player in the story, just through your electronic devices. Imagine what it would be like if you were not connected. Imagine if you didn't know what had happened when you met your friends tomorrow at lunch.

> *"I [Amanda] go in, and there's Gaby and Karina and Greg and they're sitting there looking at each other and making polite talk and I have no idea what is going on. I'm clueless. Unless somebody catches me up as to what went on.*
>
> *"Gaby says to Karina, 'Don't you like Greg's shirt?' Is she being serious? Is she being sarcastic? Did they work things out? I just don't understand anything.*
>
> *"That's why I can't not stay in touch all the time because if I don't, everything will pass me by. And, let me tell you, don't think*

for a minute that anybody is going to bother to catch me up. It doesn't work that way."

It's what's happening. And what's happening makes up the fabric of most teenagers' daily life. The way kids know and participate in what's happening is through their connection with the electronic universe.

But there is another aspect to the connection that is not about needing to always know what's going on. It is about the connection itself. Just being connected to another human, especially one with whom you are comfortable.

It is not at all unusual for a given teenager to send or receive five hundred text messages a day. Five hundred text messages? That's preposterous. What can they possibly be talking about?

Tricia texts her friend (not boyfriend) Eric:

> *"guess the number of my house on my street"*
> *"39?"*
> *"no, that's a stupid guess. much higher"*
> *"439?"*
> *"way better"*
> *"give me a hint"*
> *"the first number rhymes with LIVE"*
> *"give me more hints"*

Or the classic: James texts his friend Danny,

> *"what's going on?"*
> *"nothing. what's going on with you?"*
> *"nothing"*
> *"so why did you text me?"*
> *"i don't know. i just wanted to see if you were doing anything"*
> *"i don't know. are you doing anything?"*

It is simply about being connected at any given moment. Or if you are not at that moment connected, it's about having the immediate capacity to be connected to another person when you want to be. The beauty of both the Internet and cell phones is that they can eliminate—or at the very least keep to a minimum—the times when our kids feel that they are truly alone.

> *"Caroline, are you talking on your cell phone in the shower again?"*
> *"I'm talking to Jennifer. Do you have a problem with that?"*
> *"Yes, you already ruined two cell phones that way."*
> *"I'm holding it out of the shower spray. Okay? Please, I'm taking a shower."*

By carrying a cell phone on their person, or sitting in front of a computer screen, our kids, in effect, are running invisible lines from them to all the people in their life whom they care about, to whom they want to be connected. They are not alone.

Being alone is a very real psychological state. It is being completely separate from another human. And this psychological state of being alone is profoundly different—at any given moment—from that of being connected. When you are truly alone, you experience vulnerability in a way that you simply do not if you are not alone, if you are connected. What the constant presence of cell phones and potential Internet connection provides is a means of bypassing, during your waking hours, ever having to be alone.

This capacity to circumvent aloneness is good in the sense that connection to other humans is probably—more than anything else—the best thing that life has to offer. It is certainly not wrong or bad, when feeling alone and vulnerable, to want a connection to another person as a means of coping with those vulnerable feelings. But it is also possible that never having to be alone may create a lack of practice at, or even an intolerance for, ever being alone. Which is perhaps not so good. Maybe if aloneness, even for brief periods of time, becomes a little too scary for a child, their constant connectedness should be reconsidered.

> *"Hey, Jeannine, are you there?"*
> *"Yeah, what? This better not be one of these 'I just want to make sure I'm not alone' calls."*
> *"Well, actually it is. Thanks for being there."*
> *"Shit. Don't you dare call again within the next five minutes."*
> *"I promise I won't. Maybe."*

SETTING LIMITS

So if being connected to the electronic world all of the time presents such potential drawbacks, what would happen if we made our kids do it less? How about if we took away their connection to the electronic world? At least at times other than when they are doing legitimately school-related work? Not that you could ever make that differentiation. But let's say you could. What would happen then? Let's take a look at that scenario:

> *"Okay, Viv. No Internet. No cell phones. No video games. You can call friends, but only to make plans. And you can have an hour of TV a day. No more."*
>
> Let's see what happens.
>
> *"What is it, Doctor? Her mother and I are so concerned. She doesn't eat, and all she does is make these sighing noises and stare at her blank computer screen."*
>
> *"I'm afraid she's lost the will to live."*
>
> *"Oh, dear! Does this mean we have to give her back the Internet and her cell phone?"*
>
> *"I'm afraid so."*

Well, it was worth a try.

> *"Come to supper."*
>
> *"I can't."*
>
> *"What do you mean, you can't?"*
>
> *"I'm in the middle of something."*
>
> *"You're always in the middle of something."*
>
> *"Yeah, well, I'm in the middle of something."*
>
> *"You can't always be in the middle of something. I want you at supper."*
>
> *"I told you. I'm in the middle of something."*

So what can you do to achieve a happy medium? Especially when you want to talk to them? When you want them to clean out the tub in their bathroom, which they were supposed to have done two days ago? When you want them to come to a meal?

"Jesus, I can't believe you! I said I was in the middle of something! I'm not lying! I'm in the middle of something!"

What often works best is setting a rule that states: if you do not detach yourself from your computer, cell phone, or other electronic device upon my reasonable request, I will temporarily suspend the use of those devices for a full day. In effect, they *can* use the Internet, their cell phone, etc. It is just that they have to do it while following your rules. These rules, by the way, can include periods of time where you simply want them electronics-free—just because that's what you want. This is an effective response you can use with those teens who tend to ignore requests to unhook themselves to do what is being asked of them. If you insist, if you do not back off, and if you do follow through with your rules, kids see that you are serious. Also, because they know in their hearts that what you are asking of them is not unreasonable, more often than not they will comply. They most likely will not do it immediately. They will also probably do it begrudgingly. But far more often than not, they will abide by the general rule.

This, of course, is no different from the way it is with virtually all teenage compliance issues. You need to persist, and then, having persisted, you won't exactly win. But you won't exactly totally lose either.

> *"You didn't have to hound me so much. I said I would come to supper."*
> *"No, you didn't."*
> *"Well, here I am. I don't get what the big deal was. I told you I was in the middle of something and now I'm not in the middle of it anymore, so I can come to supper. You didn't have to keep after me like you did. I was going to come."*

Actually, she wasn't.

Teenagers and the electronic world. Where is it all going? What does it mean? What can you do about it?

Given how far we've come electronically already, it is hard to imagine that teenage kids will ever have even smoother, swifter access to others and to information than they already have. But they will. They'll be more dependent upon the electronic world than they are now. Their dealings with the world in which they live will be less directly between them and that world. Instead, through the intermediary great electronic mind that knows so much, they will be hooked up to so many more specific places and people than they could have been otherwise.

They almost certainly will have less capacity to function as a lone unit out in the world. But they may not need to. They will not necessarily know more—that is, have more information stored in their brains—but they will have quick access to more information, enough to know more at the moment when it is immediately useful to them. As I said, it will be their world.

What should you do? As a parent you won't exactly be able to control all that goes on between them and the electronic world. It simply cannot be done. But you will be part of that world too. Maybe one step behind, but that can't be helped. Your role as an incredibly important person in their lives will still continue. You cannot so much change their relationship with the electronic world. But you, as has been true all along, can continue to be a huge part of who they are and who they become. That does not change.

Fourteen

THE END OF ADOLESCENCE

Earlier we talked about how much more adoring our toddlers and tweens were before they ever became independence-seeking teens. You remember Samantha, at eight:

> *"Hi, Mommy. Look what I have for you."*
>
> Samantha hands her mother yet another note—the eleventh so far today—that says I LOVE YOU, MOMMY and has pictures of hearts and smiley faces all over it.
>
> *"I'm going to work on one with a rainbow. Would you like to see that when I'm finished with it? Won't that be nice, Mommy?"*

This, of course, is Samantha at fifteen:

> *"Hi, Samantha."*
> *"For Chrissake! I just got home."*
> *"I only said 'hello.'"*
> *"Mom, please. I've already had enough. I really don't need you being at me all the time. I really don't."*
> *"But I just said 'hello.'"*
> *"For Chrissake, Mom. Would you please not talk to me. For once."*

What did I do? I just said "hello," Samantha's mother thinks as her daughter storms past her and out of the room.

And now, looking ahead, here's Samantha just one week shy of her eighteenth birthday.

"Mom, you know those taco things that you make with the cut-up vegetables and the cheese? Could we have them sometime soon? They're really good."
"The taco things with the cut-up vegetables and the cheese?"
"Yeah, you make them really good."
"I make them really good?"
"Yeah, that's one of the best things that you make."
"That's one of the best things that I make?"
"Mom, are you okay? You're acting kind of weird."
Sobbing, Samantha's mother rushes to throw her arms around her beloved daughter, who seems to have stepped out of a time machine.
"My darling. You're back. You're back."
"Mom, you're really weird."

THE RETURN OF THE PRODIGAL CHILD

I have said it before, but it bears repeating for all of you in the thick of your child's teen years: adolescence ultimately ends. And when it does, it can seem very much like a miracle.

The allergy to parents—which is so often a part of that stage and prompts them to say such things as *"Why are you standing so close to me? Do you know how irritating that is?"*—is finally over. Finito.

Remember that the allergy happens in the first place because with the dawning of adolescence, it is no longer acceptable for teenagers to experience themselves as dependent little kids. And because they still have strong love-attachment dependency feelings toward you, just being around you makes them feel like a dependent little kid. That was okay when they were younger. They *were* a dependent little kid then. But once they are an adolescent, that is no longer the case. Unfortunately for you, when they are adolescents, your physical presence alone makes them have uncomfortable feelings.

"Must you?"
"What?"
"Be in the room."
But I haven't done anything to deserve this.

Yes, you have. You've gotten them to feel loved and protected by you. And to them, during their adolescence, that's a crime.

Adolescence forces them to turn away from the very source that has been their major supplier of well-being. Not out of rebellion, but from what they feel to be a necessity. When teens cut themselves off from their primary source of support during this time, what they are left with is just themselves and whatever other support they have gotten from the world out there separate from home and family. They become far more vulnerable. They now have to cope on their own with all the insecurities and stresses that come with adolescence. Once your child becomes a teenager—as part of their normal psychological development—they pull away.

But gradually, precisely because they have turned away, they change again. Having forced themselves to become more emotionally independent, they actually do become more emotionally independent. They begin to experience the success of surviving on their own. And the bonds with you become less than what they once were. They need you less because they have made themselves need you less. But then a funny thing happens. Being with you, interacting with you, no longer makes them feel like a dependent little kid anymore. This is true because they really aren't a dependent little kid anymore. By the end of adolescence, the strong love-attachment dependency feelings become far less of an issue for kids than what they were. They have become more emotionally independent beings. The emotional maturation work of adolescence has been completed. They can now tolerate you. Even like you.

Adolescence is real. It massively affects what goes on between you and your teenage child. But it passes.

And, because they still love you, they can now allow themselves to feel the love. To express it.

"You've been a great mom. I can't believe all the stuff that you put up with."
But the love is different from before. Not quite the same. Not the total adoration you once felt long ago.

The End of Adolescence | 343

"You sure you don't feel like making me a note or something, with maybe some illustrations. A couple of hearts, you know, maybe a smiley face? You don't feel like that a little?"

"What are you talking about?"

"Nothing. Really. Nothing."

SEEING YOU FOR WHO YOU REALLY ARE

As I said, the end of adolescence brings about a very big change. It is as though a veil has been lifted from your kid's eyes, and suddenly they see you as you are.

"You know, it's weird, but I gotta admit, you actually have been a really good mother."

"What?"

"Yeah, I mean there's stuff about you that still drives me crazy, but I was thinking how you really are a very good person. I've been lucky to have you as a mom."

"What?"

"Yeah, you've really dealt with a lot from me. And it's not just that. The way you talk to other people. I can see how you're really respectful, even with people who maybe you don't actually like. I really admire that. I hope I can be somebody like you as an adult."

"What?"

"You're doing it again. You're doing that parrot thing again. Why do you keep saying 'what'?"

"Oh, sorry. I guess I'm still not used to it."

What is going on is that they are no longer seeing you through adolescent eyes. During the throes of their adolescence, most children don't actually see their parents—they only see the role they are projecting onto you, and they seem unable to get past that role.

"Hello, I'm a person."

"No, you're not. You're my mom."

Their adolescence creates an image of you as this human being that they have to push away. Their adolescence creates a persona for you that is not so much born from the real you at all, but from their adolescent allergy. Hence the version of you whom they create:

"Mom: She is always critical. I can't do anything without her noticing. She gives me no privacy. All she wants to do is to snoop into my business. And all she likes to do—seriously—is give me orders. Also, she is completely phony. All you have to do is listen to the way she talks, and it's like it's all fake. I don't even think she really likes me. She does this good mother act for other people, and then when it's just us, she's her real self—witch woman. Oh, also she's a crazy person. Did I mention that?"

Or,

"Dad: Nothing is good enough for him. Even if I try he's always disappointed. He's not really interested in anything I say. All he wants to do is give me lectures. He's never wrong. But more than anything, he's incredibly stupid about everything. And not only does he not get it, but he thinks he's right about everything. I think he does a lot of his stupid stuff just to aggravate me on purpose. He's actually impossible to be around."

Some of these characterizations might seem familiar, even though each teen sees his or her particular parent somewhat differently. But the general personality profile most kids have of their parents is pretty similar from home to home and parent to parent. Adolescents usually think their parents are too much in their business. Critical. Phony. Stupid.

"Well, they are."

But then, with the end of adolescence, when the mask that they have projected onto you is lifted, *voilà*—there you are!

They will still see your flaws, but somehow those flaws are not so irritating. And they'll see your strengths too. Even admirable strengths.

"I mean, as you know, my mom is a total neat freak—she actually won OCD person of the year. But now, rather than it driving me crazy, I think it's sort of funny, cute even."

"Dad is really opinionated. But actually, even with me, I see how he gives his opinions, but also he really listens to what other people say. He may have strong opinions, but he gives a lot of respect."

"What Mom said to me about my friend Cynthia was really smart and helpful to me. She said that when Cynthia acts rude, and I get real hurt and offended, it's because Cynthia is actually kind of socially awkward, that a lot of stuff Cynthia says comes out rude, but she doesn't mean it

that way at all. And when I think about it, I think Mom's right. She's very sharp, Mom is."

"There was this time that Dad was picking me up from this meeting after school. But he had to sit in the car for a whole extra hour waiting for me because I made a mistake and I didn't understand that the meeting was going to be way longer than I thought. And he didn't get mad the way I've seen other kids' parents do. It wasn't like he got all blaming at me. I hope I can be like him, not always blaming everybody when something goes wrong. He's really pretty cool about that."

Also miraculously (I say "miraculously" because it is so unthinkable that they would ever say it), they see all that went on in the past and conclude that maybe, just maybe, they were not a complete victim of "abusive" parents after all.

"Remember that time I was mad—I don't actually remember what I was so mad about. But you locked yourself in your room and I kept pounding on the door, screaming, "Fuck you." I guess I did get a little out of line sometimes. Maybe it wasn't just you who was being a bitch."

THE NEW DEAL

But that's not the only way that kids change after adolescence. Listen in on just a few more exchanges:

> *"Desmond, would you please not leave your dirty dishes sitting around the house. I need you to wash them and put them away. Would you please clean them up now."*
> *"I'm busy right now, but I will, later."*
> *"No, Desmond, I need you to clean them up now."*
> *"Mom, you don't get it. I'm not your little kid who you can boss around anymore."*
> *"What are you talking about?"*
> *"Just what I said. I'm not your little kid who you can boss around anymore. In case you didn't notice, I'm not a kid. I'm an adult. A young adult."*

The other big deal that happens with the end of adolescence is that kids now see themselves officially as young adults. They actually declare their young adulthood. Often they do this prior to the end of their high school careers. Maybe well before you are even ready to officially give them that status.

> *"If I'm old enough to go into the service and die for my country, I'm certainly old enough to not have to get bossed around by my parents. I'm sorry, I love you and all, but you are no longer the boss of me."*
>
> *"But you're not eighteen yet. You haven't graduated high school. You still live in this house under our roof. You cannot just declare yourself an adult and think that we are going to abide by that."*
>
> *"Yeah, I can. And I just did."*

Even before they graduate. Even before they turn eighteen, they see themselves as having arrived at full adult status.

> *"Well, I know I'm still a high school student—at least until May twenty-eighth—that's the day of my last high school class ever. But I'm in the last marking period of my senior year. I'm certainly more of an adult at this point than I am a kid. Maybe you don't agree. But that's tough. I feel that now I am officially an adult. I've been through a lot of stuff, most of which you don't know anything about. I'm not a kid. I'm an adult. I just am. And I'm sorry if you think you can still boss me around. But that day has passed forever."*
>
> *"Now you wait a minute, mister. You still live in this house. You are still dependent on us for money. You are still our child."*
>
> *"You know what? It doesn't matter what you think. You're right. I'm still your son. I do live here. I don't have the money to support myself. But that's not my fault. You can kick me out if you want. But I have no place to go. And I'm not doing anything wrong. It is just that I'm not a little kid anymore. From now on I am going to be the person who decides what I'm going to do. You can't boss me around."*

It is not an argument that you win. Besides, they are right. The world and the culture they live in sees the end of high school as the shift from childhood to adulthood. It is just that many of them jump the gun a bit. But the reality is that by the end of high school, if not before, the whole deal changes. It just does.

Actually, it is time for an adjustment. And whether it happens before the end of high school, or once their class graduates (even without them, in some cases), the new deal now needs to be considered. It will happen soon enough anyway. Ready or not, it *is* time for a new deal around the house.

For one, you can't boss them around anymore. You do need to give them the respect of adult status, even if they continue to act like a jerky little kid. It definitely works better that way. One of the first things to change is the language:

> *"Desmond, would you please not leave your dirty dishes sitting around the house. I would really appreciate it if you would wash them and put them away. I would appreciate it if you would do it now."*
> *"I'm busy right now, but I will, later."*
> *"I really would appreciate it if you would do it now."*
> *"No, I'm busy. I will do it later."*

At that point, parents need to back off.

It's the way of the new deal. It's less bossy. Less confrontational. And with most newly adult teens, it works. Not as well as you might like, but they are far more likely to comply when they are not being ordered about. They do hear the respect for their adult status in your language. And it does have a positive influence. Also, it avoids potentially angry confrontations that you would not win otherwise.

All of this is part of a bigger and more basic change. You are no longer relating as parent to child, even though they still and forever will be your child. You are now relating as parent to adult—an adult who happens to be your child. And what that means is that it is no longer a relationship so much defined by roles. It is now a relationship, in great part, defined as any other adult-to-adult relationship is defined—by how both parties treat each other. Which means that most importantly, in the relationship going forward, each must treat the other—at least most of the time—with consideration and caring.

IS MY KID GOING TO BE OKAY?

So how can you tell what's going to happen with your teenagers? Are they going to grow up okay? Will they be fit enough to go out into the world? Are they going to be nice? Is that even possible—especially given some of the pretty terrible things that have gone on between you and them over the course of their adolescence? It is a worry many parents have.

Fifteen-year-old Vanessa screams at her mother:

"I hate you. I hate you. I'm not just saying it, I really really hate you."
So we ask her mother,
"How do you think you're doing as a parent?"
"I guess not so great."
"How do you think Vanessa's going to come out as an adult?"
"I guess, not so great to that either. I mean look at her. You want to see some videos I made?"
"Sure."
Then Vanessa's mother proceeds to play a number of brief videos, each showing Vanessa in yet another horrible scene. Many of them with Vanessa's mother herself acting pretty horribly as well.
"Mom, that's not fair. You can't show those to a stranger. They're degrading of me."
"I mean, look at her. Look at me. The videos are pretty bad, huh?"
"Yes, I would have to agree. Vanessa and you look pretty horrible."
"Mom, this is so unfair."

In the midst of these kinds of tensions it is certainly hard to tell how a teen like Vanessa will fare—or even how her mother will do in the long run. I'm not sure the answers lie in a collection of videos representing the many unpleasant scenes that occurred between Vanessa and her mother during Vanessa's adolescence. Instead I prefer to look to a different indicator.

There are two questions I like to ask, the answers to which will help predict how Vanessa is going to come out as an adult, and what the nature of her adult relationship will be with her mother. Those questions are:

"Have you, over the course of your daughter's adolescence, and in fact over the course of her whole childhood, loved your daughter and regularly shown that love? And also, have you at times been willing to make decisions in Vanessa's life that you thought were right, but which you knew would displease Vanessa?"

I believe that the answer to those simple questions, far more than any instances of unpleasant parent and adolescent child interactions, predict the final outcome.

If indeed Vanessa's mother answers yes to both of those questions, then it is fair to predict that both Vanessa—and her adult relationship with her mother—will turn out well.

It really does work that way.

DIFFERENT YET THE SAME

It is indeed a very new world that today's teens inhabit, and this book has certainly addressed just how different it is from what prior generations experienced. But in the end, the underlying issues of adolescence are still pretty consistent. Teens are more the same than not, and so is being the parent of a teenager. You will have great difficulty getting them to do what they do not feel like doing. If you say "no" to anything, they will take it badly. If you have a female child there is going to be a fair amount of drama in her life, of which you will almost certainly bear much of the brunt. If you have a male child, there may be a fair amount of drama in his life as well, but you will not get to know about it—except for that time when the police show up at your door at two in the morning.

Your aims for them are the same too. You want to keep them safe, you want to best prepare them to go out into the world, and you want to have them still love you. How parents can best accomplish this has also not changed. You react day to day—supporting them, pushing them, trying to rein them in, and worrying about them.

The good news is that they will probably turn out just fine. What is also good news is that if you love them, they are going to love you back—just maybe not right at this moment. But they will in time.

ACKNOWLEDGMENTS

I want to thank Sue Sgroi, Norah Sargent, John Meikeljohn, Sara Meikeljohn, Tim Cunard, Mary Hurtig, and Susan Sandler; also, Mary Ryan, Donna Johnson, Maria Alexander, Rich Romboletti, JoAnn Murphy, Margaret Wolf, and Nick Wolf, who read or listened to parts of the book and whose help was invaluable. I especially want to thank Joanne Cunard and Liz Klock, who read the whole manuscript and gave wonderful encouragement and advice. Another special thanks to Hugh Conlon and my beloved wife, Mary Alice, who were unbelievably available as listeners throughout the writing of this book.

I also want to thank Joe Spieler, whose vision launched my career as a writer. Thanks to Lisa Thong for her help through the process of the publication of this book. To Susan Rogers for her wise editing of the first draft of the manuscript. To Elisabeth Kallick-Dyssegaard who was responsible for the creation of this book. And last to Hope Innelli, my editor at HarperCollins, who was an extraordinary pleasure to work with and whose constant encouragement and great skill inestimably contributed to the final product of this book.